OPENING YOUR OWN RETAIL STORE

Opening Your Own Retail Store

Lyn Taetzsch

CB

CONTEMPORARY
BOOKS

CHICAGO

Copyright © 1977 by Lyn Taetzch
All rights reserved
Published by Contemporary Books, Inc.
Two Prudential Plaza, Chicago, Illinois 60601-6790
Manufactured in the United States of America
International Standard Book Number: 0-8092-7981-9

Contents

Acknowledgments

Thanks to Laura Taetzsch, CPA, for her help in the sections on record-keeping and profit and loss analysis.

Thanks to Herb Genfan, Professor of Business Administration at Ithaca College, for his help with the material on training and supervising employees.

Thanks to Mary Tilley and J.D. Gallagher, Jr., of J.D. Gallagher Co., Inc., Realtors, for their help on commercial leases.

Thanks to Hour Agency, Inc., of Ithaca, N.Y., for the promotional materials reproduced in this book.

Thanks to Julius Blumberg, Inc., for the use of commercial lease forms in Chapter 2.

Thanks to Thayer Advertising Co., of Blackwood, N.J., for use of its customer cards in Chapter 12.

Thanks to the Small Business Administration, Washington, D.C., for all its useful books and pamphlets on the various aspects of small business management.

Introduction

Opening your own little gift shop, bookstore, boutique, or whatever, has probably been a dream of yours for a long time. You love to walk into such stores and browse, perhaps even pretending it's your own shop. Maybe you've worked in such a shop as a salesperson, manager, or buyer. That was educational and interesting, but now you finally think you're ready to start out on your own.

Starting any small business is a risky, scary, exciting experience. You're staking your savings, your credit, your sweat, and your ego on the outcome: success or failure. Your own business probably will require more hard work, more time, and more personal development than any other job you might take on. Because in your own business you are totally responsible for whatever happens.

But, by the same token, you also enjoy the fruits of your own labor—you see your baby begin to grow and stand on its own feet, begin to make its first profit—there's nothing quite so thrilling as knowing *you* did it.

To reach that goal, to someday stand back and say, "Wow, it's working—and *I* did it!" you've got to be sure that you've taken every possible step to make certain it *will* work. That's where this book comes in.

Before you begin, there are many details of running a small business that you should be aware of. First read this whole book through once. Then return to those chapters that cover the specific problem you may be working on, such as choosing a location, buying fixtures, purchasing stock, planning your advertising campaign, setting up a bookkeeping system, hiring employees, and applying for a loan. You'll find this book a practical, step-by-step guide in the planning and operation stages of your new business. May it serve you well! Good Luck!

Opening Your Own Retail Store

1 What Kind of Store Should You Open?

If you take a walk through the downtown shopping section of any large city, and note each kind of retail shop, you'll find the variety almost unlimited. There are shops that specialize in all kinds of items—from tropical fish to health food to yard goods to kite supplies. Wherever there's a great enough demand for a particular product, someone eventually will open up a shop to sell it, or will expand the inventory in his or her present shop to include it.

THE BIG CITY *VERSUS* THE SMALL TOWN. New York City probably has at least one specialty shop of every type that a large, diversified population might require. But in a small town many of those shops would die from lack of customers.

Why is this? Well, all of us will need to buy shoes, clothes, and food on a fairly regular basis, but how many of us are interested in exotic pets, stamp collecting, or kite-building? As the percentage of potential customers per number of population decreases for a particular item, you need a larger population on which to draw.

So if you live in a small town, you'll be safer opening a store that sells products—including shoes, clothing, hardware, home improvement supplies, and gifts—that appeal to most people. You may complain that there are already several of each of these basic stores in your town. In this case, there are several ways to go. First, you might check around to see if one of these stores is for sale. Perhaps one of the merchants is considering retiring or relocating to another state. You might find an opportunity to purchase "an established, going" business.

BUYING A GOING BUSINESS. Some of the advantages of buying a going business are that it will save you the time and effort of setting up your own shop with equipment and stock, and that you'll probably start with ready-made customers who have grown accustomed to buying there. The previous owner should give you the benefit of his business experience, and fill you in on the daily operation of the shop. If the shop has a good reputation already, you can profit from it.

1

But be very careful before making a decision. There are possible disadvantages to buying a going business. The present owner may be asking too high a price for what he's actually offering you. If the store has a bad reputation, is in a bad or declining location, is set up poorly, or is filled with a lot of unsalable merchandise, you're going to have more headaches than you bargained for.

CAN YOUR TOWN SUPPORT ANOTHER SHOE STORE, CLOTHING STORE, AND THE LIKE? Suppose your town already has three shoe stores, five clothing stores, two gift shops, and one or more of each of the basic-needs type of shops. Can it support another one? Possibly. If you examine each clothing store in town you may find that one carries children's clothes, one maternity clothes, one men's clothes, and so on. Perhaps your town could use another clothing store that appeals especially to teenagers, or one that sells mod clothing for college students, or one that sells work clothes. Look for an area which the stores in your town do not presently cover, and for which there is a real need. Maybe a lot of people shop out of town because there is no local store that offers these items.

Gift shops are another example. There are shops which specialize in handcrafted gifts, or wedding gifts (such as china and silverware), or greeting cards, or imported gifts, and so on. You might choose a particular material, such as wood or silver, and fill your shop with a wide variety of gifts made from that material. Your town might need a gift shop that offers a wide variety of relatively low-cost gifts, or perhaps one that carries some exclusive high-priced items for the more well-to-do citizens.

MATCHING YOUR SHOP TO THE NEEDS OF YOUR CUSTOMERS. You might be dying to open up a little boutique filled with high-priced specialty clothes and accessories that appeal to upper-middle-class college students. If your town is made up mostly of lower-middle-class working families, however, and the nearest college or university is a small junior college that attracts very few of its students from the upper-middle class, then you'd better think again.

So it's vitally important to make sure you have a potential clientele large enough for your business. Even in a big city where the chances of finding customers are better, make certain your shop will be located in the proper section of the city. You should be able to pinpoint who your potential customers are—by age group, income, education, and buying habits.

WHAT ABOUT YOUR INTERESTS? In every town or city, there will be some variety in the products you might choose to sell. So in considering all of them, your own interests will be very important. After all, part of the reason you want to open your own retail store is probably that you want to be doing the kind of thing you like to do. This might include some interest in a particular product or group of products.

You may love beautiful gifts, for example, or you may have been an antique buff for years. Or perhaps you recall happy hours selling shoes in your uncle's shoe store. Whatever product you choose to sell, it should be something you can be interested in and enjoy being around. After all, you'll be spending most of your waking hours with these products—unpacking them, putting them on shelves, showing them to customers, reading about them, and looking at them. They'll really become a part of your life, so choose them with care.

UTILIZE YOUR KNOWLEDGE AND PAST EXPERIENCE. Not only is interest in a particular type of store important, but knowledge and experience will also be valuable. The more you know about the products you're going to sell, the easier it will be to sell them. For example, if you're going to open a fabric shop, it will be useful to know about the various fabrics—how each should be cared for, which ones are easier to sew with, and how to figure out the amount of material to buy for a certain pattern. You should enjoy sewing, and take an active interest in the latest developments in fabrics and the various patterns available, so that you can answer any questions your customers might have. Also, your enthusiasm for the materials will influence customers—you'll find it a lot easier to sell products that you value and enjoy.

The best experience would be to actually work in the type of store you plan to open. By working as a sales person you'll get firsthand knowledge and experience dealing with customers, handling the stock, making out sales slips, and operating a cash register. Observe your boss and the other sales people around you to see how they handle difficult customers, or how they turn a "just looking" customer into a final sale. You'll also get a chance during this time to learn about the products you're selling, to observe the changes in fashion and consumer needs, and to become aware of general buying trends.

Once you've got some experience working as a sales person, try to get a promotion to buyer in that shop—or in another shop. The buyer is responsible for making decisions about what items to purchase for stock in the store. This job is crucial to the success or failure of the operation. And of course, as the owner of your own retail shop, you'll be solely responsible for it. In most small shops the owner does all the buying. So you'll have to look for a buyer's job in a larger operation, perhaps even in a department store.

Often the buyer also does some selling, or supervises the sales people in his area. The buyer must be aware of what is selling and what isn't, now long it takes to get merchandise after it is ordered, which selling seasons are busy or slow, and how much money is available at any one time to purchase stock. Decisions will have to be made about when to mark-down items that are not selling to make space for those that will. Sales and special promotions will have to be coordinated with receipt of merchandise. Special seasonal buying, such as for Christmas, will have to be planned well in advance. All in all, any experience you can get in these areas as the buyer for another store can only help you do a better job when you eventually open your own shop.

COMPETITION. Let's say you decide to open up a small grocery store because you figure everyone needs to eat. You also have three years' experience working for a small grocery store and one in a supermarket. That experience included making purchases, dealing with suppliers, keeping stock records, and so on. You feel that you really know the small-store food business and can handle your own shop.

So far, so good. However, the neighborhood in which you decided to open your shop already has two supermarket chains and three independent small grocers. Before you open up your store, you'd better check on a few things. Is your potential market area already saturated with food stores? Can it support another one? What would your store offer customers that the others don't? Are you expecting customers to come from too far a distance?

After all, most people today do their major shopping at a supermarket chain if they have transportation to get there. You really can't hope to compete with the supermarket's prices and variety of merchandise, so you'll probably have to depend on local neighborhood traffic. How many people will be able to walk to your store from their homes? Or are you in a shopping area where people who are doing other shopping might stop in your place because they are in the neighborhood? How close are you to the next grocery store? Do you offer anything special, such as longer hours than the next place? Remember, even though everyone buys food, they only buy a limited amount, and if your neighborhood is already saturated with stores that are serving the people adequately, the competition may be too heavy for you.

It's important to analyze your competition in any location. If you're going to open up a gift shop, how many other shops are in the area, what kinds of gifts do they sell, how popular are they, how well operated are they? You may decide to open up one because you're offering a different kind of gift shop or you think you can run yours more efficiently, but be aware of the competition and decide how you'll handle it.

Don't think that the lack of any evident competition is a ticket to sure success, either. The fact that there is no craft-supply shop in your town may simply mean that your town can't support one. If you're thinking of a new kind of shop (which your town doesn't already have), first try to learn if anyone tried that type in the past and failed. Go to the nearest place with such a store and inquire how many customers come from your town. While there, you might check with the Chamber of Commerce and the local merchants to find out what demand there's been for such a store and what the possible reception for it might be. Look for these stores in other small towns and talk to the owners. How are they doing? What kind of customers do their towns have to support such a store?

If all your research indicates your town should be able to support the type of store you have in mind, then you have a fighting chance. If someone else tried such a store in the past and failed, there may be other reasons why they failed, such as poor management or poor location. Just be sure to check out everything before plunging ahead.

FADS. We've already said that people will always need to buy food, clothing, and shoes. They'll probably continue to buy cars, home furnishings, hardware, paint, toys, appliances, and other basic needs of our culture, too. But there are product areas that tend to sell better in some years than in others. Some shops depend mostly on a good economy to flourish, while others remain stable despite changes in the national economic picture. Some shops require high impulse buying to stay in business, while others develop regular customers who will walk, bus, or drive to get what they want.

For example, ask yourself what kinds of shops are in abundance today that you didn't see two, five, or ten years ago. How about the "head shop," the boutique, the health food store? How many of these shops will make it in the future? It's hard to tell how long a fad will last, or whether something new is here to stay, but you should at least consider such things. You'll also have to take into consideration what the larger businesses are doing to your market area. For example, have many furniture warehouses offering discount prices taken away customers from the standard furniture stores? If you're thinking of opening up an appliance store, study what effect such big chains as Sears and Montgomery Wards might have on your market area. Be aware of marketing trends and how they might affect you in the future.

SUMMING UP. It's important that you take the time to carefully choose the type of store you'll open. Of course you'll want to work with the kind of merchandise in which you have some interest or knowledge, or both. The more you know about the products and the more experience you've had using and selling them, the better chance you'll have for success.

But you must also take into consideration the needs of your market area. In a big city there will be more opportunity for specialization and variety of merchandise than you'd find in a small town. Additionally, you should consider the make up of the population—age, education, income, interests, and so on. Even the climate and recreational facilities are important, especially for shops specializing in sporting equipment and outer clothing.

Once you've matched your interest and experience with the needs of the community, you'll have to carefully analyze your potential competition. If your town has five gift shops barely eking out a living, a sixth one is asking for trouble unless you feel you can take enough business away from the existing shops. Finally, be careful not to open a shop at the peak of a particular fad that may either have a very short life span or may end up being smothered by discount prices at big chain stores.

2 Choosing Your Location

Matching the type of store you plan to open with the right location is an important first step. Would you do better in a neighborhood spot, a downtown shopping center, a modern shopping mall, on the highway, or within walking distance of a university or college? Costs and space, of course, will also enter into your decision. You'll want to have a large enough shop for your needs, in the best location you can afford.

WHO AND WHERE ARE YOUR CUSTOMERS? Once you've determined who your potential customers are—by age, income group, sex, and so forth—the next question is: Where do they like to shop? Will your store cater to college students, and would it best be located in the university shopping area? Or are you planning a neighborhood shop, such as a small grocery or hardware store? If you're planning a gift shop, or women's clothing store, where do most of the women in your town or city shop?

In a small town you may find that just about everyone does his and her general shopping for clothes, gifts, stationery, and shoes, in a downtown area. In a large city you may find that certain areas cater to certain types of stores—the well-to-do neighborhoods having the higher-priced stores. And one area in the city may be filled with antique shops, another with boutiques, and still another with galleries and craft shops. By having these stores clustered, the potential customer can go to that section of town to find a wide variety of that particular merchandise.

WILL YOUR STORE RELY ON IMPULSE BUYING OR ON REGULAR, REPEAT CUSTOMERS? John, the proprietor of Guitar Workshop in Ithaca, New York, has his shop located in the basement on a secondary street in the college shopping area. This location is certainly not conducive to much impulse buying. And many of his customers are not college students. In fact, many of them don't even live in Ithaca. John's rent may be relatively low, but how does he manage to attract enough customers in such a spot?

7

John sells new and used guitars and other stringed instruments. He also repairs them. He also offers something the average music store doesn't. He'll talk to you at great length about how a particular guitar was made, what kind of wood was used in it, how to take care of it, and so on. By the time he's finished, you'll feel, as he does, that you're holding a truly precious instrument. The result is that, once you've gone to John, you'll never buy a guitar from anyone else. And if you have a friend who's thinking of buying a guitar—you'll send *him* to John's shop. So John doesn't depend on walk-in traffic or impulse buying. He has slowly built up a loyal word-of-mouth clientele, that widens his area of influence and increases in number all the time.

On the other hand, a combination gift-stationery-knickknack shop would do better in a place where people could walk by and look in the window at all the colorful, attractive merchandise. The window display stops them; they look in for a few moments, see several interesting items, and decide to come in and "just browse." Before you know it, they've picked up a fifty-cent or two-dollar item they originally had no intention of purchasing.

So you should choose a location partly on the amount of impulse buying you'll need. Do you require a steady flow of traffic to pass your windows? Or are you selling the type of item for which people will come specifically to you because they need it and you've developed a reputation that assures them that they can get what they want? I'm not saying that anyone should deliberately choose an out-of-the-way spot or make it difficult for customers to get to them. The consideration, however, is how much more money in rent you'll have to pay in a prominent location than in a relatively obscure one.

DRIVE-IN OR WALK-IN TRAFFIC? Are you selling big, heavy, or bulky items, such as lumber, which the customer will want to load easily into his car or truck? If so, you'll want to make sure there's plenty of parking space close by your shop. A store on a highway or the last store in a row of stores in a shopping center might be best for you.

One example of this situation that I've seen is with a local liquor store. It's located in a downtown shopping area that used to have limited on-the-street metered parking. A customer could park his car in front of the store, pick up a case of liquor, and load it easily in his trunk. Recently this downtown area was closed off to cars and turned into an open mall for walking traffic only. This has virtually eliminated the case-load pickup business of the liquor store. So ascertain what your customers' parking need will be and make sure it will be available in your location.

SHOPPING CENTERS. Shopping centers are distinctly different from downtown or local neighborhood business areas. The center is preplanned as a merchandising unit, with careful consideration of the primary and secondary tenants. Its site has been deliberately selected for easy access, to pull customers from a particular trade area, with on-site parking that is directly related to the retail area. Some centers provide protection from the weather, and most provide an atmosphere created for shopping comfort.

There are several types of shopping centers. In a neighborhood center the leading tenant is a supermarket or a drug store. The minimum trade population is 7,500 to 40,000. In a community shopping center, the leading tenant is a variety or a junior department store. The minimum trade population is 40,000 to 150,000. In a regional shopping center, the leading tenant is one or more full-line department stores. The minimum trade population is 150,000 or more.

The smaller centers will attract the basic-needs type of store—shoes, clothing, drugs, and hardware. The larger centers, with their greater trade population, can support the more specialized shops, and in fact look for the wide variety of stores that one would find in a downtown shopping area.

WILL A SHOPPING CENTER MEET YOUR NEEDS? To help you decide if a particular center will suit your shop, investigate the following:
  1. *The trade area and its growth prospects*
  2. *General income level in the trade area*
  3. *Number of households*
  4. *The percentage of various age groups in the population*

Your location in the center will also be important. Will you be in the main flow of customers as they pass between the stores having the greatest "customer pull?" Who will your neighbors be? How much space will you have? Will this be adequate for your display and stock needs?

Also consider the total number of shopping centers and other shopping areas, including downtown, in a particular trade area. If you notice several malls of various sizes in one area, each with a few empty stores that never stay occupied for very long, you may discover this area has been oversaturated with shopping facilities for the population. It may be wiser to wait for a good space in a busy center, where all the stores are generally filled, than to quickly jump into a center with four or five spots perpetually empty or with a high store turnover. If a new mall is being planned, check the above data carefully before committing yourself to a long-term lease.

RENT. For the downtown or neighborhood store, the typical lease states that a certain amount of rent will be paid monthly for so many years, with possible increments stated after a number of years. For example, $300 a month for the first two years, $350 a month for the next five years, and so on. Or the lease may run for a specific number of years at a stated rent and be renewable for another few years at a slightly higher rent.

Most shopping center leases are negotiated. Rental expense may begin with a minimum "guarantee," which is equal to a percentage of gross sales. In addition, you may have to pay dues to the center's merchant association, contribute to maintenance costs for common areas, participate in center advertising costs, and so on. Make sure you consider total costs when considering a location in a shopping center.

FINISHING COSTS. When you rent a store, you usually get it as is. That means you'll have to pay for any finishing costs, such as light fixtures, counters, shelves, painting, and floor coverings. Some developers of shopping centers help tenants plan store fronts, exterior signs, and interior color schemes to ensure store fronts that add to the center's image. They may even offer a "tenant allowance," whereby they provide an allowance towards the cost of store fronts, ceiling treatment, and wall coverings. Be sure to check out these provisions ahead of time, and plan for any costs that might be involved.

LEASES. Retail store leases vary from simple standard forms to customized legal documents that are many pages long. Certain details, however, are common to most store leases, such as who will pay for gas, electricity, and water. Other areas covered in leases are:

1. Alterations, additions, and fixtures—who pays for them, who must approve them, and whose property they are after the lease is terminated
2. Responsibility for personal property of lessee (you), such as damage from bursting or leaking water pipes, and negligence of other tenants
3. What happens in case of damage by fire
4. What the building will be used for (i.e., what kind of goods your store will sell)
5. Defaulting on lease payments
6. Subletting

Figures 2-1 through 2-6 show a standard store lease that covers the above items, plus many additional ones. This form is reproduced by permission of the publisher, Julius Blumberg, Inc., 80 Exchange Place, New York, New York 10004. This form and other, shorter, business lease forms are available from them.

SUMMING UP. When choosing a location for your store, consider who your customers are and where they live; whether your business will rely on impulse buying or regular, repeat business; and available parking facilities. Study the benefits of shopping centers, downtown, highway locations, and local neighborhood areas before deciding on one of them. Before signing any lease, read it carefully, be aware of your responsibilities under it, and, to be even safer, have your lawyer check it.

Figures 2-1 through 2-6 (on pages 11-16) illustrate the 4-page Form A35—Lease, Business Premises, published by Julius Blumberg, Inc., 80 Exchange Place, New York, N.Y. 10004.

A **35**—Lease, Business Premises.
Loft, Office or Store. **2-65**

JULIUS BLUMBERG, INC., LAW BLANK PUBLISHERS
80 EXCHANGE PLACE, AT BROADWAY, NEW YORK

This Lease made the   day of   19   , between

hereinafter referred to as LANDLORD, and

hereinafter jointly, severally and collectively referred to as TENANT.

Witnesseth, that the Landlord hereby leases to the Tenant, and the Tenant hereby hires and takes

from the Landlord

in the building known as

to be used and occupied by the Tenant

and for no other purpose, for a term to commence on   19   , and to end

on   19   , unless sooner terminated as hereinafter provided, at the ANNUAL RENT of

all payable in equal monthly instalments in advance on the first day of each and every calendar month during said term,

except the first instalment, which shall be paid upon the execution hereof.

THE TENANT JOINTLY AND SEVERALLY COVENANTS:

FIRST.—That the Tenant will pay the rent as above provided.

REPAIRS

ORDINANCES AND VIOLATIONS

ENTRY

SECOND.—That, throughout said term the Tenant will take good care of the demised premises, fixtures and appurtenances, and all alterations, additions and improvements to either; make all repairs in and about the same necessary to preserve them in good order and condition, which repairs shall be, in quality and class, equal to the original work; promptly pay the expense of such repairs; suffer no waste or injury; give prompt notice to the Landlord of any fire that may occur; execute and comply with all laws, rules, orders, ordinances and regulations at any time issued or in force (except those requiring structural alterations), applicable to the demised premises or to the Tenant's occupation thereof, of the Federal, State and Local Governments, and of each and every department, bureau and official thereof, and of the New York Board of Fire Underwriters; permit at all times during usual business hours, the Landlord and representatives of the Landlord to enter the demised premises for the purpose of inspection, and to exhibit them for purposes of sale or rental; suffer the Landlord to make repairs and improvements to all parts of the building, and to comply with all orders and requirements of governmental authority applicable to said building or to any occupation thereof: suffer the Landlord to erect, use, maintain, repair and replace pipes and conduits in the demised premises and to the floors above and below; forever indemnify and save harmless the Landlord for and against any and all liability, penalties, damages, expenses

INDEMNIFY LANDLORD

and judgments arising from injury during said term to person or property of any nature, occasioned wholly or in part by any act or acts, omission or omissions of the Tenant, or of the employees, guests, agents, assigns or undertenants of the Tenant and also for any matter or thing growing out of the occupation of the demised premises or of the streets, sidewalks or vaults adjacent thereto; permit, during the six months next prior to the expiration of the term the usual notice "To Let" to be placed and to remain unmolested in a conspicuous place upon the exterior of the demised premises; repair, at or before the end of the term, all injury done by the installation or removal of furniture and property; and at the end of the term, to quit and surrender the demised premises with all alterations, additions and improvements in good order and condition.

MOVING INJURY SURRENDER

THIRD.—That the Tenant will not disfigure or deface any part of the building, or suffer the same to be done, except so far as may be necessary to affix such trade fixtures as are herein consented to by the Landlord; the Tenant will not obstruct, or permit the obstruction of the street or the sidewalk adjacent thereto; will not do anything, or suffer anything to be done upon the demised premises which will increase the rate of fire insurance upon the building or any of its contents, or be liable to cause structural injury to said building; will not permit the accumulation of waste or refuse matter, and will not, without the written consent of the Landlord first obtained in each case, either sell, assign, mortgage or transfer

NEGATIVE
COVENANTS

this lease, underlet the demised premises or any part thereof, permit the same or any part thereof to be occupied by anybody other than the Tenant and the Tenant's employees, make any alterations in the demised premises, use the demised premises or any part thereof for any purpose other than the one first above stipulated, or for any purpose deemed extra hazardous on account of fire risk, nor in violation of any law or ordinance. That the Tenant will not obstruct

OBSTRUCTION
SIGNS

or permit the obstruction of the light, halls, stairway or entrances to the building, and will not erect or inscribe any sign, signals or advertisements unless and until the style and location thereof have been approved by the Landlord; and if any be erected or inscribed without such approval, the Landlord may remove the same. No water cooler, air conditioning unit

AIR
CONDITIONING

or system or other apparatus shall be installed or used without the prior written consent of Landlord.

IT IS MUTUALLY COVENANTED AND AGREED, THAT

FIRE CLAUSE

FOURTH.—If the demised premises shall be partially damaged by fire or other cause without the fault or neglect of Tenant, Tenant's servants, employees, agents, visitors or licensees, the damages shall be repaired by and at the expense of Landlord and the rent until such repairs shall be made shall be apportioned according to the part of the demised premises which is usable by Tenant. But if such partial damage is due to the fault or neglect of Tenant, Tenant's servants, employees, agents, visitors or licensees, without prejudice to any other rights and remedies of Landlord and without prejudice to the rights of subrogation of Landlord's insurer, the damages shall be repaired by Landlord but there shall be no apportionment or abatement of rent. No penalty shall accrue for reasonable delay which may arise by reason of adjustment of insurance on the part of Landlord and/or Tenant, and for reasonable delay on account of "labor troubles", or any other cause beyond Landlord's control. If the demised premises are totally damaged or are rendered wholly untenantable by fire or other cause, and if Landlord shall decide not to restore or not to rebuild the same, or if the building shall be so damaged that Landlord shall decide to demolish it or to rebuild it, then or in any of such events Landlord may, within ninety (90) days after such fire or other cause, give Tenant a notice in writing of such decision, which notice shall be given as in Paragraph Twelve hereof provided, and thereupon the term of this lease shall expire by lapse of time upon the third day after such notice is given, and Tenant shall vacate the demised premises and surrender the same to Landlord. If Tenant shall not be in default under this lease then, upon the termination of this lease under the conditions provided for in the sentence immediately preceding, Tenant's liability for rent shall cease as of the day following the casualty. Tenant hereby expressly waives the provisions of Section 227 of the Real Property Law and agrees that the foregoing provisions of this Article shall govern and control in lieu thereof. If the damage or destruction be due to the fault or neglect of Tenant the debris shall be removed by, and at the expense of, Tenant.

EMINENT
DOMAIN

FIFTH.—If the whole or any part of the premises hereby demised shall be taken or condemned by any competent authority for any public use or purpose then the term hereby granted shall cease from the time when possession of the part so taken shall be required for such public purpose and without apportionment of award, the Tenant hereby assigning to the Landlord all right and claim to any such award, the current rent, however, in such case to be apportioned.

LEASE NOT
IN EFFECT

DEFAULTS

TEN DAY
NOTICE

SIXTH.—If, before the commencement of the term, the Tenant be adjudicated a bankrupt, or make a "general assignment," or take the benefit of any insolvent act, or if a Receiver or Trustee be appointed for the Tenant's property, or if this lease or the estate of the Tenant hereunder be transferred or pass to or devolve upon any other person or corporation, or if the Tenant shall default in the performance of any agreement by the Tenant contained in any other lease to the Tenant by the Landlord or by any corporation of which an officer of the Landlord is a Director, this lease shall thereby, at the option of the Landlord, be terminated and in that case, neither the Tenant nor anybody claiming under the Tenant shall be entitled to go into possession of the demised premises. If after the commencement of the term, any of the events mentioned above in this subdivision shall occur, or if Tenant shall make default in fulfilling any of the covenants of this lease, other than the covenants for the payment of rent or "additional rent" or if the demised premises become vacant or deserted, the Landlord may give to the Tenant ten days' notice of intention to end the term of this lease, and thereupon at the expiration of said ten days' (if said condition which was the basis of said notice shall continue to exist) the term under this lease shall expire as fully and completely as if that day were the date herein definitely fixed for the expiration of the term and the Tenant will then quit and surrender the demised premises to the Landlord, but the Tenant shall remain liable as hereinafter provided.

RE-POSSESSION
BY LANDLORD

RE-LETTING

WAIVER
BY TENANT

If the Tenant shall make default in the payment of the rent reserved hereunder, or any item of "additional rent" herein mentioned, or any part of either or in making any other payment herein provided for, or if the notice last above provided for shall have been given and if the condition which was the basis of said notice shall exist at the expiration of said ten days' period, the Landlord may immediately, or at any time thereafter, re-enter the demised premises and remove all persons and all or any property therefrom, either by summary dispossess proceedings, or by any suitable action or proceeding at law, or by force or otherwise, without being liable to indictment, prosecution or damages therefor, and re-possess and enjoy said premises together with all additions, alterations and improvements. In any such case or in the event that this lease be "terminated" before the commencement of the term, as above provided, the Landlord may either re-let the demised premises or any part or parts thereof for the Landlord's own account, or may, at the Landlord's option, re-let the demised premises or any part or parts thereof as the agent of the Tenant, and receive the rents therefor, applying the same first to the payment of such expenses as the Landlord may have incurred, and then to the fulfillment of the covenants of the Tenant herein, and the balance, if any, at the expiration of the term first above provided for, shall be paid to the Tenant. Landlord may rent the premises for a term extending beyond the term hereby granted without releasing Tenant from any liability. In the event the term of this lease shall expire as above in this subdivision "Sixth" provided, or terminate by summary proceedings or otherwise, and if the Landlord shall not re-let the demised premises for the Landlord's own account, then, whether or not the premises be re-let, the Tenant shall remain liable for, and the Tenant hereby agrees to pay to the Landlord, until the time when this lease would have expired but for such termination or expiration, the equivalent of the amount of all of the rent and "additional rent" reserved herein, less the avails of reletting, if any, and the same shall be due and payable by the Tenant to the Landlord on the several rent days above specified, that is, upon each of such rent days the Tenant shall pay to the Landlord the amount of deficiency then existing. The Tenant hereby expressly waives any and all right of redemption in case the Tenant shall be dispossessed by judgment or warrant of any court or judge, and the Tenant waives and will waive all right to trial by jury in any summary proceedings hereafter instituted by the Landlord against the Tenant in respect to the demised premises. The words "re-enter" and "re-entry" as used in this lease are not restricted to their technical legal meaning.

REMEDIES ARE
CUMULATIVE

In the event of a breach or threatened breach by the Tenant of any of the covenants or provisions hereof, the Landlord shall have the right of injunction and the right to invoke any remedy allowed at law or in equity, as if re-entry, summary proceedings and other remedies were not herein provided for.

LANDLORD
MAY
PERFORM

ADDITIONAL
RENT

SEVENTH.—If the Tenant shall make default in the performance of any covenant herein contained, the Landlord may immediately, or at any time thereafter, without notice, perform the same for the account of the Tenant. If a notice of mechanic's lien be filed against the demised premises or against premises of which the demised premises are part, for, or purporting to be for, labor or material alleged to have been furnished, or to be furnished to or for the Tenant at the demised premises, and if the Tenant shall fail to take such action as shall cause such lien to be discharged within fifteen days after the filing of such notice, the Landlord may pay the amount of such lien or discharge the same by deposit or by bonding proceedings, and in the event of such deposit or bonding proceedings, the Landlord may require the lienor to prosecute an appropriate action to enforce the lienor's claim. In such case, the Landlord may pay any judgment recovered on such claim. Any amount paid or expense incurred by the Landlord as in this subdivision of this lease provided, and any amount as to which the Tenant shall at any time be in default for or in respect to the use of water, electric current or sprinkler supervisory service, and any expense incurred or sum of money paid by the Landlord by reason of the failure of the Tenant to comply with any provision hereof, or in defending any such action, shall be deemed to be "additional rent" for the demised premises, and shall be due and payable by the Tenant to the Landlord on the first day of the next following month, or, at the option of the Landlord, on the first day of any succeeding month. The receipt by the Landlord of any instalment of the regular stipulated rent hereunder or any of said "additional rent" shall not be a waiver of any other "additional rent" then due.

AS TO
WAIVERS

EIGHTH.—The failure of the Landlord to insist, in any one or more instances upon a strict performance of any of the covenants of this lease, or to exercise any option herein contained, shall not be construed as a waiver or a relinquishment for the future of such covenant or option, but the same shall continue and remain in full force and effect. The receipt by the Landlord of rent, with knowledge of the breach of any covenant hereof, shall not be deemed a waiver of such breach and no waiver by the Landlord of any provision hereof shall be deemed to have been made unless expressed in writing and signed by the Landlord. Even though the Landlord shall consent to an assignment hereof no further assignment shall be made without express consent in writing by the Landlord.

COLLECTION OF RENT FROM OTHERS

NINTH.—If this lease be assigned, or if the demised premises or any part thereof be underlet or occupied by anybody other than the Tenant the Landlord may collect rent from the assignee, under-tenant or occupant, and apply the net amount collected to the rent herein reserved, and no such collection shall be deemed a waiver of the covenant herein against assignment and under-letting, or the acceptance of the assignee, under-tenant or occupant as tenant, or a release of the Tenant from the further performance by the Tenant of the covenants herein contained on the part of the Tenant.

MORTGAGES

TENTH.—This lease shall be subject and subordinate at all times, to the lien of the mortgages now on the demised premises, and to all advances made or hereafter to be made upon the security thereof, and subject and subordinate to the lien of any mortgage or mortgages which at any time may be made a lien upon the premises. The Tenant will execute and deliver such further instrument or instruments subordinating this lease to the lien of any such mortgage or mortgages as shall be desired by any mortgagee or proposed mortgagee. The Tenant hereby appoints the Landlord the attorney-in-fact of the Tenant, irrevocable, to execute and deliver any such instrument or instruments for the Tenant.

IMPROVEMENTS

ELEVENTH.—All improvements made by the Tenant to or upon the demised premises, except said trade fixtures, shall when made, at once be deemed to be attached to the freehold, and become the property of the Landlord, and at the end or other expiration of the term, shall be surrendered to the Landlord in as good order and condition as they were when installed, reasonable wear and damages by the elements excepted.

NOTICES

TWELFTH.—Any notice or demand which under the terms of this lease or under any statute must or may be given or made by the parties hereto shall be in writing and shall be given or made by mailing the same by certified or registered mail addressed to the respective parties at the addresses set forth in this lease.

NO LIABILITY

THIRTEENTH.—The Landlord shall not be liable for any failure of water supply or electrical current, sprinkler damage, or failure of sprinkler service, nor for injury or damage to person or property caused by the elements or by other tenants or persons in said building, or resulting from steam, gas, electricity, water, rain or snow, which may leak or flow from any part of said buildings or from the pipes, appliances or plumbing works of the same, or from the street or sub-surface, or from any other place, nor for interference with light or other incorporeal hereditaments by anybody other than the Landlord, or caused by operations by or for a governmental authority in construction of any public or quasi-public work, neither shall the Landlord be liable for any latent defect in the building.

NO ABATEMENT

FOURTEENTH.—No diminution or abatement of rent, or other compensation shall be claimed or allowed for inconvenience or discomfort arising from the making of repairs or improvements to the building or to its appliances, nor for any space taken to comply with any law, ordinance or order of a governmental authority. In respect to the various "services," if any, herein expressly or impliedly agreed to be furnished by the Landlord to the Tenant, it is agreed that there shall be no diminution or abatement of the rent, or any other compensation, for interruption or curtailment of such "service" when such interruption or curtailment shall be due to accident, alterations or repairs desirable or necessary to be made or to inability or difficulty in securing supplies or labor for the maintenance of such "service" or to some other cause, not gross negligence on the part of the Landlord. No such interruption or curtailment of any such "service" shall be deemed a constructive eviction. The Landlord shall not be required to furnish, and the Tenant shall not be entitled to receive, any of such "services" during any period wherein the Tenant shall be in default in respect to the payment of rent. Neither shall there be any abatement or diminution of rent because of making of repairs, improvements or decorations to the demised premises after the date above fixed for the commencement of the term, it being understood that rent shall, in any event, commence to run at such date so above fixed.

RULES, ETC.

FIFTEENTH.—The Landlord may prescribe and regulate the placing of safes, machinery, quantities of merchandise and other things. The Landlord may also prescribe and regulate which elevator and entrances shall be used by the Tenant's employees, and for the Tenant's shipping. The Landlord may make such other and further rules and regulations as, in the Landlord's judgment, may from time to time be needful for the safety, care or cleanliness of the building, and for the preservation of good order therein. The Tenant and the employees and agents of the Tenant will observe and conform to all such rules and regulations.

SHORING OF WALLS

SIXTEENTH.—In the event that an excavation shall be made for building or other purposes upon land adjacent to the demised premises or shall be contemplated to be made, the Tenant shall afford to the person or persons causing or to cause such excavation, license to enter upon the demised premises for the purpose of doing such work as said person or persons shall deem to be necessary to preserve the wall or walls, structure or structures upon the demised premises from injury and to support the same by proper foundations.

VAULT SPACE

SEVENTEENTH.—No vaults or space not within the property line of the building are leased hereunder. Landlord makes no representation as to the location of the property line of the building. Such vaults or space as Tenant may be permitted to use or occupy are to be used or occupied under a revocable license and if such license be revoked by the Landlord as to the use of part or all of the vaults or space Landlord shall not be subject to any liability; Tenant shall not be entitled to any compensation or reduction in rent nor shall this be deemed constructive or actual eviction. Any tax, fee or charge of municipal or other authorities for such vaults or space shall be paid by the Tenant for the period of the Tenant's use or occupancy thereof.

ENTRY

EIGHTEENTH.—That during seven months prior to the expiration of the term hereby granted, applicants shall be admitted at all reasonable hours of the day to view the premises until rented; and the Landlord and the Landlord's agents shall be permitted at any time during the term to visit and examine them at any reasonable hour of the day, and workmen may enter at any time, when authorized by the Landlord or the Landlord's agents, to make or facilitate repairs in any part of the building; and if the said Tenant shall not be personally present to open and permit an entry into said premises, at any time, when for any reason an entry therein shall be necessary or permissible hereunder, the Landlord or the Landlord's agents may forcibly enter the same without rendering the Landlord or such agents liable to any claim or cause of action for damages by reason thereof (if during such entry the Landlord shall accord reasonable care to the Tenant's property) and without in any manner affecting the obligations and covenants of this lease; it is, however, expressly understood that the right and authority hereby reserved, does not impose, nor does the Landlord assume, by reason thereof, any responsibility or liability whatsoever for the care or supervision of said premises, or any of the pipes, fixtures, appliances or appurtenances therein contained or therewith in any manner connected.

NO REPRESENTATIONS

NINETEENTH.—The Landlord has made no representations or promises in respect to said building or to the demised premises except those contained herein, and those, if any, contained in some written communication to the Tenant, signed by the Landlord. This instrument may not be changed, modified, discharged or terminated orally.

ATTORNEY'S FEES

TWENTIETH.—If the Tenant shall at any time be in default hereunder, and if the Landlord shall institute an action or summary proceeding against the Tenant based upon such default, then the Tenant will reimburse the Landlord for the expense of attorneys' fees and disbursements thereby incurred by the Landlord, so far as the same are reasonable in amount. Also so long as the Tenant shall be a tenant hereunder the amount of such expenses shall be deemed to be "additional rent" hereunder and shall be due from the Tenant to the Landlord on the first day of the month following the incurring of such respective expenses.

POSSESSION

TWENTY-FIRST.—Landlord shall not be liable for failure to give possession of the premises upon commencement date by reason of the fact that premises are not ready for occupancy, or due to a prior Tenant wrongfully holding over or any other person wrongfully in possession or for any other reason: in such event the rent shall not commence until possession is given or is available, but the term herein shall not be extended.

THE TENANT FURTHER COVENANTS:

IF A FIRST FLOOR

TWENTY-SECOND.—If the demised premises or any part thereof consist of a store, or of a first floor, or of any part thereof, the Tenant will keep the sidewalk and curb in front thereof clean at all times and free from snow and ice, and will keep insured in favor of the Landlord, all plate glass therein and furnish the Landlord with policies of insurance covering the same.

INCREASED FIRE INSURANCE RATE

TWENTY-THIRD.—If by reason of the conduct upon the demised premises of a business not herein permitted, or if by reason of the improper or careless conduct of any business upon or use of the demised premises, the fire insurance rate shall at any time be higher than it otherwise would be, then the Tenant will reimburse the Landlord, as additional rent hereunder, for that part of all fire insurance premiums hereafter paid out by the Landlord which shall have been charged because of the conduct of such business not so permitted, or because of the improper or careless conduct of any business upon or use of the demised premises, and will make such reimbursement upon the first day of the month following such outlay by the Landlord; but this covenant shall not apply to a premium for any period beyond the expiration date of this lease, first above specified. In any action or proceeding wherein the Landlord and Tenant are parties, a schedule or "make up" of rate for the building on the demised premises, purporting to have been issued by New York Fire Insurance Exchange, or other body making fire insurance rates for the demised premises, shall be prima facie evidence of the facts therein stated and of the several items and charges included in the fire insurance rate then applicable to the demised premises.

WATER RENT

SEWER

TWENTY-FOURTH.—If a separate water meter is installed for the demised premises, or any part thereof, the Tenant will keep the same in repair and pay the charges made by the municipality or water supply company for or in respect to the consumption of water, as and when bills therefor are rendered. If the demised premises, or any part thereof, be supplied with water through a meter which supplies other premises, the Tenant will pay to the Landlord, as and when bills are rendered therefor, the Tenant's proportionate part of all charges which the municipality or water supply company shall make for all water consumed through said meter, as indicated by said meter. Such proportionate part shall be fixed by apportioning the respective charge according to floor area against all of the rentable floor area in the building (exclusive of the basement) which shall have been occupied during the period of the respective charges, taking into account the period that each part of such area was occupied. Tenant agrees to pay as additional rent the Tenant's proportionate part, determined as aforesaid, of the sewer rent or charge imposed or assessed upon the building of which the premises are a part.

ELECTRIC CURRENT

TWENTY-FIFTH.—That the Tenant will purchase from the Landlord, if the Landlord shall so desire, all electric current that the Tenant requires at the demised premises, and will pay the Landlord for the same, as the amount of consumption shall be indicated by the meter furnished therefor. The price for said current shall be the same as that charged for consumption similar to that of the Tenant by the company supplying electricity in the same community. Payments shall be due as and when bills shall be rendered. The Tenant shall comply with like rules, regulations and contract provisions as those prescribed by said company for a consumption similar to that of the Tenant.

SPRINKLER SYSTEM

TWENTY-SIXTH.—If there now is or shall be installed in said building a "sprinkler system" the Tenant agrees to keep the appliances thereto in the demised premises in repair and good working condition, and if the New York Board of Fire Underwriters or the New York Fire Insurance Exchange or any bureau, department or official of the State or local government requires or recommends that any changes, modifications, alterations or additional sprinkler heads or other equipment be made or supplied by reason of the Tenant's business, or the location of partitions, trade fixtures, or other contents of the demised premises, or if such changes, modifications, alterations, additional sprinkler heads or other equipment in the demised premises are necessary to prevent the imposition of a penalty or charge against the full allowance for a sprinkler system in the fire insurance rate as fixed by said Exchange, or by any Fire Insurance Company, the Tenant will at the Tenant's own expense, promptly make and supply such changes, modifications, alterations, additional sprinkler heads or other equipment. As additional rent hereunder the Tenant will pay to the Landlord, annually in advance, throughout the term $......................., toward the contract price for sprinkler supervisory service.

SECURITY

TWENTY-SEVENTH.—The sum of...Dollars is deposited by the Tenant herein with the Landlord herein as security for the faithful performance of all the covenants and conditions of the lease by the said Tenant. If the Tenant faithfully performs all the covenants and conditions on his part to be performed, then the sum deposited shall be returned to said Tenant.

NUISANCE

TWENTY-EIGHTH.—This lease is granted and accepted on the especially understood and agreed condition that the Tenant will conduct his business in such a manner, both as regards noise and kindred nuisances, as will in no wise interfere with, annoy, or disturb any other tenants, in the conduct of their several businesses, or the landlord in the management of the building; under penalty of forfeiture of this lease and consequential damages.

BROKERS COMMISSIONS

TWENTY-NINTH.—The Landlord hereby recognizes   as the broker who negotiated and consummated this lease with the Tenant herein, and agrees that if, as, and when the Tenant exercises the option, if any, contained herein to renew this lease, or fails to exercise the option, if any, contained therein to cancel this lease, the Landlord will pay to said broker a further commission in accordance with the rules and commission rates of the Real Estate Board in the community. A sale, transfer, or other disposition of the Landlord's interest in said lease shall not operate to defeat the Landlord's obligation to pay the said commission to the said broker. The Tenant herein hereby represents to the Landlord that the said broker is the sole and only broker who negotiated and consummated this lease with the Tenant.

WINDOW CLEANING

THIRTIETH.—The Tenant agrees that it will not require, permit, suffer, nor allow the cleaning of any window, or windows, in the demised premises from the outside (within the meaning of Section 202 of the Labor Law) unless the equipment and safety devices required by law, ordinance, regulation or rule, including, without limitation, Section 202 of the New York Labor Law, are provided and used, and unless the rules, or any supplemental rules of the Industrial Board of the State of New York are fully complied with; and the Tenant hereby agrees to indemnify the Landlord, Owner, Agent, Manager and/or Superintendent, as a result of the Tenant's requiring, permitting, suffering, or allowing any window, or windows in the demised premises to be cleaned from the outside in violation of the requirements of the aforesaid laws, ordinances, regulations and/or rules.

VALIDITY

THIRTY-FIRST.—The invalidity or unenforceability of any provision of this lease shall in no way affect the validity or enforceability of any other provision hereof.

EXECUTION & DELIVERY OF LEASE

THIRTY-SECOND.—In order to avoid delay, this lease has been prepared and submitted to the Tenant for signature with the understanding that it shall not bind the Landlord unless and until it is executed and delivered by the Landlord.

EXTERIOR OF PREMISES

THIRTY-THIRD.—The Tenant will keep clean and polished all metal, trim, marble and stonework which are a part of the exterior of the premises, using such materials and methods as the Landlord may direct, and if the Tenant shall fail to comply with the provisions of this paragraph, the Landlord may cause such work to be done at the expense of the Tenant.

PLATE GLASS

THIRTY-FOURTH.—The Landlord shall replace at the expense of the Tenant any and all broken glass in the skylights, doors and walls in and about the demised premises. The Landlord may insure and keep insured all plate glass in the skylights, doors and walls in the demised premises, for and in the name of the Landlord and bills for the premiums therefor shall be rendered by the Landlord to the Tenant at such times as the Landlord may elect, and shall be due from and payable by the Tenant when rendered, and the amount thereof shall be deemed to be, and shall be paid as, additional rent.

WAR EMERGENCY

THIRTY-FIFTH.—This lease and the obligation of Tenant to pay rent hereunder and perform all of the other covenants and agreements hereunder on part of Tenant to be performed shall in nowise be affected, impaired or excused because Landlord is unable to supply or is delayed in supplying any service expressly or impliedly to be supplied or is unable to make, or is delayed in making any repairs, additions, alterations or decorations or is unable to supply or is delayed in supplying any equipment or fixtures if Landlord is prevented or delayed from so doing by reason of governmental preemption in connection with a National Emergency declared by the President of the United States or in connection with any rule, order or regulation of any department or subdivision thereof of any government agency or by reason of the conditions of supply and demand which have been or are affected by war or other emergency.

THE LANDLORD COVENANTS

QUIET POSSESSION

FIRST.—That if and so long as the Tenant pays the rent and "additional rent" reserved hereby, and performs and observes the covenants and provisions hereof, the Tenant shall quietly enjoy the demised premises, subject, however, to the terms of this lease, and to the mortgages above mentioned, provided however, that this covenant shall be conditioned upon the retention of title to the premises by Landlord.

ELEVATOR

HEAT

SECOND.—Subject to the provisions of Paragraph "Fourteenth" above the Landlord will furnish the following respective services: (a) Elevator service, if the building shall contain an elevator or elevators, on all days except Sundays and holidays, from   A.M. to   P.M. and on Saturdays from   A.M. to   P.M.; (b) Heat, during the same hours on the same days in the cold season in each year.

And it is mutually understood and agreed that the covenants and agreements contained in the within lease shall be binding upon the parties hereto and upon their respective successors, heirs, executors and administrators.

In Witness Whereof, the Landlord and Tenant have respectively signed and sealed these presents the day and year first above written.

....[L. S.]
                                                                Landlord

In presence of:

....[L. S.]
                                                                Tenant

State of New York, County of   *ss*:

On the   day of   19   , before me personally came
, to me known, who, being by me duly sworn, did depose and say that he resides at
; that he is   of
, the corporation described in and which executed the within
instrument; that he knows the seal of said corporation; that the seal affixed to said instrument is such corporate seal; that it was so affixed by order of the Board of Directors of said corporation, and that he signed his name thereto by like order.

State of New York, County of   *ss*:

On the   day of   19   , before me personally came
, to me known, who, being by me duly sworn, did depose and say that he resides at
; that he is   of
, the corporation described in and which executed the within
instrument; that he knows the seal of said corporation; that the seal affixed to said instrument is such corporate seal; that it was so affixed by order of the Board of Directors of said corporation, and that he signed his name thereto by like order.

State of New York, County of   *ss*:

On the   day of   19   , before me personally came
to me known and known to me to be the individual described in and who executed the foregoing instrument, and duly acknowledged that he executed the same.

State of New York, County of   *ss*:

On the   day of   19   , before me personally came
, subscribing witness to the foregoing instrument, with whom I am personally acquainted, who, being by me duly sworn, did depose and say, that he resided, at the time of the execution of said instrument, and still resides, in   that he is and then was acquainted with
, and knew   to be   the individual described in and who executed the foregoing instrument; and that he, said subscribing witness, was present and saw   execute the same; and that he, said witness, thereupon at the same time subscribed his name as witness thereto.

BUILDING..

Premises..

Landlord

to

Tenant

LEASE

GUARANTY

In consideration of the letting of the premises within mentioned to the Tenant within named, and of the sum of One Dollar, to the undersigned in hand paid by the Landlord within named, the undersigned hereby guarantees to the Landlord and to the heirs, successors and/or assigns of the Landlord, the payment by the Tenant of the rent, within provided for, and the performance by the Tenant of all of the provisions of the within lease. Notice of all defaults is waived, and consent is hereby given to all extensions of time that any Landlord may grant.

Dated,   19

....L. S.

STATE OF   COUNTY OF   *ss* :

On this   day of   , 19   , before me personally appeared

to me known and known to me to be the individual described in and who executed the foregoing instrument, and duly acknowledged to me that he executed the same.

3 Starting Up: Legal Form and Money Requirements

Once you've chosen the type of store you want to open up, and the best location for it, you'll have to decide which legal form will be best for your business: proprietorship, partnership, or corporation. You'll also need to plan carefully how much money will be necessary to start and maintain the business until it begins to make a profit. Once you decide *how* much money you'll need, the next step will be to figure out where to get it.

PROPRIETORSHIP. If you set up your business as a proprietorship, you'll be the sole owner. As far as the Internal Revenue Service is concerned, whatever profit the business makes will be considered your income. Whatever debts the business incurs will be your personal debts. In other words, you'll be personally liable for them.

Proprietorship is a simple legal form. To use the form requires the filing of a business certificate, similar to the one shown in Figure 3-1, with your local county clerk. This business certificate registers the name you'll be doing business under, such as dba (doing business as) "Bud's Duds." Call your Chamber of Commerce to find out what the procedure is in your county or state.

The problem with a single proprietorship setup is that you are solely responsible for all business debts. For example, if you sign a 15-year lease and then find that the store is unprofitable and you're forced out of business within a year, you're still responsible for paying the rent for the remaining 14 years, or for finding a satisfactory replacement tenant. If your business borrows money and cannot pay back this money out of profits, you're personally responsible. So if you choose the proprietorship form of business, be very careful about a long-term lease and any large loan commitments that you make. Check this setup with a lawyer first.

PARTNERSHIP. A partnership is similar to a proprietorship, except that more than one person shares in the business. If you have a 50/50 partnership with another person, both partners share equally in the profits of the business. Both partners are also fully liable for its debts.

17

Business Certificate

I HEREBY CERTIFY *that I am conducting or transacting business under the name or designation*

of

at

City or Town of   *County of*   *State of New York.*

*My full name is**

and I reside at

I FURTHER CERTIFY *that I am the successor in interest to*

the person or persons heretofore using such name or names to carry on or conduct or transact business.

IN WITNESS WHEREOF, *I have this*   *day of*   *19*   *, made and signed this certificate.*

....

* Print or type name.

* If under 18 years of age, state "I am............years of age".

STATE OF NEW YORK
COUNTY OF   } *ss.:*

On this   *day of*   *19*   *, before me personally appeared*

to me known and known to me to be the individual   *described in and who executed the foregoing*
certificate, and   *he*   *thereupon*   *duly acknowledged to me that*   *he*   *executed the same.*

Figure 3-1. Shown here is a New York State Business Certificate for "conducting business under an assumed name for individual," that is, for a single proprietorship.

See Figure 3-2 for a sample of the business certificate that is used for filing a new business as a partnership. Note that it's very similar to the one used for a single proprietorship business. This certificate should also be filed with your county clerk.

A partnership is no more protection against business losses than a proprietorship; in fact, it can be more dangerous. Your partner may run up large business debts that he is unable to personally back up. You will then be held responsible for them. For example, if your business becomes unsuccessful and folds, leaving a debt of $10,000, and your partner only has $200 to his name, the creditors will come and take the $5,000 you've got stashed away to help settle the debt. Depending upon the state where you live, even your home, cars, and other personal belongings may be taken to settle these debts.

So we cannot warn strongly enough that before you enter into any large commitments, such as supplies on credit, long-term leases, and bank loans, that you consider carefully the liability and risk you're taking if things don't work out as planned.

CORPORATION. A corporation is a separate business entity with a life of its own. It is a much more complex organization than the partnership or proprietorship, and will require a lawyer's help to put together. But a closed corporation may be the best bet for a small family business because it limits the liability of the owners.

This limitation of liability is a crucial point. If a corporation signs a fifteen-year lease and the business goes bust, the owners of the corporation are not personally responsible for that lease. In the same manner, if the corporation takes out a loan and is unable to repay it, the creditors can't come to the individual owners' personal accounts and assets to get their money.

The problem may be, however, that no bank will lend the corporation money unless the owners also *personally* sign notes which make them personally liable. Then you're right back where you started. So incorporating your business won't provide a magic answer to all your money problems. It's simply an alternative that offers some safeguards the other legal forms lack. Check with a reliable lawyer before making a decision about the best possible legal form for your business.

START-UP MONEY. The first step in figuring out how much money you'll need to start your business is to add up all your initial expenses. Estimated costs should be obtained for each of the following items:

1. *Initial rent payment and security deposit*
2. *Deposits for utilities*
3. *Legal and other professional fees*
4. *Initial advertising*
5. *Licenses required by state or local governments, or both*
6. *Insurance*
7. *Fixtures and equipment*
8. *Installation of fixtures and equipment*
9. *Decorating and remodeling*
10. *Supplies*
11. *Initial cash*
12. *Initial inventory*

Figure 3-2. This is a New York State Business Certificate for "conducting business as partners." (Side one, below; side two, on right.) This certificate, and the one in Figure 1, are reproduced by permission of the publisher, Julius Blumberg, Inc., 80 Exchange Place, New York, N.Y. 10004. These forms are available from them.

X 74—Certificate of Conducting Business as Partners.
Individual — Corporation.

COPYRIGHT 1973 BY JULIUS BLUMBERG, INC., LAW BLANK PUBLISHERS
80 EXCHANGE PL. AT BROADWAY, N. Y. C. 10004

Business Certificate for Partners

The undersigned do hereby certify that they are conducting or transacting business as members of a partnership under the name or designation of

at

in the County of   , State of New York, and do further certify that the full names of all the persons conducting or transacting such partnership including the full names of all the partners with the residence address of each such person, and the age of any who may be infants, are as follows:

NAME Specify which are infants and state ages.   RESIDENCE

....

....

....

....

....

....

WE DO FURTHER CERTIFY that we are the successors in interest to

the person or persons heretofore using such name or names to carry on or conduct or transact business.

In Witness Whereof, We have this   day of   19   made and signed this certificate.

....

....

....

....

....

State of New York, County of   ss.:   INDIVIDUAL ACKNOWLEDGMENT

On this   day of   19   , before me personally appeared

to me known and known to me to be the individual   described in, and who executed the foregoing certificate, and   he   thereupon   duly acknowledged to me that   he   executed the same.

State of New York, County of   ss.:   CORPORATE ACKNOWLEDGMENT

On this   day of   19   , before me personally appeared

to me known, who being by me duly sworn, did depose and say, that   he resides in

that   he is the   of

the corporation described in and which executed the foregoing certificate; that   he knows the seal of said
corporation; that the seal affixed to said certificate is such corporate seal; that it was so affixed by order
of the Board of   of said corporation, and that   he signed h   name thereto
by like order.

INDEX No.

Certificate of Partners

*CONDUCTING BUSINESS UNDER
THE NAME OF*

State of New York, County of   ss.:   INDIVIDUAL ACKNOWLEDGMENT

On this   day of   19   , before me personally appeared

to me known and known to me to be the individual   described in, and who executed the foregoing
certificate, and   he   thereupon   duly acknowledged to me that   he   executed the same.

Your local gas, water, electric, and telephone companies will be able to tell you what *deposits* are required on their utilities.

Professional fees would include lawyers and accountants used to set up the legal structure of your business, to set up bookkeeping procedures, and to offer financial advice.

For more information on *advertising* costs, see Chapter 12.

A *license* has been judicially defined as a permit granted by the governmental power to a person, firm, or corporation to pursue some occupation or to carry on some business that is subject to regulation under the police power. Thus the lawmaking body of a given governmental unit prohibits some course of action, or some use or ownership of property, unless a license is obtained, and then attaches conditions or "regulations to the granting of such a license."

A license may or may not be accompanied by a fee, an examination, or a set of rules. Basically it's a tool of regulation to control a line of business having some particularly close relationship to public health, safety, or morals. It's also a method of municipal regulation.

There is various licensing by towns, villages, cities, counties, and states. In order to find out about and comply with the type of licenses your business might be subject to, check with your local and state governments.

The amount of *insurance* coverage you'll need will depend partly on the limitations of the lease you sign. For example, if you're responsible for the plate glass window, you'll need insurance for it. If your landlord is responsible, you won't need insurance on it. Insurance pertaining to employees, such as workmen's compensation, will be necessary only if you're going to have employees. This kind of insurance is discussed fully in Chapter 14.

Other essential kinds of insurance are: fire insurance, liability insurance, and automobile insurance. If you don't own the building your store is in, you'll want fire insurance to cover your inventory, fixtures, and supplies. The following are some important points to consider about fire insurance:

1. You can add other perils—such as windstorm, hail, smoke, explosion, vandalism, and malicious mischief—to your basic fire insurance policy at a relatively small additional cost.

2. Special protection (other than that provided in the standard fire policy) is needed to cover the loss by fire of accounts, bills, currency, deeds, evidences of debt, and money and securities.

3. If you conceal or misrepresent to the insurer any material fact or circumstance concerning your insurance, the policy may be voided.

4. If you increase the hazard of fire, such as renting part of your building to a dry-cleaning plant, the insurance company may suspend your coverage even for losses not originating from the increased hazard.

5. After a loss, you must use all reasonable means to protect the property from further loss or run the risk of having your coverage canceled.

6. To recover your loss, you must furnish within 60 days a complete

inventory of the damaged, destroyed, and undamaged property, showing in detail quantities, costs, actual cash value, and amount of loss claimed. (Note that you cannot claim the retail value of your inventory, only its wholesale cost to you.)

Liability insurance is necessary to cover such things as someone slipping on the ice in front of your store or having an accident inside your store. You should consider the following points about liability insurance:

1. Legal liability limits of $1 million are no longer considered high or unreasonable even for a small business.

2. Most liability policies require you to notify the insurer immediately after an incident on your property that might cause a future claim. This holds true no matter how unimportant the incident may seem at the time it happens.

3. Under certain conditions, your business may be subject to damage claims even from trespassers.

4. You may be legally liable for damages even in cases where you used "reasonable care."

If you require the use of any automobiles, trucks, or motorcycles in your business, you'll need automobile insurance for them. When an employee or a subcontractor uses his own car on your behalf, you can be legally liable even if you don't own a car or truck yourself. Check with your insurance agent to find out if you have proper automobile insurance coverage for your needs.

Business interruption insurance can be purchased to cover fixed expenses that would continue if a fire shut down your business, such as salaries, taxes, interest, depreciation, and utilities, as well as profits you would lose. You can also get coverage if fire or other peril closes down the business of a supplier or customer and this interrupts your business. You can even get coverage for the extra expenses you suffer if an insured peril, while not actually closing down your business, seriously disrupts it.

Crime insurance will protect you against loss of inventoried merchandise, money in a safe, and damage incurred during the burglary. It can also cover losses due to theft by employees. If you're in a high-risk area and can't get insurance through normal channels without paying excessive rates, you may be able to get help through the FAIR Plan or through the U. S. Department of Housing and Urban Development. Your state insurance commissioner can tell you where to get information about these plans.

You can purchase a special glass-insurance policy to cover all risk to plate-glass windows, glass signs, glass brick, glass doors, showcases, countertops, and insulated glass panels. You can get insurance to cover not only the glass itself, but also its lettering and ornamentation.

Fixtures and equipment include such items as counters; storage shelves and cabinets; display stands, shelves, and tables; cash registers; safe; window display fixtures; lighting; outside signs; and delivery equipment if needed. Determine what your needs are and what it will cost. You may be able to save money by building some of your own fixtures, or by purchasing used ones from a store that is going out of business. Be sure to include the costs for installation of these fixtures and of other possible labor costs in getting your store in order.

Decorating and remodeling costs will depend on the condition of the store when you get it, the extent of changes you want to make, and how much of your own labor will go into the remodeling. Obviously there's a large range of possible costs here depending on the amount and quality of materials you purchase, such as paneling and rugs, plus the labor costs.

Supplies include sales receipt pads, pens and pencils, paper bags and boxes, business cards, twine, tape, and price tags. A conservative supply of these goods will be all you'll need to start. Also, allow a small amount in petty cash for the purchase of small day-to-day items.

You should have a sum put aside for *initial cash*. Some of this will be needed in the cash register in small bills and coins for change. The rest should be deposited in your business checking account to use in paying bills as they come up. Later on you'll see how to make a Cash Needs Plan in order to estimate the amount you'll need on hand until the business starts to pay off.

Your *initial inventory* cost will depend basically on the amount of gross sales you expect to make and the rate of turnover of your stock. For example, if you expect $200,000 gross sales and your stock will turn over four times a year, you'll require an initial inventory of $200,000 divided by four, or $50,000 (retail value). To figure your costs, you'll need to know the approximate percentage cost of goods sold for your line of merchandise. If it's 60 percent, the cost of your $50,000 retail inventory will be 0.60 times $50,000, or $30,000. This $30,000 is the cash that you'd need to purchase an initial inventory.

Studies have been made of the various turnover rates and cost of goods sold for different lines of merchandise. The wholesalers who will supply you, the trade associations, your banker, and other business people will be able to help you with information about your type of store. If you're buying a going business, you'll of course want information from the previous owner on gross sales, cost of goods sold, and rate of inventory turnover.

The average retail markup is 100 percent of wholesale cost. But sales, markdowns, and lines of merchandise that have a variable markup all effect the overall cost of goods sold. While you may start out marking up your stock 100 percent, by the time you account for sales, damaged goods, and theft, you will no longer be making the same 100 percent. See Chapter 8 for more details on pricing.

Your sales volume will depend on the total amount of business in the area, the number and ability of competitors sharing that business, and your own capability to compete for the consumer's dollar. Get the opinions of other businessmen and your banker, and compare them with your independent estimate of what you want in order to make the effort worthwhile to you. If you want to earn $15,000 annual net profit, and you expect a 15 percent profit on sales for your line of merchandise after all costs and expenses, then yearly sales of $100,000 will be required ($15,000 divided by 0.15).

Don't be overly enthusiastic in your final estimate of sales. A new business usually grows slowly at the start. If you overestimate sales, you're likely to invest too much money in initial inventory and equipment and commit yourself to heavier operating expenses than your actual sales volume will justify.

PLANNING CASH NEEDS. Once you've totaled your start-up costs, the next thing you should do is plan your cash needs for a full year. There will be slow periods during the year, plus an initial growth period, for which you'll want to be adequately prepared. See Figure 3-3 for a sample Cash Needs Worksheet.

To use the worksheet, first fill in the expected sales for each month. Be realistic in your estimates, taking into consideration the seasonally slow months and the fact that it will take time to build a regular clientele.

Then fill in all your expected disbursements for each month. The amount you spend on stock purchases, of course, will depend on sales. As the inventory becomes depleted, you'll order more merchandise.

Now for each month in which your disbursements are larger than your sales, you'll need to have the balance in the form of extra cash in the bank. For example, if your expected sales for the first month, January, are $5,000, and your total disbursements will be $6,000, then you'll need to start with at least $1,000 extra cash in the bank. If your disbursements are $1,000 more than sales for each of the first five months, you'll need to start with $5,000 extra cash. It's always best to allow more than the minimum cash you'll need for unexpected expenses, or for fewer sales than anticipated.

GETTING THE CASH. Now that you've determined the total amount of cash you'll need to pay for initial start-up costs, plus the cost of operating your business until it has begun to make a profit, the next question is, Where do you get the money? The first source, of course, is your personal savings, or stocks and bonds. Then relatives, friends, or other individuals might be found who would want to invest their savings in your business. But before obtaining too large a portion of the money from outside sources such as these, remember that you should be careful to retain ownership of the major part of the business in order to have control over it. If you find two other partners who put in the same amount of money as you do, they'll probably want to share in the management decisions as well as the profit. Make certain these details are understood and worked out beforehand.

Other sources of money are commercial banks, trade credit from your suppliers, small loan companies, factoring companies, and commercial credit companies. See Chapter 19 for complete details on money sources for your business.

CASH NEEDS WORKSHEET

Jan Feb Mar Apr May Jun Jul Aug Sep Oct Nov Dec

1. Cash in bank (start of mo.)

2. Expected sales

3. Total cash & receipts
   (add 1 and 2)

4. Disbursements
   stock purchases
   salary expense (your own & others)
   advertising
   office supplies and postage
   utilities
   rent
   insurance payments
   delivery expenses
   taxes (sales, payroll)
   interest on borrowed money
   losses (theft, etc.)
   miscellaneous expenses

5. Cash balance at end of month
   (subtract 4 from 3)*

*This is your starting cash balance for next month.

Figure 3-3. This "Cash Needs Worksheet" will help you plan your cash needs for your first year of operation.

4 Franchise Opportunities

While you're still in the early planning stages, you should consider the possibility of a franchise. Essentially, it's a plan of distribution under which an individually owned business is operated as if it were a part of a large chain. There are all kinds of different arrangements, with variations in cost, control, and assistance. In this chapter we'll discuss the various types of franchise opportunities, and the pros and cons of buying a franchise rather than going into business from scratch by yourself.

HOW DOES IT WORK? Basically, the supplier (franchisor) gives the individual dealer (franchisee) the right to sell, distribute, or market the franchisor's product or service by using the franchisor's name, reputation, and selling techniques. Usually the contract gives the franchisee a specified, exclusive market area in which to operate. The franchisor may also offer assistance in building, remodeling, and finding a location; in bookkeeping; in employee selection and training; in management training; in the supply of your inventory needs; in national advertising; and in similar services.

In return for this, the franchisee usually pays a set one-time fee or a percentage of sales, or both. Sometimes he simply must buy his equipment or supplies from the franchisor. In any case, the bigger the package offered to the franchisee, the more he'll probably have to pay for it.

FRANCHISE EXAMPLES.* A Snap-On Tools franchise charges no fee or royalty (percentage of gross sales) to its franchisees. It uses them merely as distributors for its products. In other words, if you went into a Snap-On Tools franchise, you'd buy all your products from it for resale. They would provide you with some bookkeeping forms and general advice, also. As a Snap-On distributor, you'd operate out of a truck selling high-quality tools to such places as auto repair shops and industrial concerns. The truck would be your "store-on-wheels," eliminating rental cost for a retail location.

Another example is a typical major oil company service station. The company owns or leases the land and building, and supplies fuel and accessories to be sold. The franchisee puts up a small fraction of the

---

*Marketing Channels

total investment, sometimes nothing, but pays for the privilege of do-ing business at a fixed rate, e.g., 1½ cents to 2½ cents per gallon of gas sold.

An Avis dealer pays a one-time fee for the use of the Avis name. This is all he gets for his fee, but he pays no royalties to the parent com-pany. Tandy Leather Company and American Handicrafts require a fee plus a percentage of gross sales. They offer a lot of assistance in the setting up and management of the store, and supply all the products that are sold in it.

ADVANTAGES OF FRANCHISING. By buying a franchise in a na-tional chain of stores that for years has proven itself to be successful, you'll be taking advantage of the franchisor's experience. A lot of the trial and error will be eliminated, and a limited background on your part will be offset by the knowledge the franchisor will pass down to you.

Buying a franchise may allow you to get started with less money than you'd need to start your own business from scratch. You may be able to pay a down payment and pay off the rest of your fee over a number of years. The franchisor also may let you delay payment of royalties and purchases in order to help you through rough times until the business gets on sure footing. Your credit standing with other sup-pliers, credit associations, and banks also will be strengthened by hav-ing the name of a well-known, successful franchisor behind you.

Another advantage is that you will be starting out with a reputation already developed, rather than having to slowly build one. If the fran-chise has a well-respected, proven name in its field, people will assume your store will offer the same quality and service. Along with this, you'll share in any national and regional promotion and publicity the franchise gets. You'll probably receive help with your local advertising, too, plus information on competition, changing times, and so forth, to keep you up to date.

Another area where you'll probably get some assistance is in the design of your store and its displays and fixtures. Through its years of experience, the parent company will know the most effective way to display and set up your products and arrange your stock. Customers will be familiar with the name of your franchise and know that when they walk into any one of the establishments they'll find the same basic store layout and range of products. Even the colors used and the style of decorating will have become familiar to customers, drawing them to your place of business.

Since the whole chain of franchises represents a much larger pur-chaser than a single store, you may benefit from savings in purchases of products, equipment, supplies, advertising materials, and other bus-iness needs. If the buying is done centrally by the franchisor, you'll also have the benefit of their purchasing agent's experience and knowl-edge of suppliers, which will eliminate the necessity of your spending a lot of time tracking down the best supplier for each item you require.

Finally, you're likely to be trained in the mechanics of the particular business and guided in its day-to-day operation until you're proficient at the job. Often this management assistance will continue on a regular basis. Record-keeping procedures will be taught and accounting assistance will be offered to help you keep track of your business's progress.

So, does all of the above sound fantastic? Like you should run right out and sign the first franchise contract you can find? Well, hold on. Franchising has its disadvantages, too, so read further before you make the big decision.

DISADVANTAGES OF FRANCHISING. Naturally it will depend upon the type of franchise you get into and the degree of controls and rules imposed by the franchisor, but one of the basic disadvantages is that you're not truly "your own boss." If you're the type of person who wants to make all his own decisions, the franchise may not be for you. With it you may have to conform to standardized procedures which you don't think are important; handle specific products which you don't think are profitable in your store; and follow other policies which may benefit the chain as a whole, but not you in particular.

Another disadvantage is that you'll have to share your profits if the franchise you choose charges a royalty on a percentage of gross sales. The harder you work and sweat to make a larger income, the more you'll be paying to the franchisor. There's nothing basically unfair about this if the royalty is a reasonable percentage—one that still allows you to make a decent income. But often the fees and royalties are way out of proportion to the profit which can be made from the business. Along these same lines, you may find that rather than saving money by buying your supplies from the franchisor, you're paying more than you would if allowed to purchase them from an independent supplier.

The franchise contract itself may impose many inequities on the franchisee. Clauses in some contracts provide for unreasonably high sales quotas, mandatory working hours, cancellation or termination of the franchise for minor infringements, and restrictions on the franchisee in transferring his franchise or recovering his investment. The territory assigned may overlap that of another franchisee, or may be otherwise inequitable. And in all of this the power balance is in favor of the franchisor because he has devised the agreement and has experience in negotiating under it, plus he has greater financial resources to back him up. This puts the franchisee at a disadvantage.

Finally, while the franchisee will enjoy the good reputation a franchisor has established, he'll also suffer the burden of the franchisor's faults. If a customer receives poor service in one store, he's likely to expect the same poor service from every store in the chain. So you'll suffer for the bad as well as the good name that the chain has established. Not only might you suffer from the chain's reputation, but you're also subject to the results of its poor management. If the whole chain goes under, you may be swept along with it.

WHERE TO FIND FRANCHISE OPPORTUNITIES. Now that we've discussed the pros and cons of buying a franchise, let's see where you can find out about them. One place to look is in the classified section of a metropolitan newspaper, under the "Business Opportunities" section. Sometimes a franchisor runs a "blind ad," in which it does not give its name but lists a box number. This way it can screen out the "shoppers" from the "buyers."

Trade publications are another source. Look in the trade magazines for the line of merchandise that you plan to sell. There are even publications devoted strictly to franchising, such as *National Franchise Reports*, published by Continental Reports, of Denver, Colorado. In addition, franchise exhibitions are held in major cities, where you can meet franchisor representatives face-to-face and compare a number of offers at one time. See Chapter 8 for more information on trade magazines and trade shows.

There are franchise marketing agencies and franchise consultants that help prospective investors locate a profitable franchise. They'll also furnish information on the reputation and profitability of particular franchisors and their franchisees. Don't rule out leads from radio, television, direct mail, and suggestions from bankers, friends, business people, and product suppliers.

Once you've narrowed your interest to several possible franchises, write directly to the companies themselves for more details. Along with a list of questions and information you desire, send them a résumé about yourself and your interest in opening such a franchise. If possible, visit a nearby franchise and talk to the franchisee about his experiences with it. Get as much information as you can before making a final decision.

EVALUATING A FRANCHISE. A franchise can be purchased for as little as a few hundred dollars, as much as a quarter of a million dollars, and even more. Therefore, it's vital that you investigate and evaluate any opportunity thoroughly. You should be able to answer "yes" to the following questions before signing any franchise contract.

The Franchisor (Parent Company)

1. Has the franchisor been in business long enough (five years or more) to have established a good reputation?

2. Have you checked Better Business Bureaus, Chambers of Commerce, Dun & Bradstreet, or bankers to find out about the franchisor's business reputation and credit rating? Were the reputation and credit rating good?

3. Does the franchising firm appear to be financed adequately so it can carry out its stated plan of financial assistance and expansion?

4. Have you found out how many franchises are now operating?

5. Have you found out the "mortality" or failure rate among franchises? Is the failure rate small?

6. Have you checked with some franchisees and found that the franchisor has a reputation for honesty and fair dealing among those who currently hold franchises?

7. Has the franchisor shown you the certified figures indicating exact net profits of one or more going operations that you have personally checked?

8. Has the franchisor given you a sample contract to study and to use when consulting with your lawyer?

9. Will the franchisor assist you with:
   a) a management training program
   b) an employee training program
   c) a public relations program
   d) obtaining capital
   e) good credit terms
   f) merchandising ideas
   g) designing store layout and displays
   h) inventory control methods
   i) analyzing financial statements

10. Does the franchisor provide continuing assistance for franchises through supervisors who visit regularly?

11. Does the franchising firm have an experienced management that is highly trained?

12. Will the franchisor assist you in finding a good location for your business?

13. Has the franchising company investigated *you* carefully enough to assure itself that you can successfully operate one of its franchises at a profit both to it and to you?

14. Have you determined exactly what the franchisor can do for you that you cannot do for yourself?

The Product

1. Has the product been on the market long enough to gain good consumer acceptance?

2. Is it priced competitively?

3. Is it the type of item which the same consumer customarily buys more than once?

4. Is it an all-year seller rather than a seasonal one?

5. Is it a staple item in contrast to a fad?

6. Does it sell well elsewhere?

7. Would you buy it on its merits?

8. Will it be in greater demand five years from now?

9. Is it packaged attractively?

10. Does it stand up well in use?

11. Is it easy and safe to use?

12. Is it patented?

13. Does it comply with all applicable laws?

14. Is it manufactured under certain quality standards?

15. Is it backed up by a guarantee?

16. If the product or products must be purchased exclusively from the franchisor or a designated supplier, are the prices to you, as the franchisee, competitive?

The Contract

1. Does the franchise fee seem reasonable?

2. Do continuing royalties or percent of gross sales payment appear reasonable?

3. Is the total cash investment required, and the terms for financing the balance, satisfactory?

4. Does the cash investment include payment for fixtures and equipment?

5. If you'll be required to participate in company-sponsored promotion and publicity by contributing to an "advertising fund," will you have the right to veto any increase in contribution to this fund?

6. If the parent company's product is protected by patent or liability insurance, is the same protection extended to you?

7. Are you free to buy the amount of merchandise you believe you need, rather than being required to purchase a certain amount?

8. Can you return merchandise for credit?

9. Can you engage in other business activities?

10. If there's an annual sales quota, can you retain your franchise if it's not met?

11. Does the contract give you an exclusive territory for the length of the franchise?

12. Is your territory protected?

13. Is the franchise agreement renewable?

14. Can you terminate your agreement if for some reason you're not happy?

15. Is the franchisor prohibited from selling the franchise out from under you?

16. May you sell the business to whomever you please?

17. If you sell your franchise, will you be compensated for the good will you've built into the business?

18. Does the contract obligate the franchisor to give you continuing assistance after you've begun operating the business?

19. Are you permitted a choice in determining whether you'll sell any new products introduced by the franchisor after you've opened your business?

20. Is there anything about the franchise or its operation which would make you ineligible for special financial assistance or other benefits accorded to small business concerns by federal, state, or local governments?

21. Did you lawyer approve the franchise contract after he studied it paragraph by paragraph?

22. Is the contract free and clear of requirements that would call upon you to take any steps which are, according to your lawyer, unwise or illegal in your state, county, or city?

23. Does the contract cover *all* aspects of your agreement with the franchisor?

24. Does it really benefit both you and the franchisor?

Your Market

1. Are the territorial boundaries of your market completely, accurately, and understandably defined?

2. Have you made any study to determine whether the product or service you propose to sell has a market in your territory at the prices you'll have to charge?

3. Does the territory provide an adequate sales potential?

4. Will the population in your territory increase over the next five years?

5. Will the average per capita income in the territory remain the same or increase over the next five years?

6. Is existing competition not securely established in your territory?

YOU—The Franchisee

1. Do you know where you're going to get the capital you'll need?

2. Have you compared what it would take to start your own similar business with the price you must pay for the franchise?

3. Have you made a business plan working out what income from sales you can expect in the first six months? the first year? the second year? Have you made a forecast of expenses, including a regular salary for yourself?

4. Are you prepared to give up some independence of action to secure the advantages offered by the franchise?

5. Are you capable of accepting supervision, even though you'll presumably be your own boss?

6. Are you prepared to accept rules and regulations with which you may not agree?

7. Can you afford the period of training involved?

8. Are you ready to spend much or all of the remainder of your business life with this franchisor, offering his product to the public?

IT'S UP TO YOU. Once you've carefully evaluated the particular franchise into which you want to buy, and have examined your own needs—financially, professionally, and emotionally—you may decide that a franchise is indeed the best way for you to open your own retail store. Franchising can offer opportunities to the small business investor that would otherwise require vast amounts of money and managerial skills. A sound franchise opportunity may be an open door to your future success and happiness.

But whether you open your own business or buy into a franchise, the primary responsibility for the success or failure of the operation will still be yours. Your return will be directly related to the amount and effectiveness of your investment in time and money. The more skill and expertise with which you operate your business, the more chance for success. So read the rest of this book carefully, in addition to learning everything else you possibly can about your business from friends, business associates, business courses, books, trade journals, newspapers, and of course, your day-to-day experience with it.

5 Basic Business Steps

In this chapter we're going to cover some basic steps you should take before opening your shop. Most of these are necessary in any business—opening a business checking account; getting a sales tax certificate; ordering business cards and letterhead; designing purchase order blanks; and establishing credit. We'll also discuss two items specific to retail shops: sales slips and packing materials. By taking care of these basic steps early in the game, you won't be bothered by them later on when you'll be too busy with other things to give them the time they deserve.

CHECKING ACCOUNTS. Before making any purchases for your new business, you should open a business checking account. It's very important to keep your personal monies separate from your business monies, and to have cancelled checks to prove payment of business supplies and services. Business checks come in an assortment of sizes, and have provisions for various pieces of information to be written on them. For example, the Holy Cow Leather check shown in Figure 5-1 has a place in the upper left-hand corner to show the date and amount of the invoice or statement that is being paid. Ask your banker to show you the various types of business checks the bank offers.

Figure 5-1. Here is an example of what a business check might look like.

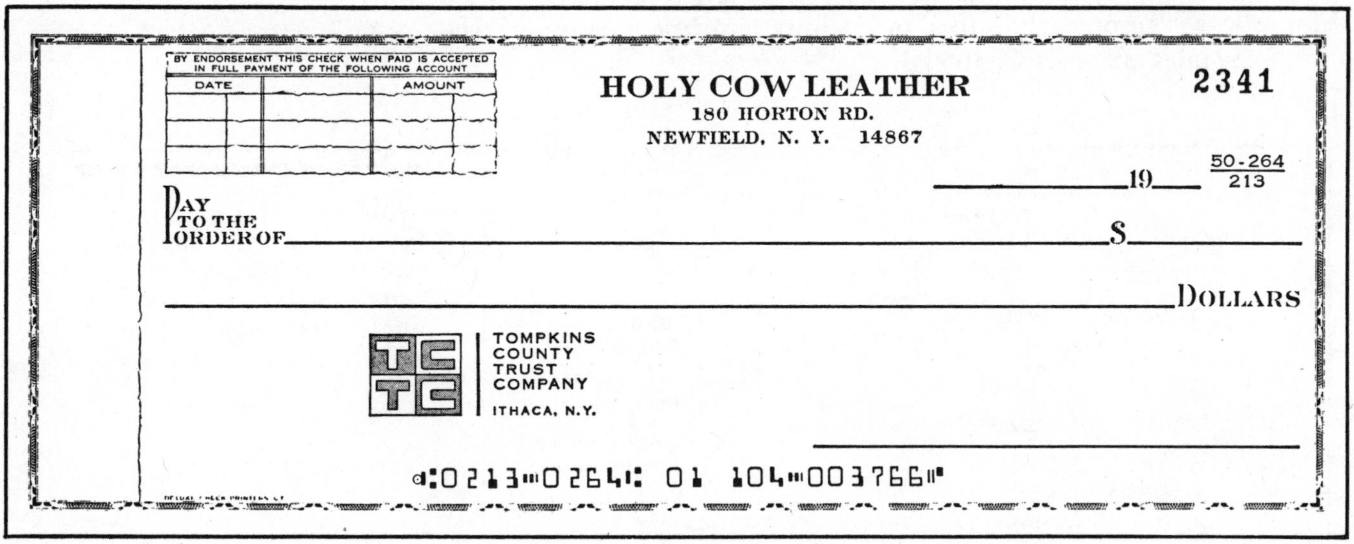

BY ENDORSEMENT THIS CHECK WHEN PAID IS ACCEPTED IN FULL PAYMENT OF THE FOLLOWING ACCOUNT

DATE		AMOUNT	

HOLY COW LEATHER
180 HORTON RD.
NEWFIELD, N. Y. 14867

2341

19__ 50-264/213

PAY TO THE ORDER OF ___ $___

___ DOLLARS

TOMPKINS COUNTY TRUST COMPANY
ITHACA, N.Y.

0213 0264 01 104 003766

If you're going to have several employees working for you, you may wish to open a separate payroll account for writing payroll checks. These checks are printed to show payroll information, and by keeping a separate payroll account, you'll have a record of all salary disbursements. This will mean, of course, that you'll have to be certain to deposit enough money in your payroll account before writing payroll checks.

SALES TAX CERTIFICATE. If you're located in a state which has a state sales tax, it'll be necessary for you to apply for a sales tax number. In Figure 5-2 you'll see a "Certificate of Authority," which was issued by New York State to Holy Cow Leather. Note the identification number in the upper left-hand corner.

A sales tax certificate has two purposes. First, it allows you to purchase goods in your state without paying a tax on them. This covers everything purchased for resale, or to use in making items for resale. As the owner of a retail shop, you'll be purchasing goods for resale. This certificate will allow you to buy them without paying the sales tax. Some suppliers may want you to fill in a "Resale Certificate," such as the one shown in Figure 5-3. If you're buying goods for resale, you'd check Box A on this form: "tangible personal property is for resale in its present form or as a component part of tangible personal property." In the box at the lower left-hand corner of the resale certificate, you'd list your identification number which was issued by your state on its Certificate of Authority.

Some items that are not tax exempt (at least in New York State) are office supplies, outer shipping cartons, and other items which are not actually resold or used in the manufacture of items to be resold. Check out your own state and local laws to learn which purchases are tax exempt and which are not.

The second purpose of getting a sales tax identification number is that you must use this number when making payments of sales taxes which you collect on goods sold in your store. If you live in a state that has a general sales tax, you must collect this tax on every item you sell unless it is exempt, such as food or clothing. For information on paying these sales taxes, see Chapter 9.

Figure 5-3. Here's an example of a Resale Certificate, which is required by some suppliers in New York State.

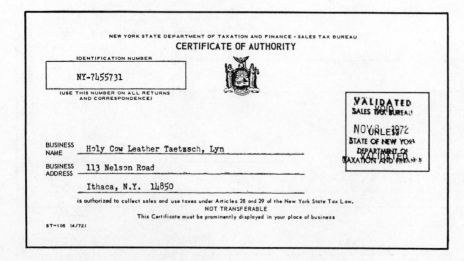

Figure 5-2. This Certificate of Authority was issued by New York State to Holy Cow Leather. Note the identification number in the upper left-hand corner.

ST-120 (1/72)   State of New York - Department of Taxation and Finance - Sales Tax Bureau

New York State and Local Sales and Use Tax

| To be completed by purchaser and given to and retained by vendor.

Read Instructions on back of this certificate. | **RESALE CERTIFICATE** | The vendor must collect the tax on a sale of taxable property or services unless the purchaser gives him a properly completed resale certificate or exemption certificate. |

NAME OF VENDOR	DATE
STREET ADDRESS	*Check Applicable Box* ☐ Single Purchase Certificate
CITY STATE ZIP CODE	☐ Blanket Certificate

The undersigned hereby certifies that he:

holds a valid Certificate of Authority to collect New York State and local sales and use tax.

is principally engaged in *(indicate nature of business)*..

....

intends that the *(check applicable box or boxes)*

A. ☐ tangible personal property is for resale in its present form or as a component part of tangible personal property.

B. ☐ tangible personal property is for use in performing taxable services where such property becomes a component part of the tangible personal property upon which the services are performed or will be actually transferred to the purchaser of the service in conjunction with the performance of the service.

C. ☐ service is for resale.

D. ☐ shipping cartons, containers and other packaging material are for resale. (see special information on shipping cartons, etc. on reverse side.)

understands that this certificate may not be used to purchase items or services which are not for resale and that he will pay the use tax on tangible personal property or services purchased pursuant to this certificate and subsequently used or consumed in a taxable manner, and that any erroneous or false use of this certificate will subject him to payment of tax plus penalties and interest.

SIGNATURE OF OWNER, PARTNER, OFFICER OF CORPORATION, ETC.	NAME OF PURCHASER
TITLE	STREET ADDRESS
Certificate of Authority Identification Number of Purchaser	CITY STATE ZIP CODE

PRINTED BY JULIUS BLUMBERG, INC., 80 EXCHANGE PLACE, NEW YORK

BUSINESS CARDS AND LETTERHEADS. Having business cards and letterheads printed professionalizes your business. It can also help communicate the desired image of your shop to actual and potential customers. Before having anything printed, decide what image you want to project to the public. If you can afford it, work with an advertising agency. The agency may be able to help you design a logo and choose a type face, colors, and so on, which will project the image you want people to have of your store. Once you come up with something good, use it on everything—on business cards, ads, letterheads, purchase orders, sales slips, and packaging materials. As more people see your logo your shop will become more familiar to the public.

Business cards can be done in plain black and white or in colors, with artwork, and even with three-dimensional effects in some of the new plastic materials. Besides your store name, address, and phone number, you may want to add such additional information as store hours, type of items sold, brand names sold, and anything special you want to get across. Figure 5-4 is an example of four different business cards. See your local printers for prices and samples.

A business letterhead can also be done in a variety of styles and colors. In Figure 5-5 you'll see a set consisting of coordinated letterhead, envelope, and business card which was designed by Hour Agency Inc., of Ithaca, New York. See Chapter 12 for more information on the value of ad agencies in your business. However, if you finally decide that you can't afford an agency, talk to your local printer about the various standard print styles and artwork that are available for letterhead designs.

Figure 5-5. The coordinated letterhead, envelope, and business card were done in black and white. Designed by Hour Agency, Inc., of Ithaca, N.Y.

Figure 5-4. The four cards illustrate some of the variety possible in designing business cards.

Waggin Tail

DOG GROOMING - ALL BREEDS
BY LISA BROWN - (201) 265-1838
320 BOULEVARD, NEW MILFORD, NEW JERSEY 07646

(914) BE 5-0034

BAGATELLE LEATHER DISCOUNT

Leathers and Suedes

NEW ROCHELLE MALL
NEW ROCHELLE, NEW YORK
LOWER LEVEL

467-1612

SHORT HILLS PERSONNEL AGENCY

350 MILLBURN AVENUE
MILLBURN, N. J. 07041

ROBERT S. KAY   THE "PERSONALIZED" SERVICE

Buy HERE!

CREDIT IS GOOD

Oriental Giftshop

INDIA BOUTIQUE
IMPORTERS OF GARMENTS
FROM INDIA, HONG KONG · COSTUME JEWELRY
INCENSES · INCENSE BURNERS · WATER PIPES
BRASSWARE · BEDSPREADS · HANDICRAFTS

2016 MORRIS AVE.
UNION, N. J. 07083

PHONE
(201) 964-4077

PURCHASE ORDER BLANKS. Because you'll be doing a lot of ordering of stock for your store, you'll need to get some purchase order forms to write up your orders on. Standard purchase order forms, such as the one shown in Figure 5-6, can be purchased in your local stationery or office supply store. There will be room at the top of the form for you to stamp in your name and address, or you may be able to order them with your name and address imprinted.

If you can't find what you want locally, purchase order sets can be bought in various sizes and styles by mail from the following companies:

PURCHASE ORDER

No. **3601**

Date_____19_____

For_____

To _____   Req. No._____

Address _____   How Ship_____

City _____   Date Required_____

Ship To _____   Terms_____

	QUANTITY		PLEASE SUPPLY ITEMS LISTED BELOW	PRICE	UNIT
	ORDERED	RECEIVED			
1					
2					
3					
4					
5					
6					

IMPORTANT

OUR ORDER NUMBER MUST APPEAR ON ALL INVOICES, PACKAGES, ETC.

PLEASE NOTIFY US IMMEDIATELY IF YOU ARE UNABLE TO SHIP COMPLETE ORDER BY DATE SPECIFIED.

Please Send   Copies Of Your Invoice With Original Bill Of Lading

Purchasing Agent

1S 144 Rediform®
Poly Pak (50 sets) 1P 144

ORIGINAL

Regent Standard Forms, Inc.
5117 Central Highway
Airport Industrial Park
Pennsauken, New Jersey 08109

Watts Business Forms, Inc.
Division of Lewis Business Forms, Inc.
Dillsburg, Pennsylvania 17019

New England Business Service, Inc.
Townsend, Massachusetts 01469

For a small extra charge, each can imprint your name and address on top of each form and number them consecutively. Write and ask for a free catalog.

You may wish to design your own purchase order and have it printed by a local printer. See Figure 5-7 for an example of a purchase order used by AR-TY, Inc. Note that there are places for the order number, the date, who to bill and ship to, the quantity, description, unit, and total price. In the bottom right-hand corner the supplier is told when the order is required, how to ship, what terms the agency will accept, and who the purchasing agent is. On the bottom left there's a section for specialized information the office will use. While it's more expensive to design and have your own purchase orders printed than to buy preprinted forms, you'll be able to customize them to your own specific requirements.

ESTABLISHING CREDIT. We've all heard the sad lament of the person who's paid cash for everything all his life. The first time he asks for credit he can't get it. Yet the person who has a record of buying things on time (credit) and borrowing money (loans), will be able to get credit if his payment record is good. So the best way to get credit is to have credit. But how do you do it when you're just starting out?

When you open a store as a proprietorship—that is, as the sole owner—your store's credit image will be based largely on your personal credit image. How much money do you have in checking and savings accounts? What are your assets? How many loans do you have outstanding and what are their amounts? What credit cards do you have? What property do you own? What is your yearly income? These are the kinds of questions that will be asked when you apply for credit. You may do this initially by applying for a loan to start your business. The bank will evaluate your personal credit situation, plus the soundness of your business plan.

If your business is a partnership, all partners will be personally evaluated. If you incorporate your business, it will probably be difficult to get a loan solely on the basis of your business assets, unless they're sizable. You may find it necessary to personally sign for loans, in which case your personal credit situation will be evaluated.

TERMS. When purchasing inventory and other supplies, certain terms are used to indicate payment. Prepaid means you pay for the goods

Figure 5-6. Here's an example of a Purchase Order form that can be purchased from your local stationer or paper supply store.

PURCHASE ORDER

AR-TY, INC.

I. B. U. E.

ROCKEFELLER BUILDING

CLEVELAND, OHIO 44113

(216) 781-5212

Holy Cow Leather
180 Horton Road
Newfield, New York 14867

No. M287

Date Aug. 23, 74 19____

BILL TO: International Brotherhood
of Union Employees
(Ar-ty, Inc.)
780 Rockefeller Bldg.
Cleveland, Ohio 44113

SHIP TO:

SAME

QUANTITY	PLEASE SUPPLY ITEMS LISTED BELOW	PRICE		UNIT
6 doz.	1 3/4" belt, assorted tooling & Colors	252	00	42.00dz

Office Use Only

Union Made _____

Imports _____

Rating _____

Invoice Paid _____

Date Required   Immediately, No B/O

How Ship   UPS

Terms   Net 30

Purchasing Agent   House

before they're shipped. COD stands for Cash On Delivery, and means that you pay for the goods when you pick up the package at the post office, or when the United Parcel Service (UPS) driver or a trucker leaves the package at your store. Most shippers will not accept checks on COD shipments until they get to know you—only cash, money orders, or certified checks (a certified check is a check which your bank certifies after making sure enough money is in your account to cover the amount of the check). There's also an extra charge on COD shipments. This charge goes to the carrier—post office, UPS, or trucker.

If a supplier wants to be absolutely risk-free, it will ship goods only on prepaid terms. COD is fairly safe, unless you refuse the goods. In this case the supplier has wasted the time needed to prepare your order and the shipping costs. If it ships COD and accepts a company check, it is taking the further risk that your check will not be good. If you're a new store, with no strong credit rating to back you up, and no experience of payment with your suppliers, they're not likely to want to take a chance on offering you open credit. You may have to start out by prepaying orders, or having them shipped COD. After the third or fourth shipment from a supplier, request a small amount of credit. Send the supplier the name of your bank and a list of local suppliers who do give you credit (if you have any). Gradually you should be able to gain more and more credit.

Open credit terms are usually based on 30-day payment, with discounts for early payment. Some examples are "3% 10, net 30," and "2% 10 E. O. M.," and "net 10 days."

"Net 10 days" means the total bill is payable within ten days after you receive the merchandise; there is no discount.

"3% 10, net 30" means the total bill is due within 30 days from receipt of the merchandise. If you pay the bill within ten days, however, you may deduct three percent of the total from your payment.

"2% 10 E. O. M." means that the bill is due the tenth of the month following shipment, and that two percent of the total may be deducted when it's paid. Usually, orders that are received after the twenty-fifth of the month are due on the tenth of the second following month. For example, if you receive merchandise on September 5, the payment will be due October 10. But if the merchandise arrives September 28, the payment will be due November 10.

"F. O. B. the factory" means you'll pay shipping charges and you'll be responsible for the goods after they leave the supplier. If goods are damaged or lost in transit, it's up to you to contact the shipper and bring a claim against them, if necessary. Sometimes a supplier will offer to pay shipping charges as an incentive to get you to buy.

CREDIT BUREAUS. There are many local and national credit bureaus or agencies that investigate the backgrounds of people and businesses, give them "credit ratings," write up credit reports, and advise their clients how much credit to offer a particular account. Dun & Bradstreet is one of the largest of such agencies. Because many suppliers rely on its reports and recommendations, it would be advisable for you to contact your nearest Dun & Bradstreet office and ask it to investigate your credit and give you a rating in its rating books. It will send you a form to fill out, and then one on which to update the information periodically. It may take time to build up the kind of credit rating that suppliers require for shipping on open terms, but it will be worthwhile.

When you place orders with suppliers, they'll often send your name and address to their own credit agency for investigation. When this happens you'll probably receive a form letter from that agency requesting such information as: names of banks where you have accounts, yearly sales, net worth, names of other suppliers, assets, and liabilities.

It will take time to develop a good credit rating. When you start out you may have to purchase most of your inventory on a prepaid or COD basis. Then you may be able to get a few suppliers to offer you limited credit (up to a stipulated dollar amount). By making all payments on time, or within the discount period, you'll gradually build up a good name and eventually be able to deal with all your suppliers on open terms.

If you ever find yourself in a situation where you must be late on a payment, call or write to your supplier and tell him about the situation. Let him know you're sorry about making the payment late, what the reasons are, that you have every intention of paying the bill, and when he can expect payment. Suppliers can be understanding about unexpected problems *if* you keep the lines of communication open. It's better to be a little late, by the way, than to write a check without funds behind it in the hopes that you'll be able to deposit enough money in a few days to make the check good. When you start doing this, your checks may travel faster than you think, or sales may not be as high as you expect, and pretty soon your checks will be bouncing. This kind of thing will only deteriorate the good relationship you've worked so hard to build with your suppliers. So if you find yourself in a tight cash situation, talk to your accountant or banker for advice on the best way to handle it. Perhaps a short-term loan from your bank will take you over the rough spot. Good planning and cash-flow analyses as discussed in Chapters 3, 16, and 17, however, can help you avoid this kind of problem.

SALES SLIPS. Unless you're selling food, liquor, or similar items where a cash register tape is all that's necessary for a customer receipt, sales slips will be required. You can get them in books containing duplicate copies and carbon paper from your local office supply or paper supply store. Figure 5-8 shows a typical sales slip. Note the room at the top where the name and address of the store can be stamped.

Register forms are a more elaborate form of the sales slip, and can be purchased from the three business form suppliers listed earlier in this chapter. These forms come with or without carbons, with duplicate or triplicate copies, and can be imprinted and consecutively numbered. There are registers (dispensers) for them available, too. Although more costly, you may wish to have customized sales slips printed with your logo and colors by your local printers.

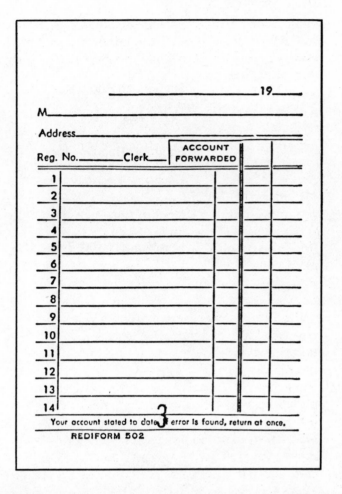

Figure 5-8. A simple sales slip, such as this example, can be purchased in books from your local stationery or paper supply store.

PACKAGING MATERIALS. Even if it's only plain, brown paper bags, you'll require some packaging materials to hold the goods your customers purchase. The type and variety of packaging materials will depend on the kind of items you sell. If you sell food you'll probably need strong, brown paper bags in several sizes. If you sell gifts, you'll probably want to have colorful bags of various sizes, and paper, boxes, and other materials for wrapping gifts.

Instead of ordering plain bags to use in your shop, consider having them imprinted with your store name and address. When the customer carries the bag around, it's a walking advertisement for your shop. If you give your customers shopping bags or plastic drawstring bags to carry their purchases, they'll be likely to save these bags and use them again. So packaging materials can be another form of promotion for your store.

To find places that sell packaging materials in your area, look in the yellow pages of your telephone directory under "Boxes," "Bags," "Paper," and "Packaging." A few suppliers are listed below for your convenience:

Federal Paper Board Co., Inc.
800 East Enterprise Dr.
Oak Brook, IL 60521

Boas Box Company
44 Greenfield Ave.
Ardmore, PA 19003

Sheboygan Paper Box Co.
Box 326
Sheboygan, WI 53081

Equitable Bag Co., Inc.
45-50 Van Dam St.
Long Island City, NY

Modern Arts Packaging
25 West 39th St.
New York, NY 10018

6 Consignment Shops

One way to open a small gift shop without a large investment in inventory is to take merchandise "on consignment." This means that you don't buy the merchandise outright, but only when it's sold. If it doesn't sell, you don't pay for it. Consignment shops are usually stocked with crafts from local or regional artisans. The shops provide an outlet for artwork and crafts that couldn't be easily distributed through a traditional method of marketing.

HOW THEY WORK. One of the first steps in starting a consignment shop is to talk to crafts people who would be interested in selling their wares through your shop. A good place to find them is at craft fairs. Look for notices in newspapers and college bulletins, and get your name on craft fair mailing lists. (See Figure 6-1 for a list of some craft fair promoters.) Other methods are to place a classified ad in your newspaper, or put notices on bulletin boards around your neighborhood. Art galleries often show crafts and might offer you a list of their exhibitors.

When you think you've got enough people to fill your shop with merchandise, the next step is to find a location. Some people begin by

Jinx Harris Shows, Inc.
RFD 1, Box 153 J
Auburn, N. H. 03032

L. Koerner
21 Fowler Ave., R-2
Peekskill, N. Y. 10566

American Crafts Expositions
P. O. Box 274
Farmington, Conn. 06032

The Crafts Report
1529 East 19th St.
Brooklyn, N. Y. 11230

Figure 6-1. Write to these craft fair promoters for information about craft fairs. The Crafts Report *is a newsletter of marketing, management, and money for crafts professionals.*

47

using part of their homes for the shop. This has the advantages of low overhead and convenience, but a possible disadvantage of poor location. As discussed in Chapter 2, location is crucial to the success of any retail store.

Once you've picked your location, your next task will be to decorate and to put up fixtures, lighting, and display cases. Since you'll be showing the wares of craftspeople and artists, you may well find some of them who have the expertise to help you design the shop and perhaps build your fixtures. Take advantage of whatever skills they offer. (See Chapter 7 for a thorough discussion of display.)

When your shop is ready, have all the craftspeople deliver their goods in time for the opening. Again, use their talents and knowledge of their own work to aid you in the proper arrangement of merchandise. Have each person sign a contract with you when they leave their goods.

CONSIGNMENT CONTRACT. There are several important items which should be covered by the consignment contract. The most obvious is the commission. Consignment commissions usually range from 20 to 33 1/3 percent. This percentage is based on the selling (retail) price of the item. For example, if a piece of pottery sells for $20, and the consignment commission is 30 percent, the shop would get 0.30 times $20 = $6, and the potter would get $14.

Another area which should be covered is liability for the merchandise while it's in your shop. Most consignment shops require the craftsperson to be responsible for his own things. This means if merchandise is stolen or destroyed by fire, the shop owner is not responsible for it. If you do decide to take responsibility for the consignment goods, be sure to get adequate insurance to cover them.

Another item of importance to cover in your contract is when craftspeople will pick up their merchandise, under what circumstances they can remove it, and under what circumstances you can remove it. For example, you don't want people coming in and removing half your stock without notice just because they want to show it at a fair. You want some guarantee that the merchandise will stay in your store for a definite period. You also don't want to get stuck storing people's unsalable goods for months or years.

Other issues to cover are dates when commissions will be paid, how prices of merchandise will be determined, standards for accepting work, and any other items special to your circumstances. Generally the craftsperson sets the prices of his own merchandise, although you may wish to recommend raising or lowering them, based on your experience in the shop.

In Figure 6-2 you'll find a sample consignment contract, which covers the basic points mentioned above. Note, also, there's a place for the craftsperson to list the items left on consignment, with the seg price of each item. The craftsperson should sign two copies of the contract, keeping one for himself.

Figure 6-2. Here's a sample Consignment Contract, which can be modified to fit your store's specific needs.

GIFT CREATIONS
111 Main Street
Ourtown, U.S.A.

CONSIGNMENT CONTRACT

I agree to leave the following items at GIFT CREATIONS at a 25% commission:

Item Name or Number	Retail Price
1. _____	_____
2. _____	_____
3. _____	_____
4. _____	_____
5. _____	_____
6. _____	_____
7. _____	_____
8. _____	_____
9. _____	_____
10. _____	_____

I understand that GIFT CREATIONS will make the final decision as to what articles are accepted for consignment and where they will be displayed in the shop. I agree to give GIFT CREATIONS 2 weeks notice before picking up my property, and to pick up items within 30 days after GIFT CREATIONS notifies me to do so. I leave all merchandise at my own risk.

GIFT CREATIONS agrees not to change any prices I have set without first getting my permission to do so. GIFT CREATIONS will send a check once a month for merchandise sold that month.

_____
M. Jones for GIFT CREATIONS

_____
(Consignor)

_____
street address

_____
city and state

_____
phone

CONSIGNMENT SHOP MARKETING. Since you'll be making a lower markup in a consignment shop than in the average retail store, it'll be even more important for you to keep costs down. Expensive advertising and promotional campaigns will probably be out of the question. But there's much that can be done.

First, make use of your local newspapers and radio stations by contacting them about the news story of your opening. Try to get on a local talk show to tell about your shop and the merchandise you'll be carrying. Encourage your featured craftspeople to have stories done about their work, of course mentioning that it can be purchased at *your* shop. Try to set up small displays of their work at local banks, with a card listing the name, address, and hours of your shop.

Another marketing aid is to offer courses in various crafts, perhaps featuring a particular craft each month or season. Make an arrangement with the craftsperson to split the fee in some equitable manner. You might offer the space, do the advertising, and enroll the students.

Utilize the talents of your craftspeople to create posters and direct mail pieces to advertise your shop. Attractive posters placed strategically around town will bring in customers. Direct mail pieces can be sent to regular customers or new prospects. See Chapter 12, on Promotion, for more information on direct mail.

Once your shop is open, you'll begin to see trends in what sells. Two or three craftspeople may actually bring in the major dollar volume. Some may sell nothing for weeks. If you give equal space to those crafts that don't sell, or sell very slowly, you'll be wasting display space and thereby losing money. You can't afford to display crafts that don't sell, and as soon as you figure out which ones don't, you'd better take them off your shelves.

This is why it's important to have a clause in your contract that allows you to make the final choice about what merchandise will be displayed, and to have craftspeople pick up unsold merchandise within a specific period. You'll also want to give the most favorable display space and the window display space to the most popular crafts.

In some cases objects won't sell because they're poorly done. Others won't sell because the market is saturated with similar items; the prospective customer can make the same thing himself too easily; or it's an odd size that doesn't fit very many people. These items can be weeded out before you even put them on your shelves. Sometimes an item is well done, attractive, and original—except the price is too high. When you have some experience you may be able to advise the craftsperson to lower his prices. Or you can feed back remarks from customers after the high-priced article sits on the shelf for awhile. Finally, if the craftsperson refuses to budge and the item still doesn't sell, remove it.

RECORD-KEEPING. To keep track of the consignment goods in your shop, and the money due craftspeople, it's necessary to set up a record-keeping system and use it daily. To begin, each article should be tagged with the retail price, craftsperson's name, and article number or name. See Figure 6-3 for sample tags. These should be attached as soon as the articles are brought in.

Figure 6-3. These sample tags give the price of the article, the craftsperson's name, and the product's name or number, or both.

When a consignment article is sold to a customer, a sales slip should be made out listing the date of sale, price, craftsperson's name, and article name or number. If desired, you may also write in the name of the customer and his address. (This is a good way to develop a customer mailing list.) A sample sales slip can be seen in Figure 6-4. It should be filled out in duplicate—the original for the customer, the copy for your records.

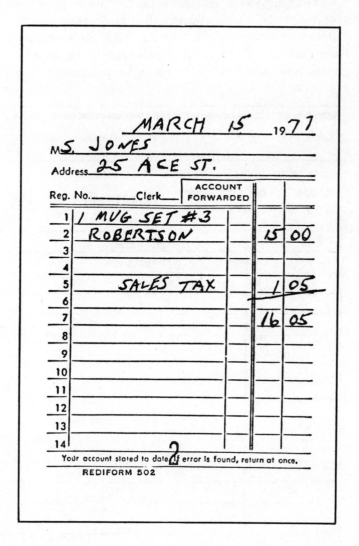

Figure 6-4. Fill out sales slips in duplicate and give a copy to your customers.

Two five-by-eight-inch card files should be kept on craftspeople—one to keep track of sales, the other to keep track of stock. A sample sales card is shown in Figure 6-5. Note there's a place to fill in the date of the sale, the article number or name, and the amount of the sale. At the end of each day use the sales slips from that day to get the sales information for these cards. Periodically (monthly is typical) add up all sales, compute and deduct your commission, and write a check to the craftsperson for the balance. Once you've written the check, mark that total "paid," as shown in Figure 6-6.

The stock card file should be set up as shown in Figure 6-7. The items are entered when the craftsperson brings in his things. Periodically, the goods sold should be subtracted to ascertain what stock is left. See Figure 6-8 for an example of how this should be done. In the beginning, do the stock cards once a week, or when you notice a particular craftsperson's inventory of crafts getting low. You may find it necessary to do the stock cards only once a month, but periodically the stock actually in the shop should be counted and matched against the figure on the card. Utilize the information on the cards to inform the craftspeople what's selling best and what articles you need the most.

Matching the information on the stock cards with the actual inventory will also show you whether any articles have been stolen or misplaced. Another function of the stock cards occurs when the craftsperson wants to remove his goods from your shop. The stock card will show how much of his merchandise you have.

Figure 6-6. Once you've written a check to the craftsperson, mark his or her card "Paid," as shown.

Figure 6-7. Here's an example of how you might set up your stock card file on each craftsperson.

Figure 6-8. Periodically update your stock card file, as shown.

Figure 6-5. Keep a sales card, such as this one, on each craftsperson.

JANE ROBERTSON 255 LEXINGTON	Phone: 572-9033	SALES CARD # 1
DATE	ITEM	PRICE
2/5	MUG SET #3	15.00
2/8	SUGAR BOWL	6.00

JANE ROBERTSON
255 LEXINGTON   PHONE: 572-9033   SALES CARD #1

DATE	ITEM	PRICE
2/5	MUG SET #3	15.00
2/8	SUGAR BOWL	6.00
2/9	BOWL #5	10.00
2/15	VASE #2	18.00
2/21	MUG SET #1	16.00
2/25	MILK PITCHER	8.00
	PAID 3/10/76	73.00

JANE ROBERTSON
255 LEXINGTON   PHONE: 572-9033   STOCK CARD #1

DATE	ITEM	In Stock	IN	OUT	TOTAL
2/5	MUG SETS		3		3
	SUGAR BOWL		1		1
	BOWLS		6		6
	VASES		2		2
	MILK PITCHER		1		1

JANE ROBERTSON
255 LEXINGTON   PHONE: 572-9033   STOCK CARD #1

DATE	ITEM	In Stock	IN	OUT	TOTAL
2/5	MUG SETS		3		3
	SUGAR BOWLS		1		1
	BOWLS		6		6
	VASES		2		2
	MILK PITCHER		1		1
2/30	MUG SETS	3		2	1
	SUGAR BOWL	1		1	—
	BOWLS	6		1	5
	VASES	2		1	1
	MILK PITCHER	1		1	—
3/10	MUG SETS	1	3		4
	BOWLS	5	—		5
	VASES	1	2		3
	PLATES		3		3

WHY START A CONSIGNMENT SHOP? Some people start consignment shops because they're looking for an outlet for their own crafts. This way their earnings include profits from the shop, plus what they make on the articles they produce themselves. Other people simply like handmade articles and enjoy providing an outlet for them. Still others do it so they can go into business with a very small investment.

The problem with consignment shops is that they're more likely to provide a hobby than an income. With the lower markup and the dependence on local craftspeople to supply all the shop's merchandise, there's simply less profit potential. You also have to cope with the possible capricious pricing and production practices of the craftspeople. You may be selling some craftsperson's leather like crazy for months, building up a solid reputation for it among your customers, then one day he walks in and tells you he's taking off for Colorado!

In addition, if you want to make a monetary success of your consignment shop, you'll still need a sizable investment to assure the best location, display, and promotional campaign. If you're going consignment strictly to save the cost of an initial inventory, I suggest you reconsider everything involved. If going consignment means you won't have top-notch stock with which to draw customers, it's not worth spending money on rent, fixtures, and so forth.

AN ALTERNATIVE. An alternative to a straight consignment shop is to combine consignment merchandise with regular goods. You might purchase your basic gift inventory outright from wholesalers, and supplement your stock with crafts on a consignment basis. This allows you to offer your customers more variety than either a straight retail or straight consignment shop.

7 Decor and Display

When planning the decor of your store, first decide what image you want to project. Do you want to present your store as a modern, exquisitely elegant, high-style women's wear shop? Or as an airy, light-filled, green-thumb, jungle of a plant shop? Whatever image you choose, your wall and floor coverings, color scheme, lighting, fixtures, signs, and displays should all be coordinated to put this image across.

THE BALCONY. This gift shop in Schenectady, New York, is located in an old house in a residential area. The proprietor, Mrs. Irwin, has created an intimate atmosphere of peace and trust. Shoppers are encouraged to browse in its various rooms, which are filled with soft music, floating incense, and flickering candles. Each room in the house is a separate boutique. For example, bath items are displayed in the bathroom. The furnishings in the rooms are for sale, but until sold are used as display fixtures. On a table in the women's room is a small card which states, "Please handle our merchandise—you'll like it." Ms. Irwin's customers come from afar to enjoy this unharried atmosphere, where they can leisurely browse among the many beautiful gift and craft items so tastefully displayed.

TRAFFIC. When planning the arrangement of various departments, or of types of merchandise, and the placement of fixtures in your store, first decide what the overall traffic pattern should be. First of all, your main aisle should be wide enough for customers to move rapidly through the store. Secondary aisles should allow enough room so customers can comfortably examine the merchandise on counters, shelves, and racks. If the merchandise will be tried on right there, more space will be needed.

In planning departments or the location of a particular type of merchandise, place the big drawers furthest from the entrance In like manner, place the slow movers or "on-sale" merchandise near the entrance or in another high-traffic area. Your slow moving and close-out items need to get the most exposure, so they require playing up in a prominent area.

Group your merchandise to move logically from one type of item to the next. For example, various women's accessories should be near each other, not at opposite ends of the store. Also plan your groupings to inspire impulse buying. Consider who your customer is and what type of merchandise he or she is likely to buy.

DISPLAY. Display is an invitation to your customers to buy. According to a survey by the National Retail Merchants Association, one out of four sales is made because of the way merchandise is presented in displays. A display makes its total effect through fixtures, lighting, color, props, arrangement, the merchandise for sale, coordination with other displays, and its location in your store. The trick is to make your displays decorative, yet functional, with enough variety and density to create interest without clutter.

On the practical side, you want a display that makes it easy for the customer to find what he wants. Each item should be shown according to its use. For example, if a wallet's use is not apparent when closed, display it open so the customer can see the credit card holder and the change pocket.

Coordinate items in a display. For example, if you have a mannequin wearing a dress in the dress department, add jewelry from the jewelry department, put a handbag from the handbag department over the arm, and shoes from the shoe department on the feet. Then put it against a decorative background and use props to make it really attractive. These could be as simple as a colored backdrop and posters and stuffed animals.

Show off the intrinsic qualities of your merchandise. Place shiny metal against the patina of wood, or put glassware on a glass shelf with light shining through to make it sparkle. Use the various merchandise in your store to set up coordinated displays that enhance each other; for example, fine tableware on a linen tablecloth.

To break up your store into separate areas for different types of merchandise, vary the lighting and coloring effects to create separate feelings or identities. Change the floor and ceiling heights, and vary the fixtures to match the moods you want to create.

SPECIAL DISPLAYS. When you have a slow mover, you've got to make a special effort to sell the item before marking it down. You can give it a glamorous name, and extra advertising. Then give it a special spot in your store—make it a part of the window display, place it on a rack or counter near the cash register, or put it in some other high-traffic area. See section on lighting feature displays, elsewhere in this chapter, for tips.

WINDOW DISPLAYS. Open window displays should take the entire store into account. This means you've got to consider not only the merchandise which is actually in the window, but how the whole store appears to the person looking in from outside.

All window displays should be changed often and follow the same image as the rest of the store. This is your first chance to grab a passerby and turn him or her into a customer, so you want your window to please the eye and entice the person to step inside. Use the same care that you would in your interior displays, coordinating merchandise, lighting, color, and props for total effect. See section on show window lighting elsewhere in this chapter.

SALESPEOPLE ARE DISPLAYS. What kind of image do your salespeople reflect? Do you have a man in a conservative suit selling mod clothes? Or a woman in dungarees selling wedding gowns? The point is, your salespeople are part of your store's image and should reflect it as closely as possible, within reasonable limits.

If you sell clothing, jewelry, shoes, or other items that can be worn, you might offer your salespeople a generous discount if they'll buy and wear merchandise from your store. You can also set up dress requirements that you feel are important to maintain your image. It may not be necessary for the salesperson to actually wear your merchandise, but simply to be fashionable and neat. For example, a salesman wearing dirty, ragged, scruffed-up sneakers wouldn't make a good impression selling shoes. So you might simply require him to wear any pair of shoes that are clean and in good condition.

FIXTURES. Fixtures include tables, racks, shelving units, and floor stands—anything which is used to hold and display merchandise. The type of fixture you choose will depend upon the kind of merchandise each is going to hold. You'll want fixtures that both stimulate buyer attention and at the same time make selling easy.

Choose a fixture which offers the best possible sales volume per square foot of display space. Because of the high costs of doing business these days, more density (amount of merchandise per square foot of space) is required to make a profit than in previous years.

Consider a fixture's storage space and restocking ease, also. Will you have to restock a number of sizes? Will you have to change the types of merchandise as the seasons change? Will the fixtures be flexible enough to handle this?

Fill the space in your store properly. Utilize every possible display area you can. For example, large pieces of merchandise can sit on the floor. Planters and mobiles can hang from the ceiling. And wall fixtures will hold twice the merchandise that a floor fixture will.

Consider your salespeople's needs in designing placement of fixtures. Put cash registers where a minimum amount of walking is necessary to get to them. Arrange open stock so salespeople can keep their eye on it. Also, be aware that you'll require more sales labor to sell merchandise that is in enclosed cases than you will with self-help tables and counters.

When you purchase merchandise, ask your supplier (wholesaler or manufacturer) what kind of fixtures he recommends to sell his products. He may even supply fixtures free or at low costs, such as a rack for displaying earrings if you buy a minimum quantity.

If you're handy and require a special kind of fixture to fit the specific motif of your store, you may want to make your own. For example, some western stores that want to capture the "olden days" appearance use wagon wheels, potbellied stoves, old church pews, and antique store counters to enhance this feeling in their shops. One even made an "outhouse" dressing room from barnwood and cut a crescent in the door.

In choosing your store fixtures (whether you buy or make them), cost will of course be a consideration. But bear in mind that a well-designed, efficient fixture, which gives maximum exposure of goods, is cheaper in the long run than a lower-priced fixture that does not allow effective display. The efficient fixture helps to bring the biggest sales turnover.

LIGHTING. Buying decisions are the result of seeing. Proper lighting can make common merchandise appear more attractive, while improper lighting can make the finest merchandise look dull. When planning your store lighting, first choose the overall room lighting, then the lights for displays, showcases, window displays, and so on. See Figure 7-1 for a chart showing the recommended illumination levels for various parts of a store.

RECOMMENDED ILLUMINATION LEVELS FOR STORES

The following lighting levels for various merchandising areas are recommended by the Illuminating Engineering Society.

	Footcandles*
Circulation areas	30
Merchandising areas	
Service	100
Self-service	200
Showcases and wall cases	
Service	200
Self-service	500
Feature displays	
Service	500
Self-service	1000
Fitting rooms	
Dressing area	50
Fitting area	200
Alteration rooms	
General	50
Pressing	150
Sewing	200
Show windows (daytime or nighttime)	
Main business districts	
General displays	200
Feature displays	1000
Secondary business districts or small towns	
General displays	100
Feature displays	500

*A footcandle equals the illumination falling on a surface 12 inches by 12 inches in size from a candle one foot away.

Figure 7-1. This chart shows the recommended illumination levels for various parts of a store. From "Pointers on Display Lighting," by Charles B. Elliott, Small Business Administration, Washington, D.C.

In room lighting, beware of bright overhead fixtures that distract a shopper's attention. Also watch out for overhead lamps that reflect into glass tops of showcases and make it difficult for customer to see. And be careful that your overhead lights don't cast shadows.

FLUORESCENT LAMPS. Fluorescent lamps come in various wattages and sizes, and are used for general room lighting, large-area display lighting, and for specialized lighting of shelves and showcases. A wide range of shades is available for enhancing the colors of merchandise and the atmosphere of the store.

Warm white and deluxe warm white fluorescent lamps create a "warm" atmosphere and blend well with incandescent lamps. Deluxe cool white fluorescent lamps produce a "cool" or neutral environment that blends with daylight. They give colors a bright, clear, natural appearance and flatter customers, employees, and store decor.

Colored fluorescent lamps—blue, green, cool green, gold, pink, and red—produce dramatic effects and colorful backgrounds. Ultraviolet fluorescent lamps can be used in areas of reduced general light level to create unusual "blacklight" displays.

If you use only fluorescent lighting in your store, however, the overall atmosphere may appear dull and uninteresting. You can avoid this impression by combining fluorescent and incandescent lighting.

INCANDESCENT LAMPS. Incandescent lamps have sharply defined beams which are easily directed to emphasize merchandise. They come in a great variety of types, shapes, beams, wattages, and colors.

Reflector lamps are most widely used for spotlighting interior displays. The reflectors are sealed-in and never need cleaning. They are available in 75, 100, 150, and 200 watts, and in spot and flood beams. For higher intensities, 300-watt lamps are available to produce spot, medium flood, and wide flood patterns.

Color spot lamps of 150 watts with integral dichroic-coated lenses produce concentrated beams of amber, green, blue, yellow, and red light. They can be used at increased distances from the merchandise.

Cool reflector lamps are good to reduce deterioration of perishable displays, fading or discoloration of merchandise, and to boost customer and clerk comfort. A dichroic coating on the built-in reflector of this lamp removes most of the heat from the light beam yet retains high light output and good beam control.

The tungsten-halogen lamp is ideal for lighting many window and wall displays because it's small yet powerful. A 250-watt lamp isn't much bigger than a cigarette and delivers a beam of intense light. It can be used in compact inexpensive fixtures. This type of lamp resists moisture and has a self-cleaning action.

The white metal halide lamp features beam control, long life, and excellent color rendition. It gives a natural daylight beam, which can be used for general lighting as well as display. Certain phosphor-coated mercury lamps that flatter red colors may also be used.

Because of their lower lamp efficiency, shorter life, and high heat load, incandescent lamps aren't recommended for general lighting where cost is an important factor.

USE DISPLAY LIGHTING TO INCREASE ATTRACTIVENESS.
Glassware, small appliances, and similar items look better when free of
distracting shadows. Shadows can be eliminated by individually lighting each open shelf. Use thin fluorescent lamps with shields and locate
them just under the front edge of each shelf. A more elaborate method
would be to use double translucent glass shelves. Between the two
panes of glass is a thin strip-type lighting fixture, which is shielded by
a narrow, semiopaque front pane. Use large area lighting fixtures plus
incandescent downlighting to avoid heavy shadows when displaying
major appliances and furniture.

Tinted light and lamps with a complete light energy spectrum can
help bring out the true colors of merchandise. Color tints can also be
used to create various atmospheres and dramatic displays. But make
sure the customer can examine the merchandise under a light that
brings out the true color of the item. For example, if lipstick is displayed under a romantic pink fluorescent light, the customer may pick
the wrong shade because she'll be wearing the lipstick under the incandescent lights of her home or in the sunlight.

Mirror lights should illuminate the figure from head to toe. The
angle of the light beam is critical, because the wrong angle will throw
long shadows that emphasize both wrinkled apparel and complexions.
Fluorescent lamps flatter skin tones, and incandescent or tungsten-
halogen lamps are good for lighting mirrors. The light on mirrors
should show the true color of merchandise, however, so the customer
won't be disappointed when he gets the garment home.

Bring out the sparkle and luster of hardware, toys, auto accessories,
highly polished silver, and other metalware by using a blend of general light and concentrated light sources (spotlights). Use concentrated
beams of high-brightness incandescent sources to add brilliant high-
lights to jewelry, gold and silver, or cut-glass.

Highlight the colors, patterns, and textures of rugs, carpets, uphols-
tery, heavy drapes, and bedspreads by using oblique directional lighting plus general low-intensity overhead lighting.

Heighten the appeal of men's wear by using a cool blend of fluorescent and incandescent, with fluorescent predominating. For women's
wear—especially the bright, cheerful colors and patterns—use Natural
White fluorescents blended with tungsten-halogen.

To bring out the tempting colors of meats, fruits, and vegetables, use
fluorescent lamps rich in red energy, including the deluxe cool white
type. Cool reflector incandescent lamps also may be used for direct type
lighting.

LIGHTING FEATURE DISPLAYS. Extra lighting is the key in building feature displays—ones that sell new items, remind customers of
products that carry a high markup, or help to move closeouts quickly.
These displays can be made with regular merchandising fixtures, such
as wall cases or tables. The secret is using light that is 2.0 to 2.5 times
stronger than the light you use on regular displays.

In using such spots of brightness, vary their location from time to
time. You want to give your customers something new to look at—to

attract their attention. This is all important in retailing. In fact, one chain of department stores gets 50 percent of its sales volume from special displays.

SHOW WINDOW LIGHTING. Display lighting in show windows of open-front stores is fairly simple. The lights in such windows (and in store interiors) should be strong enough to overcome the reflections from outside objects, such as parked cars and buildings. At night, additional light on overhead marquees and projecting cornices can make the window area look larger.

A high-level general illumination is the first requirement for a closed-back window. An exception would be when you want to achieve dramatic effects, perhaps by using some spotlights in a darkened window.

Massed window displays are often lighted with overhead fluorescents that are supplemented by closely spaced clear incandescent lamps. Metal halide lamps can also be used. They have a highly contrasting light with many of the best display features of a combination of fluorescent and incandescent systems. Certain phosphor coated mercury lamps, which flatter red colors, may also be used.

The more direct lighting of tungsten-halogen lamps is especially effective on high-style displays. Dichroic and other color filters may be used to produce colored light from lamps with white beams. Eye-catching mobile color effects can be provided by automatic dimming of switching cycles. If you center each principal display between two or more adjustable lights, you can achieve the extra illumination for emphasizing the display and for overcoming reflections on the glass.

Use miniature portable spotlights to accent small display areas, price cards, and specific items in a massed display. Compact footlights help relieve shadows near the bottom of verticle displays.

COLOR. In the most effective interior display, color—and the atmosphere that it helps to create—must be considered from the start. The colors of walls, overhead, and floor and fixtures must blend into the display or, if done effectively, contrast with it.

Usually strong contrasts and loud colors should be avoided. Bright shades get attention, but they also can overpower the merchandise. Background colors should suit and blend with the merchandise. For example, use beige, cream, and ivory, with brown.

If you sell ready-to-wear, fashion accessories, or home furnishings, you have a special need for careful color planning. Color enhances high-fashion and high-quality merchandise and is vital in motivating the shopper to buy. You may want to feature one color that has been dictated by the current fashion trend. Sometimes you may want to highlight a family of colors.

Color can give the illusion of greater size and can offset objectionable physical factors. For example, light shades add depth to a small space. Dark shadows help to make a large space look smaller. In general, soft pastel shades are popular for overall store decor, with darker colors favored for accents.

In experimenting with color, you'll want to keep in mind that higher-priced merchandise is best displayed in more refined color arrangements, such as blues, greens, grays, and blacks. And if you're handling low-priced bargain items, the vivid shades of yellow, orange, and red, in combinations with whites are best for achieving the right decorative touch.

Change the color schemes in your displays from bright to soft, wild to subtle, and so on. Use color to add drama and excitement to special displays or types of merchandise. And of course, let colors herald the seasons—purple and yellow for Easter, for example. Coordinate color with lighting to draw your customer's focus where you want it.

SIGNS AND TAGS. Use outer signs to identify your store and attract people to it. Make sure your signs are large enough, well-lighted, and of professional quality. Once again, consider the image you're trying to project and use the lettering style, colors, and design or illustration that will reflect this image.

Small signs and tags do the talking for a display inside your store. They give significant details about the article, such as size, style, color, and price. Make these signs informative, compact, and as professional looking as possible. There are sign and price tag machines available for making your own.

Change your signs often to keep them timely. Replace dirty or marred signs and tags, and check periodically to make sure tags are attached to the proper merchandise. Attach tags so the customer can easily see the price, size, and other pertinent information about an item.

Try to make your signs sell customer benefits, rather than things. Signs for clothes, for example, should sell the neat appearance, style, and attractiveness, rather than the utility. For furniture, they should sell home life and happiness, rather than just lamps and tables.

PROFESSIONAL HELP. If you can afford it, professional help in planning your store decor, lighting, fixtures, and displays can be of great service. Advertising agencies, contractors, and freelance display experts may be able to help in the planning and purchasing for a total store design.

Lighting assistance may be available from electrical utilities, contractors, and lighting equipment manufacturers. Several lamp companies publish brochures, which key their production features into specific merchandising areas. Some lighting distributors often employ personnel who can help in upgrading or planning store lighting.

Suppliers of consumer goods generally offer display assistance, materials, props, and fixtures. Sometimes suppliers will even give advice on specific display needs and techniques, especially when doing special promotions or when installing displays in your store.

Keep in mind also, that manufacturer-supplied displays are the result of talented design and engineering. Color is expertly chosen to set off the merchandise. Such displays are available free or at limited cost to retailers.

Still another source for assistance is the local or nearby supplier of display materials and fixtures. He or his representative can often give you ideas and supply you with the latest materials—items ranging from inexpensive artificial flowers to specially built displays. In large cities these companies often maintain showrooms in which you can look for ideas and materials. See Figure 7-2 for a list of suppliers.

FIXTURE SUPPLIERS

Berg Company
1911 S. Stoughton Rd.
Madison, Wisc. 53701
(608) 222-5566
(local rep is available for consultation service)

The Baker Store Equipment Co.
18976 Cranwood Parkway
Cleveland, Ohio 44128
(216) 475-5900
(total store planning)

Abstracta Structures, Inc.
101 Park Ave.
New York, N.Y. 10017
(212) 532-3710
(ask for 13mm *Abstracta* catalog)

The Columbus Show Case Co.
849 W. Fifth Ave.
Columbus, Ohio 43212

Figure 7-2. Ask these companies to send you catalogs and related information on their fixtures and other display materials.

8 Purchasing

This chapter will cover your basic function as a buyer for your store. Where can you get product information? How much stock should you purchase? When should you reorder? How should you request orders to be shipped? How can you take advantage of various selling seasons? Read on to find the answers to these questions.

WHO ARE YOUR POTENTIAL CUSTOMERS? There's no point in purchasing merchandise your customers won't want, so your first step is to determine who your customers are and what their needs are. Do you expect to cater to low-income families, teenagers, or high-income professionals? Will your niche be low-cost work clothes, one-of-a-kind gift originals, far-out boutique, high-fashion coats, home-remodeling supplies for do-it-yourselfers, or something else?

You need to determine not only what type of product line you'll carry—such as gifts, hardware, and clothes—but also the price lines and specialty areas within that broad framework. It's better to carry a full selection of a limited product line than a sparse selection in a complete line. If a customer comes in expecting your store to carry a particular item, and you don't have it, he will go elsewhere. If it happens enough times, you'll probably lose that customer. There's more chance of this happening if you offer a wide variety of product lines sparsely stocked, than if you concentrate on a narrow area which you can completely cover.

For example, you may want to open a shoe store. You could open a family shoe store and try to stock shoes for children, teenagers, men, and women. If your store space and capital were small, you wouldn't be able to stock a full assortment of styles and sizes for each type of customer. If you took the same capital and store space and used it to stock one type of shoe—children's shoes, perhaps—you'd be able to offer more styles, brands, and sizes. Since customers would only come to your store to buy children's shoes, they wouldn't expect you to carry men's shoes or women's shoes. The result would be fewer disappointed customers or, looking at it positively, more satisfied customers.

HOW TO FIND SUPPLIERS. Once you've carefully chosen your product area, the next step is to find suppliers of this merchandise. The best places to find them are at trade shows and in trade magazines. Once you're in business for awhile, they'll also be making the effort to find you, and you'll be contacted by salespeople from various sources. As mentioned earlier in this book, working for a retail shop similar to the one you plan to open can be very helpful. You'll get firsthand experience seeing what brands sell and which suppliers are the most reliable. This is one way to develop a list of potential suppliers for your store.

To find the names of trade magazines for your product lines, look them up in the *Guide to Periodical Literature* in your public or school library. Also ask the owners of shops with similar product lines what magazines they read. Subscriptions to many of these magazines are free to retail shop owners. Manufacturers and wholesalers that advertise in them want them to reach as many retail outlets, or potential buyers of their merchandise, as possible.

Besides offering ads by suppliers, trade magazines often offer news about the industry, merchandising hints, articles on retail management, information on new products, stories about successful retail shops, display information, and announcements of upcoming trade shows. This is why you'll want to subscribe to all the trade magazines that relate to your kind of store.

When you leaf through the trade magazines, make a list of all the suppliers who might have the kind of merchandise you'll need in your shop. Write each one a letter, on your store letterhead, asking for catalogs and other information. See Figure 8-1 for an example of how your letter might look. Make sure to ask for information on prices, discounts, minimum orders, delivery schedules, and credit requirements.

TRADE SHOWS. At trade shows, groups of related suppliers rent booths to display their merchandise to retail buyers. There are regional trade shows, national trade shows, and international trade shows. You'll probably have to go to New York, Chicago, or Los Angeles to see a national trade show. International trade shows are held all over the world and regional shows are held in all sections of the country.

While admission to these shows is usually free to buyers, there will be expenses for traveling, food, and possibly lodging. You may wish to try a regional show first to get a feel for what the shows are all about. Be sure to wear comfortable shoes, because you'll be doing a lot of walking and standing.

Some national shows have over 1,000 exhibitors, which means that even if you manage to see them all it's certainly not going to be easy to keep them sorted in your memory. Most shows last two to five days, which allows time for initial screening of all exhibits, plus returns to those of interest. On your first trip around, jot down the booth numbers of all those suppliers you think you might be interested in. Most exhibitors give away free literature and even samples, which you can pick up along the way.

The booths will be run by trained salespeople who will be happy to talk with you about their products. If possible, come prepared with a

aged or late, it may be the carrier's fault. And you're the one who will suffer lost time and money because a shipment is late or damaged. You'll probably pay for shipping costs, too, so you have an important interest in how your merchandise gets to you. Therefore, you should exert every influence you can on the supplier to have goods shipped in the cheapest, most efficient manner.

There are four ways to have your goods shipped: parcel post, United Parcel Service (UPS), motor freight (truck), and rail freight (train). Parcel post and UPS are used for small shipments weighing under 100 pounds. Of the two, we recommend UPS as it is generally cheaper and more efficient. Packages are automatically insured for $100 at no extra charge, and every shipment can be traced. Parcel post can only be traced if it's insured, and there is an extra charge for all insurance. UPS also picks up and delivers packages, although there is no Saturday service.

Motor and rail freight are used for large shipments (over 100 pounds). A bill of lading must be filled out by the shipper, listing the classification of goods to be shipped. Since the rates are based on the classification used, be sure to find out from the carrier what the proper classification is for the goods you're ordering, and make sure your supplier uses that classification.

Once you're in business for awhile you may notice that some trucking companies give you better service than others. When you do, request your supplier to ship via these companies. For example, I had experience with one local trucker who used to keep my merchandise in his warehouse for several days because he only made trips into my town once a week. Other truckers in the area came in daily. So naturally we requested our suppliers not to use the weekly trucker. It isn't always possible to get the carrier you want, since one company will pick up the merchandise, take it part of the way, and turn it over to another carrier for final delivery. But when you get to know the various routing methods of the carriers, you can have some influence over what happens.

FILLING OUT A PURCHASE ORDER. Once you know what you want to order, who you want to order it from, and when you want it delivered, you're ready to write up a Purchase Order. Even if you do your ordering by phone, all orders should be confirmed with a written Purchase Order. This will keep your records straight and help the supplier fill your orders properly.

See Figure 8-2 for a sample Purchase Order. As much detail about the merchandise as possible should be listed, *i.e.*, style, number, description, size, and color. Be sure to fill in the price. Otherwise, if there has been a price change, the supplier can ship you the merchandise without notification of the new price. It's important to fill in the date you want the goods shipped and what the deadline is for receipt. If you list a deadline, then you can justifiably refuse shipments that come too late.

The Purchase Order is also the place to list your preferred carrier, packaging instructions, whether or not you'll accept partial shipments

PURCHASE ORDER

GROVER'S GIFTS
100 Main St.
Someplace, U.S.A. 11111

No. 3603

Date *March 15* 19*76*

For _____

To _____ *Charm Corp.* _____

Req. No. _____

Address _____ *1011 State St.* _____

How Ship _____ *UPS* _____

City _____ *Hope, Calif. 90000* _____

Date Required *May 20, 1976*

Ship To *Above* _____

Terms *Net 30*

	QUANTITY				
	ORDERED	RECEIVED	PLEASE SUPPLY ITEMS LISTED BELOW	PRICE	UNIT
1	10 DZ		Style 52 Gift Paks Asst'd Colors	30 00	3/DZ
2	3 DZ		Style 11 Crazy-Shirt		
3			1 Dz each Sizes S, M, L	36 00	12/DZ
4					
5			NOTE: DO NOT SHIP LATER THAN MAY 25, 1976		
6					

IMPORTANT

OUR ORDER NUMBER MUST APPEAR ON ALL INVOICES, PACKAGES, ETC.
PLEASE NOTIFY US IMMEDIATELY IF YOU ARE UNABLE TO SHIP COMPLETE ORDER BY DATE SPECIFIED.

Please Send   Copies Of Your Invoice With Original Bill Of Lading

Alar Jones

Purchasing Agent

1S 144 Rediform
Poly Pak (50 sets) 1P 144

ORIGINAL

or substitutions, and possibly credit information. The problem with partial shipments is increased paperwork and higher freight costs. If you're ordering from a new supplier, you may want to list your credit references or state that COD shipments are acceptable.

REORDERING. Once your store is in operation, you'll have to decide what and when to reorder. The inventory control discussed in Chapter 9 will of course be a valuable tool in this task. The obvious goal of reordering is to have a fast-selling product come in just before its stock is depleted. And, of course, items which do not sell, or sell very slowly, or sell only after being marked-down considerably, should not be reordered.

Another important tool for making buying decisions is customer feedback. Keep track of items the customers ask for that you don't stock. If several customers ask for the same item, or brand, or size, or color, perhaps you should order it.

You'll also have to keep track of changes in styles and tastes in order

Figure 8-2. Here's an example of a Purchase Order filled out by a typical retail store.

to keep up with trends. Read trade journals, fashion magazines, and newspapers to become aware of new and passing fads, consumer tastes, new products, and the state of the economy. When considering a new product, however, keep in mind not only the needs of your present customers, but how this product might attract new customers.

Use your sales records to plan future buying. But add-in an additional margin for increased sales. In other words, if your record shows you sold $75,000 during the previous year's Christmas season, plan $80,000 or $90,000 sales for the next Christmas season. Plan for slow but steady growth in your business.

SEASONS. Every retail store has seasonal selling patterns. Clothing stores will have a certain season for selling bathing suits, another for sweaters. While hardware may sell all year round, gardening tools and seeds will sell better in the spring. Swimming pool maintenance supplies will sell best in the summer.

Pre-Christmas is a busy selling season for any kind of merchandise that can be purchased as a gift, and this includes practically everything. Other gift-giving times are June (weddings and graduations), Mother's Day, Father's Day, and St. Valentine's Day. It's important to plan for these peak selling times so you don't run out of stock in the middle of them, or end up with too much stock left when they're over.

When planning purchases for a particular season, take into consideration these factors: sales estimates for that season, the type of merchandise which will sell best during it, the required delivery time (with extra time allotted during peak seasons), and the expected percentage of cancellations. Every supplier may not always come through with your order, so you'll have to plan for this possibility.

At the end of each season put seasonal merchandise on sale in order to make room for the next season's merchandise. Once you've gone through a particular season, use this experience and the sales records to plan for the following year. Be sure to coordinate advance advertising, extra help, and longer selling hours for busy seasons.

9 Behind the Scenes

This chapter covers a variety of behind-the-scenes work that is necessary in the operation of a retail store. This includes pricing, inventory systems, receiving merchandise, paying invoices, and sales records. While these tasks may sound like a lot of work, your effort in these areas will be well rewarded because they'll directly affect the profits of your store.

PRICING. The average beginning retail markup is 100 percent of wholesale price (or 50 percent of retail price). This means if you purchase an item for $5 from your wholesaler, you'll tag it with a $10 retail price. As we continue to talk about markup in this chapter, we'll be referring to a percentage of the retail price.

Some stores use higher beginning markups: 55 or 60 percent, or more. Others use lower markups. Some product lines are normally sold by all stores at a particular markup, so, to be competitive, your markup will have to be about the same. Usually your supplier will be able to advise you what the standard markup is for his line of products. Some suppliers even preticket merchandise with the retail price. This is especially true when it's a brand of nationally advertised products that have been promoted by the manufacturer at a particular price.

To use markup percentages which will benefit your particular store, you'll have to customize your pricing according to your individual needs. Your prices should be based on these four factors:

1. The price *your* customers will be willing to pay for the item.
2. The particular additional costs of that article, such as freight, advertising, and overhead.
3. The cost of the item itself.
4. The profit needed to be made.

Put a higher markup on items that take more effort and cost more to sell, or on items that, from your customers' point of view, are worth the higher markup.

When figuring markups, you don't need to make the same profit on every item, but the overall profit mix should average out to what you need. When figuring initial markups, take into consideration the marking down you'll be doing on some items later on. In other words, if your original average markup is 50 percent, your gross margin will be less than 50 percent after some items have been marked down for sales. You may end up with an average ending gross margin of 40 percent. This is okay if the 40 percent margin will provide you with enough profit, but make sure you've considered this factor in your original pricing.

MARK-DOWNS. The purpose of marking-down a price is to help a slow-moving item move faster. Or to use the item as a "loss-leader" to get people into your store to buy other items. Marking down should never be done frivolously. Every effort should be made to first sell the item through other methods, such as special display or promotion.

Once a decision is made to mark-down items and have a "sale," however, the first mark-down should be enough to move at least 60 percent of the merchandise. This is especially true if you're trying to move out seasonal goods at the end of their season. You want to get rid of them as quickly as possible to make room for the next season's merchandise. But don't make your first mark-down so great that 100 percent of the merchandise is scooped up in the first day of your sale. This would indicate you're taking too much of a loss. You may have to take several mark-downs before the total stock is depleted.

When you mark down a nonseasonal item because of a special sale, be sure to mark the price back up on all unsold items after the sale period. Every item sold at a marked-down price when it didn't have to be means money out of your pocket. The customer who walks in after the sale is over doesn't expect to get the item on sale. He expects to pay the original price. So get your full markup whenever possible. By the same token, merchandise that sits eternally on your shelves isn't making you any money either, so don't be afraid to mark down prices when necessary.

INVENTORY SYSTEMS. The purpose of an inventory system is to tell you what you have in stock, how fast it's moving, and when to reorder. Depending on the size and type of shop you open, more or less paperwork will be necessary. In some small shops with limited product lines, you can tell when to reorder by a periodical checking of your shelves. Since every shop should have its display units stocked and checked daily, this would be a good time to jot down any items which are getting low.

If you can't keep track of your stock visually, a stock-control sheet will be useful. First take a complete physical inventory of all the stock in your store. This should be done initially and then periodically by every retail shop, no matter what size. See Figure 9-1 for an example of a typical inventory sheet and how it might be filled out. These forms can be purchased at your local office supply store. Note that different sizes and colors are listed separately on the sheet.

Under "price" you can list the wholesale or retail price of each item,

Figure 9-1. Here's a sample inventory sheet for use in taking a physical inventory of your stock.

CHECK	QUANTITY	DESCRIPTION	√	PRICE	UNIT			EXTENSIONS							
	24	Panties, Style 43		23	ea				5	52					
		6 Size 2, 3 Size 3, 5 Size 4,													
		8 Size 5, 2 Size 7													
	15	Stretch Hats, Style 202		1	09	ea			1	6	35				
		2 green, 3 red, 1 blue, 1 pink													
		3 yellow, 2 white, 3 black													

INVENTORY June 30 1976 Folio

Sheet No. 1
Department Children's Clothes
Called by
Entered by L. Smith
Location
Priced by
Extended by
Examined by

Amount Forward

as long as you're consistent. If you use wholesale prices, you have to decide whether to use the actual price you paid for that particular item on the shelf, or the current price of similar merchandise at the time the inventory is taken. Once again, be consistent. Using the retail price may be more useful to you in the management of your store, but you'll have to list the wholesale value of your year-end inventory at income tax time. See Chapter 18 for more information on this.

Once you've taken a physical inventory, make up a stock control sheet for each product, similar to the one shown in Figure 9-2. Use information from sales slips, sales records, or a visual count so you can periodically update your stock control sheet as shown in Figure 9-3. Note that in the example the sheet has been updated every week. After awhile, the stock control sheet will tell you how fast a particular item is moving. In our example, an average of ten scarves were sold each week. It takes three weeks from the date of ordering for these scarves to be delivered, so as soon as the supply gets down to 30, the scarves should be reordered. This was figured out by multiplying the three weeks reorder time by the 10 scarves sold per week. Having a stock of 30 will take care of three weeks' sales.

Figure 9-3. (Right) *In this example, the Stock Control Sheet has been updated weekly. Whenever the supply of scarves got close to 30, a new supply was ordered.*

STOCK CONTROL SHEET

Item: _Silk Multicolor Scarves, Style #6-4_

Delivery Period: _3 Weeks_

DATE	SALES	ON FLOOR	IN STOCKROOM	ON ORDER
2/6		15	36	

STOCK CONTROL SHEET

Item: *Silk multicolor Scarves, Style # G-4*

Delivery Period: *3 weeks*

DATE	SALES	ON FLOOR	IN STOCKROOM	ON ORDER
2/6		15	36	
2/13	9	18	24	
2/20	11	19	12	60
2/27	10	15	66	
3/6	10	17	54	
3/13	12	17	42	
3/20	8	15	36	
3/27	10	17	24	
4/3	9	20	12	60

Figure 9-2. (Left) *Set up your Stock Control Sheet as shown in this example.*

Make up a stock control sheet to fit your store's needs. If you carry assortments of colors and sizes, you may need to keep track of your stock by size and color to make sure you reorder the proper assortment. Before setting up any record-keeping systems, ask yourself what information you'll need to know in order to reorder effectively—then set up a system which will give you this information. Don't make up such complex, time consuming systems that you'll never have the time to keep them up-to-date. A system is worthless if it's not utilized efficiently.

RECEIVING MERCHANDISE. When merchandise comes into your store, it should be processed quickly and efficiently. Most packages will come with a packing slip attached to the outside, or just inside, the carton. The packing list tells you what is in the carton, or at least what's supposed to be in the carton. See Figure 9-4 for an example of what a packing list looks like. It's usually a carbon copy of the invoice, but without the prices listed.

When a package arrives, bring it into the stockroom for processing. Never open packages in the store itself during open hours. It looks messy, and stopping to wait on customers will interfere with the efficient processing of the merchandise. If you're in the store alone, wait until after hours to open the package.

When you do open the carton, check the contents carefully against the packing list. Make note of any missing or damaged articles. Then get out your original Purchase Order to check that everything you ordered has been delivered. Staple the papers together so they'll be ready when the invoice arrives from the manufacturer or distributor. Put the stock away and make a note of it on your stock control sheet.

PAYING INVOICES. Most suppliers mail an invoice a day or two after the package is shipped. Some send the invoice in the carton with

Invoice

HOLY COW LEATHER
180 HORTON RD.
NEWFIELD, N. Y. 14867
(607) 564-9022

INVOICE No. ✳ 1336

INVOICE DATE 2/16/77

SHIPPED TO

Holly's Leather Shop   SAME
100 Main St.
Somewhere, U.S.A.

OUR ORDER NO.	YOUR ORDER NO.	SALESMAN	TERMS	SHIPPED VIA	Ppd. or Coll.
N1234	306		3%10 EOM	UPS	

QUANTITY	DESCRIPTION	PRICE	AMOUNT
2 dz	3/4" belts, asst'd colors and sizes	XXXXXXX	XXXXXXXX
6 dz	keyrings, asst'd	XXXXXXX	XXXXXXXX
6 dz	wristbands, 2 dz. ea. Sm., M & L.	XXXXXXX	XXXXXXXX
		XXXXXXX	XXXXXXXX
		XXXXXXX	XXXXXXXX
		XXXXXXX	XXXXXXXX
		XXXXXXX	XXXXXXXX
		XXXXXXX	XXXXXXXX
		XXXXXXX	XXXXXXXX
		XXXXXXX	XXXXXXXX
	PACKING LIST	XXXXXXX	XXXXXXXX
		XXXXXXX	XXXXXXXX

the merchandise. The invoice should be matched against the original Purchase Order and packing list to be sure amounts and prices are correct. If the supplier offers you a two percent discount for paying within ten days, make sure your check is in the mail by the tenth day. If the invoice total is $100, this two percent will save you two dollars. Every bit saved in this manner means increased profits. It also builds a good relationship between you and your suppliers when you pay your bills within the discount period.

SALES RECORDS. Counting sales by the perpetual method means keeping track of sales when they're made on a per-item basis. If your sales volume gets large (over $200,000 annually), you should explore the possibility of using a computer service center to count sales and create up-to-date stock records. It might be more economical than maintaining the records manually.

Cash registers are made to differentiate sales by item or department. For example, if your register has ten classifications, you can keep track of ten separate categories. Each time a sale is made, that category or department code is hit. The register totals sales in each department to give you an idea how these departments are doing at the end of each day. Some electronic registers can count 200 different items or classifications.

In a small store, sales records can be developed by using sales slips or price tickets. The tickets can be coded with a key for item, department, size, and color. If you use sales slips for this purpose, fill out the necessary information on each slip every time a sale is made.

At the end of each day, the sales information should be summarized and recorded on a Sales Record Sheet similar to the one shown in Figure 9-5. Note that a daily total is kept of sales for that day. Even if you don't itemize sales, you should keep this information on a daily basis (see the Daily Summary in Chapter 16).

At the end of each week, use your Sales Record Sheet to fill in the amount of goods sold on your stock control sheet. If you don't keep an itemized perpetual sales record, take a physical count of stock to get the information for the stock control sheets. However, not all the shortage may be due to sales—some may be due to theft.

Remember that the purpose of stock control is to maintain a balanced assortment, and to assure that excessive working capital isn't tied up in merchandise. The kind of stock control you should use depends on the type of merchandise you carry. In a delicatessen, for example, you'll require no paperwork because your stocks are controlled visually. Many deliveries are daily and others are quite frequent. Your suppliers have a self-interest in keeping your stock fresh, and will often replace stale items for credit. You should still make periodic stock checks yourself, however, especially to be sure you're keeping up with the change in customer demands.

Figure 9-4. A packing list might look like this example.

WHAT IS THE VALUE OF THESE SYSTEMS? The systems mentioned above will only be valuable if you use them. For example, when you see certain items selling too slowly, it's time to put them on sale

SALES RECORD SHEET

date	item	pieces sold	$ amount	daily total	weekly total
8/2	Model LX10 Refrigerator	1	315.00		
	" 332 Mixmaster	2	50.00		
	" 517 Washer	1	250.00		
	" 518 Dryer	1	200.00	815.00	
8/3	" 104 Blender	3	60.00		
	" 513 Washer	1	300.00		
	" X14 Freezer	1	225.00	585.00	
8/4	" 332 Mixmaster	1	25.00		
	" 104 Blender	2	40.00		
	" 52 Coffeepot	1	30.00		
	" LX10 Refrigerator	1	315.00	410.00	
8/5	" 103 Blender	1	18.00		
	" 512 Washer	2	750.00	768.00	
8/6	" 103 Blender	2	36.00		
	" 104 "	1	20.00		
	" 519 Dryer	1	225.00		
	" 520 Washer	1	300.00		
	" 331 Mixmaster	2	60.00	641.00	
8/7	" LX10 Refrigerator	1	315.00		
	" 003 Compactor	1	165.00		
	" 103 Blender	3	54.00		
	" 512 Washer	1	325.00		
	" 513 Dryer	1	275.00		
	" 331 Mixmaster	4	120.00		
	" 013 Toaster	2	40.00	1294.00	4513.00

Figure 9-5. Here's an example of a Sales Record Sheet. Note that a column has been added to keep track of weekly sales totals.

and get them moving. When you notice an item moving more quickly, it means you should order in larger quantities. Use your records to discover which sizes move best, and which brands are most popular. Once you've determined which lines move fastest and make you the most profit, stock more of these items and eliminate slow movers.

At the beginning of each sales season, make predictions of expected sales. Later, match what actually happens against your predictions. Once you've been in business awhile, use your sales records for information about slow times so you know when to have special promotions to offset them.

The purpose of a system is to give you information upon which to base future decisions. You'll be able to generate more profit if you do a better job of managing your inventory and utilizing sales records in your planning.

10 Customer Relations and Services

Today, with increased competition, customers can choose merchants who offer them the best service. They don't have to shop in dirty stores where they're treated indifferently by rude, ignorant clerks. They have a wide choice of conveniently located shops accessible by walking, bus, subway, or driving. So they're going to choose the ones that offer them the services, the courtesy, and the personal attention they require.

A poll of 10,000 shoppers determined the five things they considered most important in a retail store. The results:

1. *cleanliness*
2. *courtesy*
3. *selection*
4. *quality*
5. *price*

In this chapter we're going to discuss the general atmosphere of your store and personnel, and the effect these have on customer relations. We're also going to cover specific services, such as check cashing, use of national charge cards, in-store accounts, and lay-away plans. Some of the areas overlap promotion and selling, but are important enough to deserve special mention in this chapter.

SALES CLERK COURTESY. Whether you or an employee is waiting on a customer—courtesy, friendliness, and interest in the customer are all important. Greet each customer when he comes in the door with a friendly remark, such as, "Good afternoon. That's a bright sun out there today, isn't it?" If at all possible, greet and address the customer by name. This means you'll have to make an effort to remember faces. Whenever a check is written or a charge card used, try to connect that face with the name for future use. Make sure your employees do this also.

Never allow salesclerks to sit around talking to each other or reading newspapers, when customers are in the store. A customer will be reluctant to break up a chatty group of salesclerks, and the clerks won't be alert to the signs of a customer needing help. While it's not necessary to breathe down a customer's back, sales personnel should be ready to help as soon as they see it's needed.

Always be friendly, polite, and patient with your customers. If you must leave them to answer a phone or take care of some other momentary business, leave with a remark such as, "Excuse me while I answer that phone. I'll be back in a moment." Be courteous to everyone who comes into your store, whether they purchase something or not. You never can tell when a "just looking" type will turn into a regular customer.

PRODUCT KNOWLEDGE. Product knowledge will be discussed in more depth in Chapter 11, on Selling, but it also needs to be mentioned here. If a customer asks a question about a product and your sales clerk replies, "I dunno," you're about to lose that customer. It's important for you and all your employees to know as much as possible about the products you sell. If a clerk does not know the answer to a question, the correct response would be, "I'm sorry, I don't know that, but if you'll wait a moment I'll check with my manager," or, "I'll look it up for you." Sales clerks should not only know their products, but store policies on refunds, store hours, and information about special sales.

TELEPHONE MANNERS. Everyone who calls your shop is an actual or potential customer. They should be treated with the same courtesy and friendliness as someone who walks in the door. Have your sales clerks answer the phone with a friendly, "Good morning," or, "Good afternoon," and get them to put a sparkle in their voice. Keep clippings of special sales and other important information near the phone so employees will have the material handy to answer questions.

Instruct employees how to handle long phone conversations when they're in the middle of serving a customer in the store. This should be done by politely asking the phone customer if you can have his number and call back later with the information. Just as another customer in the store would have to wait his turn if you were busy with someone else, so should a telephone customer.

COMPLETE STOCK. Although stocking and reordering problems were discussed in Chapter 9, we want to discuss here the impact these have on your customer relations. For example, suppose a woman comes into your woman's shoe store after seeing a pair of shoes she likes in the window. She asks for them in size nine. You check your stock and find that you don't have them in size nine, and tell her this. She asks if you'll be getting them in soon. You tell her to try again in two weeks. Two weeks later she comes back and you still don't have size nine. She then asks if size nine is on order. After twenty minutes in the back room you come out and say, "No, size nine is not on order. But we'll order them for you if you still want them." She says, "*No* thanks!" and walks out of your store forever.

There were several things handled poorly in the example above. First, if you didn't carry the shoe in the size the customer wanted, you should have offered to show her similar styles in size nine. You might have satisfied her right there and she would have walked out a happy customer. The second thing to consider in this example is whether you need a wider size range in your initial stocking. Were you simply out of size nine in that style, or had you never carried it? If you get a number of calls for this size, perhaps you should consider stocking it on a regular basis.

The third thing that occurred in the example was really unforgivable. You told a customer to come back for something in two weeks and then you still didn't have it. Don't think this example is too far out, either. I have gone to stores that did precisely this type of thing. I don't shop at them anymore. So before you tell a customer to come back on a particular date, make certain you order the item and that it will arrive by that date. There are situations beyond your control, of course; the manufacturer may be out of the item or the carrier may be late in making the delivery. In this case, call the customer before she comes back and tell her there will be a delay, so she doesn't waste a trip to your store.

SELF-SERVICE PROBLEMS. If your store is set up on a self-service basis, be sure to make it easy for the customer to serve himself. Have merchandise tagged properly so customers can find the size and price easily. Be sure you have enough signs that are visible and clearly worded. Keep aisles clear, have an adequate supply of workable push-carts, and arrange store layout so customers can easily find what they want. Also, be sure to have enough help during busy hours so customers don't have to wait in long lines at check-out counters.

PLEASANT SURROUNDINGS. Note that cleanliness was at the top of the list of customer requirements at the beginning of this chapter. Keep your store, stockroom, counters, and restrooms clean. Keep restrooms stocked with supplies. Have adequate space and lighting in your dressing rooms. Keep the temperature in all rooms at a comfortable level. Replace worn and dirty signs, dust and sweep (or vacuum) every day, and restack merchandise that's gotten into a messy heap from handling.

If you're going to have music in your store, gear it to the desires of your customers. Blaring rock will most likely be appropriate only if all your customers are teenagers, and even they might enjoy shopping in a more peaceful atmosphere. A constant high noise level will also be difficult for you and your employees to work under all day without strain and fatigue, so consider this when planning your store's musical background.

STORE HOURS. When you decided to open a retail store, one of the reasons may have been that you didn't want to go to a nine-to-five job every day. If that was your main reason, you'd better think again. You'll probably work closer to 60 or 80 hours a week in your own business than the mere 40 you worked on a job.

Store hours should be planned to suit your customer, not yourself.

In states where it's allowed, some stores are open 24 hours a day. We're not suggesting you do this, but do plan your store hours to catch the times when most people like to shop. This usually means being open six days a week, and at least one night. During Christmas season many stores are open every night. Your hours will also depend on the type of store you have, and the hours of the stores around you. If you're in a shopping mall, all the stores will probably keep the same hours. If you have a small food store, you may open at 8 o'clock in the morning, whereas a clothing store might open at 10 o'clock. The important issue, again, is to be open at your customers' convenience.

COMMUNITY RELATIONS. As a retail merchant in your community, you can improve your standing in the community and become known as a responsible citizen by working on such problems as zoning, urban redevelopment, parking, street beautification, air pollution, and juvenile delinquency. After all, your store isn't isolated. If the neighborhood deteriorates around it, people won't want to come there and shop. By supporting local improvement, you're actually helping your own business.

Besides the physical improvements for your business, the more people who get to know you as a caring and responsible citizen, the more potential customers you'll have. And on the negative side, if you're known as an old sorehead who's always against everything the community is trying to accomplish, this won't do your reputation much good. Unless you're fighting for a worthwhile principle, it's better to cultivate good will by conforming to the consensus of the community.

CHECK CASHING. Today many customers don't like to carry cash while shopping. They prefer to pay by check. If you refuse to cash any checks, you'll turn off some customers. If you cash checks indiscriminately, you may end up getting some bad checks. The solution is to set up a check-cashing policy and stick to it. When cashing checks, look for these key items:

1. *Date.* Examine the date for accuracy of day, month, and year. Don't accept a check if it's not dated, if it's postdated, or if it's more than 30 days old.

2. *Nonlocal banks.* Use extra care in examining a check that's drawn from a nonlocal bank, and require the best type of identification. Some stores refuse to accept checks from out-of-state banks.

3. *Amount.* Be sure that the numerical amount agrees with the written amount.

4. *Legibility.* Don't accept a check that's not written legibly. It should be written and signed in ink, and must not have any erasures or written-over amounts.

5. *Payee.* Have the customer make his check payable to your store. Use special care in taking a two-party personal check. Many stores refuse to take two-party checks.

6. *Amount of purchase.* Personal checks should be for the exact amount of the purchase. The customer should receive no change.

7. *Checks over your limit.* Set a limit on the amount you'll accept on a check. When a customer wants to go beyond that limit, your salesclerk should refer him to you.

Require Identification

When you're satisfied that the check is okay, make sure the person holding the check is the right person. Requiring identification will help certify this, although a crook can always forge identification. Some useful types of identification are drivers licenses (be sure they're current), automobile registration cards, charge cards, government passes, and student cards. Some types of identification that are not useful (too easily forged, and so forth) are: social security cards, business cards, club or organization cards, bank books, work permits, insurance cards, learner's permits, letters, birth certificates, library cards, initialed jewelry, unsigned credit cards, and voter's registration cards.

When you ask for identification, compare signatures carefully. If the identification includes a photo of the person, check the likeness to be sure it is the same person. Take down telephone numbers and license numbers for future use if a check bounces.

Refusing a Check

You're not obligated to take anyone's check. Even if a stranger presents satisfactory identification, you don't have to take his check.

In most cases you'll take a check when the customer has met all your identification requirements, because you want to make the sale. But don't take a check if the customer is intoxicated or acts suspiciously. If you have doubts, tactfully and courteously refuse to take the check.

Payroll Checks

Some stores offer a payroll check cashing service for their customers who work in the local area. This is fairly safe because you'll know the names of the companies in your area; payroll checks are easy to identify (they'll usually be typed or printed, and often say "payroll" right on them); and you can require the usual identification you do on other checks.

Cashing payroll checks is the kind of extra service that will bring people into your store to shop. And just think of the advantage of having them in your store at the time they get their paychecks cashed. While all may not purchase merchandise every time, your store will leave a favorable impression on them.

If your store is small and you don't have adequate cash on hand to cash payroll checks, then of course it wouldn't be feasible to do this.

NATIONAL CHARGE CARDS. Most stores today will honor national charge cards, such as BankAmericard and Master Charge. It will cost you about five percent of your sale, but will probably bring in enough extra business to make it worthwhile to you. For example, a customer who knows he can only spend cash or write a check for his purchases is likely to keep a tight money limit on what he buys in your store. If, on impulse, he sees something that he'd like but doesn't have the money for, he can't buy it. But if he can use a charge card, he can get the impulse item and pay for it later. Some customers shop only with their charge cards, and simply won't patronize your store at all if you don't accept them.

Other than the five percent or so charge on sales, there's really no risk in accepting charge cards. The charge card company will make good on bad cards. For you to help them track down phony and stolen cards, however, they'll supply you with a list of "bad" numbers and even offer rewards for helping them catch a bad card. Outside of that, your basic obligation is to check the signature on the card with the one on the charge slip, and to be sure the card is current.

IN-STORE ACCOUNTS. A study was done that showed a store's most loyal customers were the ones who had charge accounts. They came in more often and spent up to 20 percent more than cash customers. This is certainly a way, then, to develop a group of loyal, regular, buying customers.

The problems with keeping in-store accounts are several. First, it means more paperwork for you, and added costs in printing, postage, and bookkeeping. But the biggest problem is customers who pay late or not at all. Unless you can keep your percentage of losses very low, having in-store accounts will eat away at, rather than increase, your profits.

Your first step in offering in-house accounts is to carefully scrutinize the credit background and potential of your prospective charge customers. You'll need to ask them for information about their employment, family size, bank accounts, present loans, and other charge accounts. Check all references. Find out how they've been paying their other bills. If they have a long record of good credit, have a good, permanent job, and are not overloaded with debts, chances are they'll make a good risk. For help in analyzing credit risks, contact your local credit bureau. For a fee they'll help you evaluate potential charge customers, and then help you collect on future bad debts if necessary.

LAY-AWAY PLAN. A lay-away plan is another customer service that can help to increase sales. This is the way it works: Your customer sees an item he wants, but which costs more than he wants to spend at that time. He puts down a deposit, $10 or $20, or whatever, and you put aside the article for him. Within a specified period—two weeks, a month, two months—the customer returns, pays the balance due on the article, and takes it home.

This method is fairly risk-free, because you keep the article until it's completely paid for. If the customer never returns, you've got his deposit. But be sure to make the time limit clear—even have it stamped or printed on the receipt you give the customer for his deposit, if possible. And take enough of a deposit to make the customer care if he loses it or not.

THE CUSTOMER IS YOUR BOSS. Throughout this chapter we've been pointing out ways you can please your boss—the customer. For when he leaves your store with a smile, he'll enter the next time with confidence. And when conversations with his friends and neighbors come around to stores that are good to shop in—your store will be brought up with praise.

11 Selling

No matter how fantastic the location of your store is, and how desirable your merchandise is, you'll be losing out on a lot of sales if you just wait for the merchandise to sell itself. Even in a strictly self-service operation, customers will come into contact with clerks at check-out counters, and occasionally they'll need help finding merchandise. How you and your clerks interact with your customers is crucial to the success or failure of your business.

PERSONAL APPEARANCE. Regardless of what your personal tastes are in dress, when you're in your store you represent the store and the merchandise you sell. Dress according to the image you are trying to project. If you sell fine quality merchandise, you should be dressed in fine clothes. If you sell mod clothes, you should try to dress in the latest fashions yourself. If you're opening a "head" shop selling roach clips, papers, and other smoking accessories, then you can dress much more casually.

When you go shopping, take note of the appearance of sales clerks in the various shops. Which ones seem to best "represent" their shop? Which ones appear sloppy or out of place? Think about the kind of customer you expect to come to your store. What kind of salesperson will attract that customer and put him at ease?

I'm not saying that every salesclerk must wear a suit and tie, or a dress, stockings, and high-heeled shoes. Informal clothing may be quite appropriate, as long as it's done in good taste. No one likes to run around in old jeans and sneakers more than I do, but I'd be kidding myself if I thought this kind of personal appearance would help sales in most retail stores.

CUSTOMER COURTESIES. This subject was discussed in Chapter 10, but it deserves to be mentioned again. Every possible courtesy should be shown to *every* customer who enters your place of business—whether or not they buy anything. All customers should be greeted with some friendly remark, and walked to the door after they've made a purchase. If a customer has heavy packages, offer to help carry them to the car. If this is impossible, at least open the door.

Be polite and friendly to every person who enters your shop. If possible, try to learn customers' names and call them by name when they come in. It's important to make every possible effort to build repeat business, and getting to know your customers is one way to do it. Repeat customers are the best word-of-mouth advertisements.

KNOW YOUR PRODUCT. This is one of the most important areas in any kind of selling. Find out everything you can about the products you sell. Read product labels, guarantees, and other information put out by the manufacturer. Read trade journals, consumer reports, and the literature distributed by your suppliers' representatives. Find out everything you can about the products your competitors sell. Be able to answer customer questions about the materials your products are made of, how long they'll last, how they perform, what guarantees the manufacturer or your store offers, and how to take care of them.

It certainly helps if you're personally interested in the type of merchandise you sell. For example, if you're selling boats, it would help if you're a boat enthusiast. If you're selling fabrics, you should enjoy sewing. The more interest you have in the products you sell, the more this enthusiasm and knowledge will come across to the customer.

This is one area where the small merchant has an advantage over the large department store. In a large store, the individual sales clerks may be working there because they need the job. They may find themselves selling shoes, or children's clothes, or handbags, with no real interest in the items they're selling. As the owner of a small shop, however, you've probably chosen the type of store you have *because* of your interest in it. You're selling gifts because you've always loved to browse through gift shops yourself; or selling sporting goods because you love sports.

A couple of years ago I wanted to buy a classical guitar. First I checked out the regular music stores in town. They carried all kinds of instruments, including classical guitars in various price ranges. The sales clerks showed me all the classical guitars they carried—but nothing else. Then I went to Guitar Workshop, a little shop that specializes in guitars. In addition to selling guitars, John, the proprietor, also repairs them. When he showed me his stock of classical guitars, he immediately pointed out the models he considered to be the best buy for the money. He talked about the difference in construction, the type of wood that was used to make each one, and the possible disadvantages and advantages of each model. Where do you think I bought my guitar?

USE YOUR PRODUCT KNOWLEDGE. Having all the knowledge in the world won't help if you don't use it. If you wait around for the customer to start asking you questions, they may leave the shop without ever discovering your vast store of information. It's true that some customers will ask, but many won't. It's up to you to start the ball rolling the minute they show an interest in some item on your shelves.

The words, "May I help you?" don't really work, either. If a customer isn't sure he wants to make a purchase, he's likely to answer "no thank you, I'm just looking." At that point you've cut off possible conversation. Therefore, it's better to start right in with some information about the product. If a customer walks over to a slack rack, for example, you might say, "Those slacks just came in last week. They're made of that new glorbydook fabric, which is so easy to take care of. What size are you looking for?" The question at the end is a good lead-in to continue the conversation. Once you help the customer find her size, you might ask if she'd like to try them on. You can also point out other styles and colors that you carry. Once she's looked at several types, you can point out the differences in materials, style, and quality.

If you find it difficult to walk up and start talking to customers about your products, think of it this way: What's the worst that could happen? The customer will ignore you? The customer will tell you to shut up? The customer will walk out and not buy anything? Well, if she was going to do that, she probably would have walked out without buying anything, even if you had said nothing. But much more likely, if she isn't interested in buying slacks, or even trying them on, she'll probably say something like, "Thanks for the information. I just wanted to look around today. I may be back another time." And she just might be.

About a year ago I was contemplating purchasing a winter coat, but not until I had saved enough money to do it. One day I happened to pass a coat store. I decided to go in and just look around to get an idea about the kind of coat I might like to buy later on when I had the money. Well, thanks to a very competent saleswoman, I ended up buying the coat that day. After we reached the point where I knew I liked a particular coat, I confronted her with the fact that I had no money to buy one that day. She immediately told me about their lay-away plan, and I bought the coat. Now, if she had left me alone when I informed her initially that I was "just looking," and walked off to the other end of the store, I would have walked out of the shop without making a purchase.

The point is, when someone is making a decision about whether to purchase an item, they want to feel they're making the right decision. They want to feel good about what they're doing. By pointing out the quality of the item, its serviceability, and how well it looks on the customer, you're helping the customer feel good about buying your product. He'll walk out of the store much more confident and happy. Even the most independent shopper certainly won't object to your approval of his purchase.

PHONY ADVICE. I must add one word of warning about overdoing your praise of the products you sell. If you tell a man who comes into your shop that *every* suit he tries on makes him look like Robert Redford, he's going to feel that your comments are phony, and resent them. If you make exaggerated claims about a particular lawn mower to a customer, she may purchase it. But when the machine fails to live up to your claims, she may bring it back, stop patronizing your store, and criticize your store when talking to her friends and neighbors.

In the area of product information, be factual and accurate. While you don't have to run down everything that's wrong with a product, you certainly shouldn't initiate false claims about its worth. Dealing with customers when they try on clothes, shoes, hats, or jewelry is a little more delicate. While you certainly don't want to insult your customer, try to tactfully point out which articles flatter him the most. Rather than saying, "That shirt makes you look sick!" you can say, "I think this blue shirt is much more flattering on you than the red one." Even if you have to lose a sale, don't talk a customer into buying something he won't be happy with when he gets home. It's better to lose a single sale than risk bad publicity and a customer's ill will.

SELL CUSTOMER BENEFITS, RATHER THAN PRODUCT FEATURES. When at all possible, you should point out how the product will enhance the customer's life. For example, when talking about the kind of materials that clothes are made of, you can emphasize how easy they'll be to take care of, how they'll save the customer money because they're long-lasting, or how they'll enhance the customer's appearance. If you're selling a plant, you can discuss how easy it will be for the customer to take care of the plant, and how decorative it will look in his home. If you're selling sewing machines, the customer wants to know how it will help him to sew better and more easily. While you can point out the construction of the machine, the horsepower of the motor, and the number of attachments that come with it, you'd better tie in these facts with customer benefits to achieve an impact. The point is this—the product has value only because it fits your customers' needs, and this is why people buy things.

MAKE THAT "EXTRA" SALE. When a customer has chosen the particular article he wants to purchase, it's time to try to sell him something "extra" if at all possible. For some kinds of products you can easily suggest an accessory: a hat with a coat; stockings with a pair of shoes; tennis balls with a tennis racket; a cage and food with pets; music books or pitchpipe, or both, with a musical instrument. This list can go on endlessly. Some items, however, don't lend themselves as easily to an accessory sale. In those cases you might simply suggest some new item that has recently come into your shop, or some article that's now on special sale, or find some other reason for mentioning it. In any case, don't let the customer out the door without at least mentioning some other item. The best time to catch him is while he's still looking around as he begins to walk to the cash register. If his eye falls on a particular counter, mention the items on it. Another spot to get an extra sale is at the check-out counter. Keep impulse items displayed there for that last-minute purchase. In the beginning it may be difficult, but practice *always* attempting to make that extra sale. If the customer says, "No thanks, this is all I need today," you haven't lost anything. And every time it works you'll be putting additional money in your cash register.

SELL QUALITY. When a customer comes in looking for a particular product, you'll normally have two or three items in various price ranges to show her. She may walk in with a price in mind, perhaps one she's seen advertised. You could let her walk out with the low-priced item. But by utilizing your product knowledge, you'll often be able to sell a better quality item than the one the customer originally planned to purchase. Once a customer realizes the added value of the higher-priced item, she'd often rather buy that one because in the long run it will be worth it to her. So whenever possible, try to sell better quality.

ADDRESS YOUR CUSTOMER'S NEEDS. Each customer who walks into your store is a different person. He or she has different tastes, a different personality—different *needs*. Rather than trying to sell to a generalized image you have of what a customer is and wants, deal with each customer personally, finding out each one's particular needs and wants. This means you'll have to ask questions, and you'll have to listen. Don't concentrate so hard on your own spiel that you ignore what the customer is saying. If you address yourself to the things that you think are important about a product, or that the last ten customers thought were important about a product, you may be missing the needs of this particular customer. Maybe he or she wants the product for entirely different reasons.

Two women walk into your store to buy shoes. One is looking for the latest style. She wants to be "in fashion," and if the shoe fits that need, and is her size, she'll love it. The second woman walks in. You start to talk to her about the latest styles, the "in" thing—but she doesn't care about that. She's looking for a shoe to wear at work, where she stands a good part of the day. Her needs are entirely different from the needs of the first woman. You must stop and listen to her. Find out what she needs. Then you'll be able to help her and make a sale.

This brings us to another potential problem—talking too much. If you continuously ramble on without giving the customer a chance to express her opinions and desires, you won't learn what she needs and you won't be able to properly serve her. While it's good to show friendliness by making some small talk, don't get carried away with it. Don't let useless conversation interfere with the job at hand—which is the buying and selling of merchandise. Too much unrelated conversation will distract the customer from her thoughts about the product, waste her time, and therefore add up to fewer sales for you.

In line with idle chattering, also avoid poor mannerisms that might distract the customer and lose sales. Things to watch out for are talking fast or loud, or both, tapping the fingers or foot, and giggling. Observe yourself and your sales clerks, and eliminate these things if they occur.

SELF IMPROVEMENT. In any business or profession, there's always more to learn and ways to improve. Continue to read everything you can related to your business, observe other businesses, take courses in marketing and management, and work at the things in your sales personality that need improvement. At the end of each day or week, review what happened and ask yourself where you might have done better. Was there some customer who could have been handled differently, which would have made the difference in landing a sale? Was there some product you didn't know enough about to adequately answer a customer's questions? Were there certain customers you didn't feel comfortable with? Keep working at the trouble spots and practicing good selling techniques every day.

NINE-STEP SELLING PLAN. The following steps will help you focus on the stages of a selling transaction from beginning to end:

1. *Greet your customer.*
2. *Make some general, friendly remark.*
3. *Find out what the customer's needs are.*
4. *Explain how the product will fill those needs.*
5. *Close the sale.*
6. *Try to make the "extra" sale of an accessory or other item.*
7. *Thank the customer for shopping in your store.*
8. *Walk your customer to the door.*
9. *Invite the customer to come back soon.*

By focusing on these nine points, and the transition from one to the next, you'll avoid getting sidetracked in nonrelated conversation, or missing an important step. Remember, your function and that of your salesclerks is to make sales. Keep that goal as your prime target, and work at improving sales methods continuously.

12 Promotion

Promotion is more than just advertising—it's developing an image and communicating that image to the public. Just about everything you do in the operation of your store affects promotion: the location you choose, the decor of your store, the merchandise you stock, the customer services you offer, and the way you sell your merchandise. In this chapter we're going to focus on some additional promotional techniques you can use to bring people into your store and keep them coming back.

IMAGE. I've talked about image before and I'll continue to talk about it throughout this book. What is the image or identity you want your store to project? What do you want people to think of when someone mentions your store: high quality, name brands, extra services, imported gifts, the latest in fashion? Once you choose the image you want to project, push it in all your promotions.

The advantage of having a small store means you can sell individualized products to the increasing number of identity-striving buyers. A small business can do this effectively because you, yourself, make the decisions and your store can therefore be more flexible than many large stores can. Decide who you're going to appeal to: the status seekers, searchers for high quality, or the fashion conscious. Then build your entire identity to appeal to such a group.

ADVERTISING. Once you've chosen the image you want to project, it should be reflected in all your advertising. Even if you've got the best location and your customers have given you a fantastic reputation by word-of-mouth, you'll probably still need some advertising to survive and grow. The problems to consider in planning your advertising are: how much should you advertise, when should you advertise, and what should you advertise. While there are no cut and dry answers to these questions, there are facts to take into consideration before making these decisions.

HOW MUCH ADVERTISING. Some retail shops use formulas to compute how much advertising they'll do. They take a percentage (from two to six percent) of retail sales or projected retail sales. For example, if they use three percent and the projected sales for the year are $100,000, they'd spend $3,000 in advertising for the year. This plan has its drawbacks. How do you know what projected sales will be? Also, new shops may need more advertising, initially, until they become known. And finally, what percentage is "proper" for your store?

A more goal-oriented approach is to decide what you want your advertising to do, and then learn how much it will cost to do it. Of course, with this approach, you need to be able to measure results so you can find out if the advertising has done its job. You also may find you can't afford all the advertising you'd like to do.

If you do have a figure in mind for your first advertising budget, you might contact an ad agency and ask them what they suggest. They may be able to devise a comprehensive advertising plan for you. Since they're aware of the various media and the costs involved, they should be able to give you some accurate information.

If you're working within a very limited budget, first try the low-cost promotional methods mentioned later in this chapter. Consider carefully the possible media available, and try to plan the most impact for your money. There are ways a small store can promote itself without spending huge sums on large newspaper ads or TV spots.

WHERE SHOULD YOU ADVERTISE? Before choosing the media you'll advertise in, you should answer the following questions:

1. To whom do you want to advertise? Who are the people who need what you sell, or who influence what others buy?

2. Where are these people? From how far away do you expect people to come to your shop?

3. What kind of advertising message do you want to deliver? Would it be told best in print, radio, or television?

Each medium has its own characteristics. Newspapers, for example, reach people of both sexes and all ages, of different income and educational levels, and with varied interests, but within a limited geographical area. Radio, on the other hand, is usually a fragmented medium, with different stations appealing to different audiences. Other differences in media are limits on the length of the message, and visual or audio presentations.

You'll get the best results from advertising if you limit the number of media you use to one, or possible two. If you spread yourself too thin, the advertising will lose impact. In whatever media you select, your advertising should be frequent and regular. When you step up your advertising at Christmas and other peak seasons, it will bring in more sales if you've advertised consistently throughout the year, than if you've only advertised sporadically.

PLAN YOUR ADVERTISING. Before placing any ads, set up a full year's advertising schedule. You can make revisions later on as needed, but you need a guide to start with. Your plan should show the following:

1. Each newspaper, radio station, TV station, or other medium you've decided on.
2. The dates your advertising will appear.
3. The cost.

Choosing your medium properly is the first step in a good advertising plan. But what you offer and how well you present the offer will also affect the response your advertising brings.

HOW TO DESIGN ADS. If you decide to design your own ads, the first thing to do is study ads in newspapers and on radio and TV. Which ones attract your attention? What kind of an impression do they make? What kind of information do they get across? Do you go out and buy the product or shop in the store after you see or hear the ad?

The first job of an ad is to get the reader's or listener's attention. If this isn't done, it doesn't matter what the message is—it will be overlooked. This is why it's important to have your ad in the right section of a newspaper. What pages are your customers most likely to read— sports, news, recipes? What programs do they listen to on radio and watch on TV? In a newspaper ad, artwork, placement, size of the ad, and style and size of lettering can be used to draw the reader's attention. On radio you can use voice, music, and the message itself to get the listener interested. TV utilizes both visual and audio effects, so it has unlimited possibilities—or problems, depending upon how you look at it.

In newspapers, one way to get people to start recognizing your ads is the use of the same logo, type style, or basic design in all your ads. People will associate that logo with your store. On radio ads, use the same program, announcer, and musical introduction in all your ads.

Generally, it's better to pick one or two particular products to feature in your ads, rather than running general ads on all your merchandise. If possible, show a photo or illustration of these products. Emphasize the quality, rather than the price. On radio, you can give a full description of the articles, even though they can't be shown.

One way to see obvious results from your ads is to print a coupon which the customer redeems in your shop for a free gift or a special price on an item. If you use radio ads you can have the customer come in and mention a special he heard on the air.

SAMPLE ADS. In Figure 12-1 the ad by Robinson & Carpenter, Inc., uses large bold letters at the top to draw the reader's attention. The words "red tag sale" are printed on a slant at varying levels—another attention getter. Note that three specific articles are featured with illustrations and a brief description. The ad lists the sale price and the original price of these items. If you simply list your sale price on an item, the customer may not realize what the savings is if he doesn't know the original price.

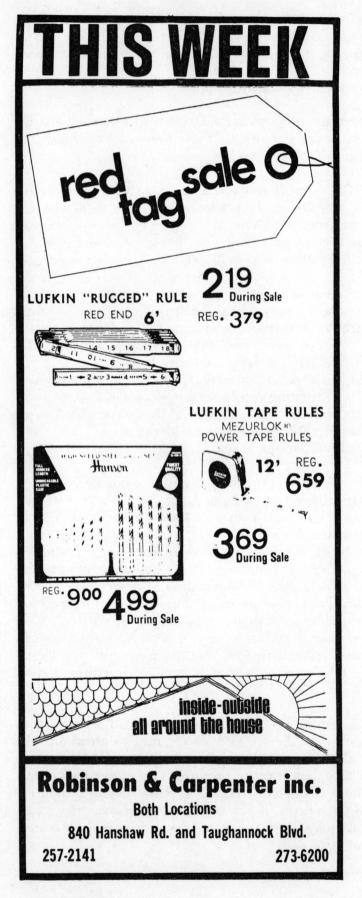

Figure 12-1. A sample newspaper ad for Robinson & Carpenter, Inc.

The ad for Nippenose Equipment Company in Figure 12-2 catches the reader's attention whth its beautiful ink drawing. The company uses similar drawings in all its ads, which helps the reader to immediately identify them. Note that specific brand names familiar to outdoor enthusiasts are stressed in the ad.

The ad in Figure 12-3 features one of the store's gift items, writing instruments, with an illustration and full description stressing quality and beauty. The Hallmark crown and script are used to identify the store, Charjan's, with this well-known card and gift line.

Figure 12-4 is an interesting example of an attempt by a food chain to do something different in its ads. Most supermarket ads are simply full pages of specials and coupons for the week. The Great American chain has used a clever gimmick to get the reader's attention, amuse him, and convince him that Great American is somehow different from the rest of the supermarket chains. It's establishing an identity with these humorous ads, which contains a different "Un-great American" story each week.

Figure 12-2. (Below) *Note the beautiful ink drawing in this ad for Nippenose Equipment Co.*

Figure 12-3. (Right) *In this ad, note the use of the Hallmark trademark.*

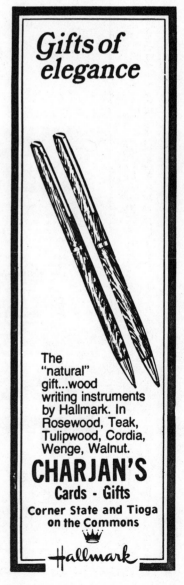

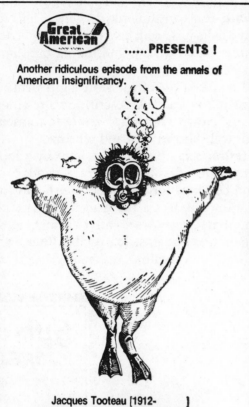

Figure 12-5 is an ad designed by Hour Agency, Inc. The stylized ink drawing gives an aura of elegance and quality. The language used immediately suggests to the reader the feeling she'll get once she dons this pantsuit. It sets the precise mood that Euphoria wishes to communicate.

ADVERTISING AGENCIES. What can an advertising agency do for you? Basically it will carry out the following functions:

1. Plan your advertising.
2. Select media and contract for space and time.
3. Prepare the advertising, including copy layouts, and other creative work.
4. Produce finished ads in the form required by different media.
5. Take care of record-keeping, accounting, and other details involved in the advertising.

Most small retailers handle their own advertising to save the cost of using an agency, but this doesn't mean that more local businesses wouldn't benefit from having agencies. Even though the agency services increase advertising costs, they can also increase advertising effectiveness. Without an agency there'll still be a cost in time and money, even if you handle the advertising yourself. But whether the cost is less, the same, or more, if you put your advertising in the hands of an agency, you'll get expertness and coordination. At least it's worth looking into.

HOW TO CHOOSE AN AGENCY. As a retailer, you'll want an agency with experience in newspaper, radio, and direct mail advertising. To find out what agencies are available in your area, look in the Yellow Pages of your telephone directory under "Advertising Agencies." If you live in a small town, look in the directories of nearby cities.

Once you've prepared a list of possible agencies, let each one know you're looking for an agency and ask them to give you information about their work. You may wish to ask them to fill out the questionnaire shown in Figure 12-6.

After you've narrowed your list of agencies, interview each one. After you've been shown samples of its finished advertisements, ask about the thinking that went into the planning and preparation of the ads shown. You might also ask whether the people who planned and prepared the ads are still with the agency.

Before you tell an agency that it's your final choice, be sure you and the agency agree about how your advertising will be handled. Know for what things you'll be charged and how you'll be billed. Don't take anything for granted.

COOPERATIVE ADVERTISING. Cooperative advertising means a manufacturer and retailer share the cost of local advertising. The manufacturer gets more advertising per dollar, because the local rates a retailer pays for ad space are lower than the national rates a manufacturer must pay. For the retailer, it's an incentive to stock and advertise brand-name products. The most common ratio for sharing costs is 50-

Figure 12-4. (Far left) *This ad uses humor to amuse and attract the reader.*

Figure 12-5. Here's an ad designed by Hour Agency, Inc., of Ithaca, N.Y.

50, and the total funds allocated by the manufacturer are based on a percent of dollar purchases by the store.

If you're going to sell brand-name products, check out the cooperative advertising plans that may be offered by your suppliers. If the manufacturer sets aside cooperative advertising money, you should utilize it, since the "factory share" is included in the wholesale price you pay for the goods anyway. It's worth putting in your share to benefit from this advertising. Ads telling people that they can buy brand-name products at your store increase traffic for sales of other merchandise, too.

SUGGESTED AGENCY QUESTIONNAIRE

1. _____   _____
   Name   Phone

   _____
   Street and number   City   State   ZIP

2. Proprietorship _____ Partnership _____ Incorporated _____

3. Who has control? _____

4. Media recognition _____

5. How long have you been in business? _____

6. Billings: Now _____ 2 years ago _____ 5 years ago _____

7. Present accounts (Attach list showing name and address, type of business, and number of years with your agency.)

8. Three largest active accounts:

   Name   Percent of your total billings

   _____   _____

   _____   _____

   _____   _____

9. Percent of total billings you place with each medium:

   Newspapers ___   Consumer magazines ___   Directories ___
   Business papers ___   Radio ___   Direct mail ___
   Farm papers ___   Television ___   Other ___
   Business magazines ___ Outdoor ___   (Explain)

10. Accounts lost during last 5 years. (Attach list showing name, type of business, dates with your agency, and reason for termination.)

11. Number of full-time salaried employees:

    Executive and professional ___
    Clerical ___

12. Account executive who would be assigned: _____

    Experience and other qualifications: _____

    _____

    _____

Figure 12-6. This suggested questionnaire for ad agencies is from Selecting Advertising Media, *Small Business Administration, Washington, D.C.*

TIE-IN WITH OTHER MERCHANTS. Very often merchants who share the same neighborhood will run ads together. For example, shopping centers often will run ads promoting the whole center. Each individual shop will contribute to the cost of the ad. Sometimes special promotions are planned, and all the shops will keep longer hours, have sales, and advertise together. One such example is "Midnight Madness," promoted by a group of local shops in a section of Ithaca, around Halloween. All the shops stay open until midnight and offer sales on special items or general discounts on all merchandise. All the merchants in the area chip in for group ads, and usually run their own special ads as well.

DIRECT MAIL ADVERTISING. Direct mail advertising is any advertising that is sent through the post office. It's the most selective and flexible of all media. It's selective because you advertise only to people who can use what you sell. You can send it to a few people or to many, to a small geographical area or the whole country. Direct mail is flexible because the sizes and shapes of your ad are up to you. Your presentation can be simple or elaborate, and be distributed when you choose.

Direct mail advertising can be used in the following ways:
1. To announce new lines, models, designs, or changes in products.
2. To notify your customers of price increases or decreases.
3. To welcome new customers.
4. To help regain lost customers.
5. To thank all customers for their business at least once a year.
6. To create an image for your business.
7. To remind customers of seasonal or periodic needs.
8. To make the most of special events, such as feature sales.

If you doubt you're reaching all customers and prospects through other advertising media, direct mail gives you another chance. If you're already reaching them, direct mail adds to the impact.

The cost of direct mail advertising will be based on the following:
1. Cost of preparing the folder or other literature to be enclosed.
2. Cost of processing a letter.
3. Cost of the envelope.
4. Cost of addressing the envelope, inserting the enclosures, and sealing.
5. Postage, either first or third class.
6. Cost of a mailing list if you buy one (you can develop your own list, or use telephone directories).

Direct mail is the most costly advertising medium in terms of dollars spent versus size of audience or readership. But because of the high percentage of returns, it can be one of the cheapest in terms of results. The true measure of the cost of advertising is the cost *per inquiry* or *per sale*.

For more information about direct mail advertising, talk to your advertising agency. It can help you prepare direct mail promotions.

IMPRINTED CARDS. One form of direct mail advertising is the use of preprinted cards. Thayer Advertising Company puts out several styles that can be imprinted with your store name and address. Figure 12-7 shows the front and inside of its "Thank You" card. This is an easy way to show your customers that you appreciate their patronage. Purchase the number of cards you need and mail them to your recent customer list. Or, each time a new customer opens an account in your store or makes a large purchase, send him or her a card.

Figure 12-8 shows the front and inside of Thayer's "We'll do anything for you" card. This one should be sent to customers who have stopped patronizing your store. For samples and price information on these cards, write to: Thayer Advertising Company, P.O. Box 100, Blackwood, N.J. 08012. (Note: these cards are copyrighted by Thayer Advertising Company.)

Figure 12-8. This is a card put out by Thayer Advertising Company to send to lost customers.

CLASSIFIED ADVERTISING. Classified advertising is often over-

Figure 12-7. These "Thank You" cards are available from Thayer Advertising Co., P.O. Box 100, Blackwood, N.J. 08012. (Note: these cards are copyrighted by Thayer Advertising Co.)

We're Happy to have you as a Customer

Thank you so much for your patronage. We genuinely appreciate you as our customer and you have our assurance that we shall make every effort to maintain the friendly type of relationship so necessary for your continued confidence and good will.

You will find all of us eager to serve you in every possible way.

Once again, our sincere thanks.

Sincerely yours,

YOUR IMPRINT HERE
ADDRESS

Thank you

We'll do anything for you.

We Are Looking
Forward to Seeing
You Again

*I*t seems like a long time since you have taken advantage of our services. We've missed you and want you to know that it has always been our genuine pleasure to serve you.

If there is any reason for dissatisfaction, please let us know. Your friendship and patronage are important to us and we want you to know that we are here to do all we can to insure your complete satisfaction.

Sincerely yours,

YOUR IMPRINT HERE
ADDRESS

looked by businesses, but it can be an especially effective and inexpensive method of advertising. Many people who never stop to look at display or space ads in a newspaper will carefully read the classified section from top to bottom. Since it costs very little to place a classified ad, you can run them often in your local newspapers. If you can't find a specific heading to place your ad under, put it in "Articles for sale."

For a small shop with a limited advertising budget, a repeated classified ad will probably bring more results than a small, occasional display ad. If your store offers some service, such as repairing the articles you sell, or giving lessons, advertise this in the appropriate section of the classified ads.

NEWS RELEASES. The news release is the workhouse of the publicity field, and publicity means promotion. You can write them up on your regular store letterhead, or have a supply of special forms printed featuring the words "News Release" prominently at the top. Each release should include the following information:

1. Date of release.
2. Date that information can be used by the media (this will normally be "for immediate release").
3. Your name or name of someone who can give further information.
4. Phone number.
5. A short headline in the center of the page.
6. Double-spaced copy answering the questions: who, what, when, where, why, and how.

Generally one typed page will be adequate for your news. A release can be sent out whenever you have something newsworthy to say—normally four or five times a year. If you send them out too often, you'll wear out your welcome. Newsworthy items could include: your store's opening, relocation, remodeling, new manager or promotion of employees, and major change in product lines. To get more ideas about newsworthy items, read the business section of your newspaper.

Once you've written your release, send it to all media that might conceivably be interested in what's happening in your store. This includes all local newspapers, magazines, trade magazines, radio and TV stations, and columnists. If you've got a big story, such as the opening of your store, local newspapers may want to include photos as well as a story.

News releases are a way to put a small dollar cost to good use. This promotion tool has in practice produced hundreds of times the amount of its cost in actual traceable sales volume.

DISPLAY BOOTHS. Many banks have display booths or windows that their business customers can use for display without charge. Find out if your bank has such a service. You can also rent display booths at airports, hotels, and motels. By making an attractive display with a card giving your store name and address, you can attract tourists and other visitors when they come into your area.

CHARITY. Once you're in business, many local charities will contact you for donations. While you may give each one a small sum, it can add up to a sizable amount by the end of the year. A way to get this public service to promote your store is to pick one charity each year and donate the total amount to it. Usually an announcement of this gift will be made in the local paper and at the charity's board meetings.

Another idea is to sponsor a local team, perhaps a team on a junior baseball league. When you purchase the uniforms, they can be in your store colors and have your name printed on them. This promotes good will toward your store at minimal cost.

PROMOTE YOUR CUSTOMERS. One way to promote customers is to keep a birthday-list card file of your customers, or of their children. Design a gift certificate, write in your customer's name, and send it out two or three days before his or her birthday. By having the gift certificate redeemable in your store for merchandise only, you can offer a $5 gift certificate for only your $2 or $3 wholesale cost. While you shouldn't set a minimum purchase figure, most customers will buy more than the value of the certificate. By consistently sending these gifts you'll develop a loyal group of customers, with the actual costs and time involved fairly minimal.

PROMOTE YOUR EMPLOYEES. Just as people like to shop in familiar stores, they like to know the salespeople they're dealing with. If you have several employees, give each a name tag to wear in the store. Have a professional photographer take a portrait of each employee and put one in the window each week with a slogan, such as "Employee of the Week." Have the employee's name printed under the photo in large letters. This will improve the selling atmosphere in your store as your customers get to know the salesclerks' faces and names. It will also improve employee morale by making them feel they are an integral part of your store.

POSTERS AND BILLBOARDS. Posters are a low-cost method of local advertising. Have a freelance artist, friend, or student design an attractive poster for you. The more artistic and pleasing the poster, the less it is likely that it'll be torn down. After printing 50 or 100 of them, distribute them around town wherever it's legal to post them. This includes schools, supermarket bulletin boards, and laundry centers. Every so often, update your poster to keep it fresh, and replace those that are worn or have been torn down.

CLASSES. Holding classes is another way to promote your store. The classes themselves may earn profit, too, but if they just break even or cost a little, they're worth the promotion. Some ideas are: craft classes if you sell craft supplies; gardening classes if you sell gardening supplies; cooking classes if you sell food, utensils, or cookbooks; sewing classes if you sell fabrics; interior decorating classes if you sell home improvement supplies; art classes if you sell art supplies; modeling classes if you sell high-fashion clothes.

Actually, with a little creativity you could think of courses to offer for any type of merchandise. If you have the space, conduct the classes in your shop. Otherwise try renting local public space—in schools, for example. You might even consider offering a class in conjunction with your local adult-education school. You might supply the materials while they supply the space and the teacher. In any case, be sure to get all the publicity you can out of this by sending a news release on it to all the local media.

SUMMING UP. Whether your store is small or large, your advertising budget ample or severely limited, there are ways and means available to you to promote and advertise your shop. Give careful thought to all the possible avenues open to you. Plan your program carefully. And follow through to ascertain the results of each campaign. Modify and improve your plans as you discover what works most effectively and efficiently in your business.

13 Employees

If you're opening a small retail store and have several members of your family, or partners, to help you operate the shop, you may not need to hire employees. But if you're trying to run the business yourself, you'll probably need help, at least during busy times. Just how many employees you need will depend upon the size of your store, how busy it is, how much help the customers require, and so forth. Once you decide you need help, the next steps are recruiting, interviewing, hiring, training, and paying employees. We're going to cover these procedures in the rest of this chapter. The legal and bookkeeping responsibilities that accompany employees will be handled in Chapter 14.

RECRUITING. Finding *an* employee is fairly simple, no matter where you're located. It's finding the *right* employee that may be tough. In order to increase your chances of finding the right employee, it's important to have a choice of several applicants to choose from. You may find people who just walk in your store and ask for a job. But if you use only this method to find employees, your selection will be quite limited.

One of the best ways to contact prospective employees is to put an ad in the "Help Wanted" column of your local newspaper. This is where people looking for jobs go to find out about them, so it works very well. In your ad list the pertinent information about the type of work you have and the kind of applicant you're looking for. Remember, however, that it's illegal to discriminate in hiring because of age, sex, race, religion, or nationality. You don't have to state in the ad what the salary will be, although most applicants will ask this when they call about the job. By listing your phone number you can screen some people on the phone and waste less interviewing time.

Figure 13-1 shows an example of what your ad might state. It includes all the important items: what the job is, whether it's full- or part-time, how the person will be paid (salary, tips, or commissions), what kind of person should apply, who to contact for further informa-

111

Salesclerk wanted for downtown shoe store. Part time. Salary + commission. Must be personable and dress neatly. Call Joe at 843-2971.

Figure 13-1. You might place an ad similar to this example in the "Help Wanted" section of your newspaper.

tion, how to contact them. If you want only experienced sales clerks to apply, state this in your ad.

Other ways to contact potential employees are: through your local employment agencies, state and private; through placement agencies of schools; by placing notices on bulletin boards; through word of mouth; through friends and relatives. The way the unemployment situation is these days, it's an employer's market, and you shouldn't have any problem finding a number of people to apply for the job.

JOB DESCRIPTION. Before interviewing any applicants, you should have a clear idea of what the employee's duties will be in your shop. Will he be expected to handle customers on the floor, work with stock in the back room, operate the cash register, make any purchasing decisions, answer the phone, clean the shop, take out the garbage, deliver packages, do any record keeping? Who will be his immediate boss—you, your spouse, an assistant manager under you?

Once you've decided exactly what you'll expect from your new employee, write a brief job description listing these items. Also list the person to whom the employee will "report" or be responsible. It's better to have each employee report to one person. Otherwise, confusion may result if conflicting orders are given. For example, you tell Bob, your new employee, to spend the morning cleaning up the stockroom. Your spouse comes in at 11:00, sees Bob in the stockroom when the store is full of customers, and yells at him, "Why aren't you on the floor selling?" You can just imagine this leading up to a whopper of a family argument, can't you? We'll get into the problems of family businesses in more detail in Chapter 20. The point we want to make here is that family or no family, it's tough for any employee to be responsible to more than one person, and conflicts are bound to occur.

SELECTING EMPLOYEES. What kind of person should you hire? This question has stumped employers for ages, and even the professional personnel departments of large corporations that administer ability tests and psychological tests, and that also check references, ten years' experience, and fingerprints, still can't be fail-safe in their choice of applicants. "If that's the case," you might say, "why don't I just hire the first person who answers the ad?" Well, while no system is perfect, you can at least increase your chances of finding a good employee with a few simple procedures.

First, you should decide what kind of person will be able to handle the job you have. Most likely his main function will be selling— dealing with customers. This means you'll want someone who likes dealing with people, someone who is friendly and easy to get along with. It doesn't mean he must be an extrovert, or a stand-up comedian, but he shouldn't be quick-tempered, express prejudices against groups of people, or get into arguments easily.

You'll also want to hire someone with whom *you* can get along. After all, you'll be working with him, so the more comfortable *you* feel, the more chance there is that the relationship will work out. If you have other employees, you'll also have to consider how he'll get along with them. Will your staff be able to function cooperatively, or will they let personal differences interfere with their jobs?

Next, you'll want someone who's reliable. If you need him or her on Friday night because the store will be busy, you want to be able to count on the person to be there. Someone who regularly comes in late, is absent, or doesn't call in when sick, will be more of a liability than an asset to you. Also, you want someone you can trust not to put cash or merchandise in his pockets when your back is turned.

Finally, you want someone who either knows how to do the job when you hire him, or can learn it fairly quickly with your training. You want him to take an interest in your customers and the merchandise, to learn from you and his daily experiences in the store, and to do a good job, consistently. The kind of person who does a good job and works at improving his performance is usually someone who also enjoys that job and takes pride in his work. We'll talk about ways you can help this happen later on in the chapter.

EMPLOYEE APPLICATION FORMS. Well, now that you know all the qualities you want in an employee, how do you go about finding out which applicant has them? One way to begin is by having each applicant fill out an employee application form. You can have your own specialized form printed, or purchase one like the example in Figure 13-2 at your local office supply store. These standard forms allow the applicant to methodically list all the pertinent information you might want about their education, experience, and personal background.

THE INTERVIEW. When the applicant has filled out the application form, the next step is the interview. This should be a two-way conversation, in which you can find out about the applicant and she or he can find out about you and the job. Remember, however, that the applicant may be a bit nervous about the interview, so a few friendly words at the beginning will help put the person at ease.

You can begin by telling the applicant about the job, what his duties will be, with whom he'll be working, the salary, store policies, and hours. Then try to get the applicant to talk about himself. Ask him about the previous jobs he held—what he did, why he left. Ask him what his interests are, his future plans, why he wants the job, and so on. Try to ask questions that can't be answered with one word. By talking with the applicant you'll get a feeling about how he might fit into your organization, and how he might interact with customers. Use the application form as a starting point for questions. For exam-

Figure 13-2. A standard application form, such as this, can be purchased at your local office supply store.

APPLICATION FOR EMPLOYMENT

PERSONAL INFORMATION

Date _____ Social Security Number _____

Name _____ Age _____ Sex _____
    Last   First   Middle

Present Address _____
    Street   City   State   Zip

Permanent Address _____
    Street   City   State   Zip

Phone Number _____ Own Home _____ Rent _____ Board _____

Date of Birth _____ Height _____ Weight _____ Color of Hair _____ Color of Eyes _____

Married _____ Single _____ Widowed _____ Divorced _____ Separated _____

Number of Children _____ Dependents Other Than Wife or Children _____ Citizen of U. S. A. Yes O No O

If Related to Anyone in Our Employ, State Name and Department _____ Referred By _____

EMPLOYMENT DESIRED

Position _____ Date You Can Start _____ Salary Desired _____

Are You Employed Now? _____ If So May We Inquire of Your Present Employer _____

Ever Applied to this Company Before? _____ Where _____ When _____

EDUCATION	Name and Location of School	Years Attended	Date Graduated	Subjects Studied
Grammar School				
High School				
College				
Trade, Business or Correspondence School				

Subjects of Special Study or Research Work _____

What Foreign Languages Do You Speak Fluently? _____ Read _____ Write _____

U. S. Military or Naval Service _____ Rank _____ Present Membership in National Guard or Reserves _____

Activities Other Than Religious (Civic, Athletic, Fraternal, etc.) _____
EXCLUDE ORGANIZATIONS, THE NAME OR CHARACTER OF WHICH INDICATES THE RACE, CREED, COLOR OR NATIONAL ORIGIN OF ITS MEMBERS.

(Continued on Other Side)

Form 660-26 U. S. A. WILSON JONES   APPLICATION FOR EMPLOYMENT

(side margin labels: Last, First, Middle)

FORMER EMPLOYERS (List Below Last Four Employers, Starting With Last One First)

Date Month and Year	Name and Address of Employer	Salary	Position	Reason for Leaving
From				
To				
From				
To				
From				
To				
From				
To				

REFERENCES: Give Below the Names of Three Persons Not Related To You, Whom You Have Known At Least One Year.

	Name	Address	Business	Years Acquainted
1				
2				
3				

PHYSICAL RECORD:

List Any Physical Defects _____

Were You Ever Injured? _____ Give Details _____

Have You Any Defects In Hearing? _____ In Vision? _____ In Speech? _____

In Case of Emergency Notify _____

Name   Address   Phone No.

I authorize investigation of all statements contained in this application. I understand that misrepresentation or omission of facts called for is cause for dismissal. Further, I understand and agree that my employment is for no definite period and may, regardless of the date of payment of my wages and salary, be terminated at any time without any previous notice.

Date _____ Signature _____

DO NOT WRITE BELOW THIS LINE

Interviewed By _____ Date _____

REMARKS: _____

Neatness		Character	
Personality		Ability	

Hired _____ For Dept. _____ Position _____ Will Report _____ Salary Wages _____

Approved: 1. _____ 2. _____ 3. _____

Employment Manager   Dept. Head   General Manager

ple, if the applicant lists under "education" that he had one and a half years of college, you might ask why he left, and whether he plans to go back.

In any job interview situation, you're not going to get the absolute truth from the applicant, and he's naturally on best behavior because he wouldn't be there if he didn't need or want the job. Maybe he hates the thought of working in your store, but can't find a job in the field of his interest. Or maybe he's just looking for something to fill in until he goes back to school. Maybe he doesn't know if he'll like working for you, but wants to give it a try. Some people are more skilled than others at job interviews, so the interview method of choosing employees is fallible. But it's better than nothing, and the more skilled you become at interviewing, the more chance you'll have of successfully choosing applicants through the use of this method.

CHECKING REFERENCES. No matter how great an applicant seems to be at the interview, don't make a decision until you've checked his references. If he's worked for other companies, write each one a letter asking about the applicant's work record. See the example in Figure 13-3. Be sure to enclose a stamped, self-addressed envelope to make it easy for him to reply. You might also want to ask the person for personal references and write to them, although practically anybody can get friends to write a good recommendation. If the applicant has no work record, ask him for the names of several teachers, and ask them for recommendations.

Although previous employers usually will not give a really bad reference on anyone, you'll at least be able to confirm that the applicant actually worked for that company when he said he did. You'll also be able to note the difference between a really great reference and a mediocre one.

JUDGING THE APPLICANT'S APPLICATION. While no system is perfect, it's been found that the applicant who neatly answers every question on his application form (or hands you a beautifully typed resume), will probably work out better than the one who leaves out a lot of information, fills out the form incorrectly, and does it sloppily. Also the applicant who shows a spotty work record—short periods of employment at many jobs with long lapses of unemployment in between—will also tend to be a poorer choice for you. These are only generalities, and there will be many exceptions, but utilizing these guidelines can help you increase your chances of successfully choosing the right employee.

WHAT DO YOUR EMPLOYEES EXPECT FROM YOU? Once you've chosen the right employee, you want to keep him or her on the job. There are many things that are important to employees besides their paycheck at the end of the week. The more you're aware of your employees' needs, the more you'll be able to satisfy them and maintain a happy, efficient staff.

One thing everyone wants to feel is that their work is appreciated.

Figure 13-3. Here's a sample letter used to check an applicant's previous work record.

Holy Cow Leather

180 HORTON ROAD
NEWFIELD, NEW YORK 14867

PHONE: (607) 564 - 9022

June 16, 1976

Mr. Raymond Smith
XYZ Company
100 Main St.
OK, USA

Dear Mr. Smith:

Ellen Jones has given your name as a reference on her
job application with our company. We'd appreciate
your answering the following questions and returning
this form in the enclosed stamped, self-addressed
envelope.

Thank you.

                              Sincerely,

                              HOLY COW LEATHER

                              Jeff Jinx
                              Jeff Jinx

Above mentioned employee, Ellen Jones:

1. worked for us from _____ to _____

2. job title_____

3. duties _____

4. quality of work _____

5. lateness and absenteeism: (circle one)

        excessive   average   low

Let your employees know when they're doing a good job. Make them feel that they're an important part of your team, and that what they do counts. One way to do this is to use employee name tags and photographs, as suggested in Chapter 12. Another way is to discuss future plans, special sales, and advertising with them. Ask them for ideas. Listen to their suggestions. By involving them in the store's operations, they'll become more interested in their jobs, and identify with your store.

Most employees will appreciate good working conditions and resent bad ones. Good conditions include clean restrooms, adequate workspace, good lighting, parking space, and so forth. After all, they're spending a major part of their lives on the job. No one wants to live in a dirty, dark, dingy place. Employees are people, and they have people problems. It's not always easy to turn off, robotlike, all your personal problems when you get to the job. A little sympathy and personal understanding from the boss and fellow employees can go a long way toward making a person feel good about his work.

TRAINING EMPLOYEES. Even if the new employee you hire has had previous selling experience in a similar retail store, you'll still want to train him in your methods. Whether the task he is hired for is handling a customer, processing shipments, arranging stock, or operating the cash register, there's a training procedure to follow.

First, tell your employee what's to be done and how it should be done. Then show him how to do it while you explain it again. Then ask him to tell you how it should be done. Finally, have him do it. When he's finished, point out areas in which he might improve. Watch him again. Then leave him alone to practice for a while. Check in periodically—more often at first—to make sure he's still doing it right.

This training plan is basic to all situations, although it'll have to be modified in some instances. For example, you can follow it exactly to train an employee how to operate a cash register. But in handling customers, you might try it this way. First, discuss the procedure you expect him to use in handling customers (see Chapter 11, Selling). Then let him observe you on the floor dealing with customers. When you get a chance to be alone with him again, ask him to tell you how you handled the customers. Point out any details he might have missed, such as the initial greeting of the customer or trying to make the "extra" sale. Then give him a chance to handle a few customers himself. Don't hover over him, however, because you'll only make him nervous. Give him some breathing space, but be near enough to casually observe what happens. Once again, when you're alone with him, point out anything he might have missed or could improve on in his customer contacts.

The important thing in coaching your employees is to do it rationally, consistently, and tactfully. By rationally, I mean you should only expect from your employees what you've requested of them. Be clear about what their duties are and how you expect them to behave. Consistency is necessary, because if you're strict about requirements one day and let anything happen the next, the results of training will be just as inconsistent. Tact is important so the employee can maintain his self-respect. Never criticize him in front of customers or other employees. Always wait and do it privately.

EMPLOYEE NEWSLETTERS AND SALES MEETINGS. Monthly employee newsletters and sales meetings can help your sales staff coordinate sales efforts and improve employee performance. Write up a short letter with several relevant subjects. For example: selling tips, new products, special promotions, and product information. Distribute the newsletters about a week before the sales meeting. Tell your employees that they should read the newsletter and then jot down their comments and ideas for discussion at the meeting.

At the sales meeting discuss the items in the newsletter. Ask your sales clerks specific questions to get their ideas, opinions, and feelings. "What do you think is the reason sales were down last week?" "How do you think we should display this new product line?" "Do you like your new work schedule?"

Distribute copies of trade magazines and literature from suppliers to your staff and ask them to read the material. Discuss important marketing trends and product information at the meetings. Talk about the advertising that's going to be done, and make sure everyone is aware of special promotions. If problems have occurred, such as with shoplifting or waste, discuss these situations with your staff and enlist their aid for solutions. Keep your employees informed about how they're doing, and consequently, how the store is doing.

PAYING EMPLOYEES. There are several ways you might consider paying your employees. You could pay them salary, or commissions and bonuses, or both. There are advantages and disadvantages in each system. The advantage of straight salary is that it's simple, and the least clerical work is involved. The disadvantage is that all sales clerks are paid the same no matter how they perform. There's no incentive to do well.

On straight commission the sales clerk who sells the most gets paid the most. The misfits are weeded out and high sales volume is encouraged. The problem is that sales clerks will tend to concentrate on items easiest to sell, and there may be a temptation to high-pressure customers. It's also difficult to use straight commission if you expect salesclerks to have other duties, such as cleaning or working in the stockroom.

Probably the best arrangement is a combination of salary plus commission, or salary plus a bonus on sales over a certain quota, or salary plus a share of the profits of the business. This way you've eliminated the problems of the straight commission plan without destroying the incentive to sell more merchandise.

The exact dollar amount of salary to offer, and what percentage of commission or bonus, will vary depending upon your location, the supply of workers, and what your competition pays. Check out other retail stores in your area to learn what the going rate is and figure your own. You want to be able to attract and keep the best employees possible. This means offering a competitive salary, with the possibility of getting raises or increased future earnings through commissions or bonuses.

SUPERVISION. Supervision is an ongoing proposition. You can do the best job of hiring the right employee and training him, but you can't stop there. While you shouldn't be constantly on your employee's back, don't ignore him either. He needs feedback about the kind of job he's doing. That means praise when he's doing something right, and a tactful reminder when he's doing something wrong. So you've got to observe what he's doing in order to know whether he's doing it right.

While some people are what you would call "self-starters" and require little supervision, they're the exception, rather than the rule. And even they like to know that they're appreciated. Since your store is your business and you make the profit off it, naturally you've got the most interest in its success. You simply can't leave your business to employees while you go off for days or weeks or months and expect things to run properly. The only way to do this successfully would be to hire a manager for your store, train him in that management, pay him for doing a manager's job (perhaps offering him a share in the profits), and still it would be necessary to supervise what he's doing, even if you do so through the records of sales and profit and loss.

FIRING EMPLOYEES. This is one step that no employer enjoys doing, and it's especially hard the first time it happens. Unfortunately, you'll probably have to face it sooner or later in your business. Since your selection procedures are not perfect, and some people who seem right for the job just don't work out, occasionally it may be necessary to fire someone. This isn't a tragedy, and you shouldn't feel responsible for that person's life. Your business would eventually fail if you continued to pay salaries to unproductive employees, and once your business failed, everybody would suffer, including you and your family.

Before you fire an employee, however, be sure you've done everything possible to help him succeed in his job. Have you told him what he does wrong? Have you asked him to improve, and suggested ways he might? Always give a definite time limit within which you expect these things to be accomplished. After you've done this and there's still no improvement, issue a final warning. Then follow through and keep your word.

SUMMING UP. Employees can make or break your business. This is why recruiting, selecting, training and supervising your employees should be taken seriously. Hire the best person you can for the job. Train him thoroughly. Then use a competitive reward system and communicative supervision to keep that employee top notch. Your efforts will be rewarded twofold, with a satisfied staff and a profitable business.

14 Payroll

Whether you have one or 20 employees, you'll be required to comply with federal, state, and local requirements on withholding taxes, social security, workmen's compensation insurance, disability, and safety laws. There will be payroll records to keep, forms to fill out, and monies to deposit with various agencies. Before hiring any employees, check with your local agencies to find out which laws apply to you and how to comply with them.

DO YOU HAVE TO GO THROUGH ALL THIS? The only way to avoid these responsibilities is to have only partners or stockholders in your business. This is why some people prefer family businesses, but that's not always possible or even desirable. By setting up complete records at the beginning and conscientiously depositing monies and filing forms as they become due, the handling of your payroll responsibilities will become routine. If you feel it's too much to handle by yourself, hire an accountant or experienced bookkeeper on a part-time basis.

WHAT WILL IT COST YOU? When figuring the cost of hiring an employee, you'll have to consider more than his base salary. There are laws governing overtime payment that must be complied with, and minimum wage laws to govern the hourly rate you pay. In addition, employers are required to pay social security taxes, federal unemployment insurance, possibly state unemployment insurance, and in some cases workmen's compensation and disability insurance. All these costs, plus the bookkeeping time involved, should be considered when hiring an employee. Extras, such as pension plans and medical insurance coverage, add to the cost. The important thing is to know what each of your employees will cost you and to be able to justify this cost in the overall operation of your store.

REGISTER WITH TAX AGENCIES. Before you hire, notify all your local tax agencies that you're a new employer. The Internal Revenue

Service will send you a form to fill out to obtain an Employer's Identification Number. This permanent identification number should be used on all federal, state, and city tax forms. The IRS will also send you a current *Employer's Tax Guide,* which will give you all the information you need about how and when to deduct and pay federal withholding taxes, social security taxes (FICA or FOAB), and federal unemployment taxes. It'll also send you the necessary forms for deposits and reporting.

Next, call your state agencies and advise them you'll soon be a new employer. They'll send you all the necessary forms and information about withholding and unemployment taxes. If your local community has withholding taxes, get in touch. You'll find the addresses and phone numbers of these agencies in your phone book. Internal Revenue Service is listed under United States Government, state tax agencies under your state government, and city tax agencies under your local government. If you have difficulty finding any of these agencies, ask your local Chamber of Commerce for help.

To get information about workmen's compensation and disability insurance, contact your insurance agent. Every state has its own laws, and your agent will be able to help you comply with them. The rates are usually based on the number of employees you have and the type of work they do. The purpose of workmen's compensation is to protect employees who get hurt on the job. It pays the medical costs of work-related injuries and a percentage of their salaries while out of work due to these injuries. Naturally the more dangerous the work your employees do, the higher the insurance rates will most likely be.

EMPLOYEE FORMS. Whenever you hire a new employee, have him fill out a Form W-4 or W-4E, Employee's Withholding Allowance Certificate (see Figures 14-1 and 14-2). On it he should list the exemptions and additional withholding allowances he claims. This completed certificate is your authority to withhold income tax in accordance with the withholding tables issued by the IRS. If an employee fails to furnish a certificate, you're required to withhold tax as if he were a single person with no withholding exemptions.

Figure 14-1. Here's an example of how your employee might fill out a W-4 form. The back (not shown) has a worksheet for determining withholding allowances for itemized deductions.

Figure 14-2. (Below) Here's a sample W-4E form that is used by employees who expect not to be liable for income taxes that year. This means you deduct no withholding taxes from their pay.

Form **W-4E** Department of the Treasury Internal Revenue Service	**Exemption From Withholding** (of Federal Income Tax) For use by employees who incurred no tax liability in 1974 and anticipate no tax liability for 1975	**1975**

Type or print full name JIM WARREN	Social Security Number 130-20-1287	Expiration date (see instructions and enter date) 5/30/76

Home address (Number and Street)   300 MAIN ST.

City, State, and ZIP Code   OURTOWN, USA 10000

Employee.—File this certificate with your employer. Otherwise he must withhold Federal income tax from your wages.	**Employee's certification.**—Under penalties of perjury, I certify that I incurred no liability for Federal income tax for 1974 and that I anticipate that I will incur no liability for Federal income tax for 1975.
Employer.—Keep this certificate with your records. This certificate may be used instead of Form W-4 by those employees qualified to claim the exemption.	Jim Warren (Signature) 4/3/75 (Date)

Employee's Withholding Allowance Certificate

The explanatory material below will help you determine your correct number of withholding allowances, and will indicate whether you should complete the new Form W-4 at the bottom of this page.

How Many Withholding Allowances May You Claim?

Please use the schedule below to determine the number of allowances you may claim for tax withholding purposes. In determining the number, keep in mind these points: If you are single and hold more than one job, you may not claim the same allowances with more than one employer at the same time; If you are married and both you and your wife or husband are employed, you may not claim the same allowances with your employers at the same time. A nonresident alien other than a resident of Canada, Mexico or Puerto Rico may claim only one personal allowance.

Figure Your Total Withholding Allowances Below

(a) Allowance for yourself—enter 1 .... | **1**
(b) Allowance for your wife (husband)—enter 1 ....
(c) Allowance for your age—if 65 or over—enter 1 ....
(d) Allowance for your wife's (husband's) age—if 65 or over—enter 1 ....
(e) Allowance for blindness (yourself)—enter 1 ....
(f) Allowance for blindness (wife or husband)—enter 1 ....
(g) Allowance(s) for dependent(s)—you are entitled to claim an allowance for each dependent you will be able to claim on your Federal income tax return. Do not include yourself or your wife (husband)* .... | **2**
(h) Special withholding allowance—if you have only one job, and do not have a wife or husband who works—enter 1 ....
(i) Total—add lines (a) through (h) above .... | **3**

If you do not plan to itemize deductions on your income tax return, enter the number shown on line (i) on line 1, Form W-4 below. Skip lines (j) and (k).

(j) Allowance(s) for itemized deductions—If you do plan to itemize deductions on your income tax return, enter the number from line 5 of worksheet on back ....
(k) Total—add lines (i) and (j) above. Enter here and on line 1, Form W-4 below .... | **3**

*If you are in doubt as to whom you may claim as a dependent, see the instructions which came with your last Federal income tax return or call your local Internal Revenue Service office.

See Table and Worksheet on Back if You Plan to Itemize Your Deductions

Completing New Form W-4

If you find that you are entitled to one or more allowances in addition to those which you are now claiming, please increase your number of allowances by completing the form below and filing with your employer. If the number of allowances you previously claimed decreases, you must file a new Form W-4 within 10 days. (Should you expect to owe more tax than will be withheld, you may use the same form to increase your withholding by claiming fewer or "0" allowances on line 1 or by asking for additional withholding on line 2 or both.)

▼ Give the bottom part of this form to your employer; keep the upper part for your records and information ▼

Form W-4 (Rev. Aug. 1972) Department of the Treasury Internal Revenue Service

Employee's Withholding Allowance Certificate

(This certificate is for income tax withholding purposes only; it will remain in effect until you change it.)

Type or print your full name **KAREN JONES**

Your social security number **130-40-3682**

Home address (Number and street or rural route) **200 MAIN ST.**

Marital status ☒ Single ☐ Married
(If married but legally separated, or wife (husband) is a nonresident alien, check the single block.)

City or town, State and ZIP code **OURTOWN, USA 10000**

1 Total number of allowances you are claiming **3**

2 Additional amount, if any, you want deducted from each pay (if your employer agrees) .... $

I certify that to the best of my knowledge and belief, the number of withholding allowances claimed on this certificate does not exceed the number to which I am entitled.

Signature ► *Karen Jones* Date ► **3/2/76** 19____

Figure 14-3 illustrates the front and back of Form IT-2104, the New York State Employee's Withholding Exemption Certificate. If your state or local government has withholding taxes, your employees will be required to fill out similar forms. Before December 31 each year, you should ask your employees to file new exemption certificates for the following year, if there has been a change in their exemption status.

PAYROLL BOOK. Using a payroll book is the simplest way to keep track of your employees' salaries and deductions for various taxes. These books, available in office supply stores, come in various sizes, depending on the number of employees you have (see Figure 14-4). Note that there are columns to list hours worked, rate of pay, overtime, other earnings, deductions, and net pay. If you pay commissions or bonuses, as well as an hourly or weekly rate, these can be listed under "other earnings."

Figure 14-4. (Right) *Here's a page from a typical payroll book that can be purchased from your local office supply store.*

Figure. 14-3. (Below) *This is the front and back of Form IT-2104, New York State's Employee's Withholding Exemption Certificate. Your state and city may have similar forms.*

IT-2104 (1/72)
State of New York
Dept. of Taxation and Finance

NEW YORK STATE - EMPLOYEE'S WITHHOLDING EXEMPTION CERTIFICATE

Print full name ...... KAREN JONES ...... Social Security No. 130-40-3682

Print home address ...... 200 MAIN ST., ... City OURTOWN State USA ZIP Code 11000

EMPLOYEE:

File this exemption certificate with your employer if you choose to claim New York State withholding tax exemptions different from those used for Federal withholding purposes.

EMPLOYER:

Keep exemption certificates with your records. Certificates may be on this form, or a similar form. If the employee is believed to have claimed too many exemptions, notify the Director, Income Tax Bureau.

HOW TO CLAIM YOUR WITHHOLDING EXEMPTIONS

1. Personal exemption for yourself. Write "1" if claimed................   1
2. If married, personal exemption for your wife (or husband) if not separately claimed by her(him). Write "1" if claimed........................   ....
3. Special withholding allowance if claimed on Federal Form W-4. Write "1" if claimed .   ...
4. Exemptions for age and blindness (applicable only to you and your wife but not to dependents):
   (a) If you or your wife will be 65 years of age or older at the end of the year, and you claim this exemption, write the figure "1"; if both will be 65 or older, and you claim both of these exemptions, write the figure "2".................   ....
   (b) If you or your wife are blind, and you claim this exemption, write the figure "1"; if both are blind, and you claim both of these exemptions, write the figure "2"...   2
5. Exemptions for dependents. Write the number of such exemptions claimed.........   ....
6. Withholding allowances for itemized deductions claimed on Federal Form W-4 (See instructions on other side)............................   ....
7. Add the number of exemptions and allowances claimed above and write the total   3
8. Additional withholding per pay period under agreement with employer .... $ ....

I CERTIFY that the number of withholding exemptions claimed on this certificate does not exceed the number to which I am entitled.
(Date) ...... March 2 ...... , 19 76   (Signed) Karen Jones

IT-2104 (Back) (1/72)   Page 2

**HOW TO CLAIM ADDITIONAL WITHHOLDING ALLOWANCES
FOR ITEMIZED DEDUCTIONS**

If you claimed withholding allowances for itemized deductions on Federal Form W-4 you may also claim such allowances at item 6 of this form for New York State withholding purposes.

The number of such allowances may not exceed the corresponding claim on a Federal Form W-4 filed by you with your employer for the period for which this certificate is filed. You may, however, claim fewer allowances on this form than you did on Federal Form W-4.

If you file a new certificate on Federal Form W-4 reducing the additional withholding allowances for itemized deductions for the current year or for a subsequent year you must file a revised New York State Form IT-2104 unless the total number of exemptions and allowances on the new Federal certificate equals or exceeds the number claimed on the New York State form currently used by your employer.

MUTUAL NO. SS-12   *PAYROLL WEEK ENDING* _____ *19* ____

• NAME OF EMPLOYEE	• DAYS AND HOURS						TOTAL		• WAGES				• EMPLOYEE DEDUCTIONS						TOTAL DEDUCT.		• NET AMOUNT PAYABLE
							REG. TIME	OVER TIME	WAGE RATE	REGULAR WAGES	OVRTIME WAGES	TOTAL WAGES	FED. O.A.T.	FED. WITH. TAX	STATE WITH. TAX	CITY WITH. TAX	SICKNESS DISBLTY				
1																					
2																					
3																					
4																					
5																					
6																					
7																					
8																					
9																					
10																					
11																					
12																					
13																					
14																					
15																					

SUMMARY OF EARNINGS & TAX DATA

	• TOTALS FIRST QUARTER							• TOTALS SECOND QUARTER					
	TOTAL WAGES	FED. OLD AGE	FED. WITHHOLD TAX	STATE WITHHOLD TAX	CITY WITHHOLD TAX	SICK DISB. TAX		TOTAL WAGES	FED. OLD AGE	FED. WITHHOLD TAX	STATE WITHHOLD TAX	CITY WITHHOLD TAX	SICK DISB. TAX
1													
2													
3													
4													
5													
6													
7													
8													
9													
10													
11													
12													
13													
14													
15													

Once you've figured an employee's total earnings for the week, the FOAB (also known as FICA, or social security taxes) is computed by multiplying a set percentage rate times the earnings. This rate, presently 5.85 percent for employees, may change over the years. A table is provided in the *Employer's Tax Guide*, which saves you the trouble of computing the tax. The same FOAB rate is used no matter what the exemptions or marital status of your employee.

Tax tables are provided in the *Employer's Tax Guide* to compute federal withholding tax. There are separate tables for married and single employees—the fewer the exemptions, the larger the deduction. Follow the tax tables carefully, to find the employee's proper federal withholding tax deduction.

State and city withholding deductions, similarly, are found in the tables provided, and are usually based on the number of exemptions. Once you've computed all the deductions, subtract them from total earnings to get the employee's net pay—the amount to be shown on his paycheck.

PAYING EMPLOYEES. When paying your employees, you should provide them with a listing of their wages, deductions, and net pay. If you use a separate payroll checking account, the checks come with stubs prepared for filling in this information. If you have only a few employees, however, this really isn't necessary—simply write all the information on a piece of paper as shown in Figure 14-5. Then staple the paper to the employee's paycheck.

Many employees discard this piece of paper or payroll check stub after looking at it. But for those who want to keep track of their taxes and check the totals at the end of the year, these stubs provide the necessary information. You, of course, will have a permanent record in your payroll book.

RECAPITULATIONS. Depending upon the total amount of taxes you withhold, you'll be required to deposit taxes either monthly, quarterly, or yearly. Generally, if the amount of taxes due is large you'll be required to pay them more frequently than when the amount is small. Figure 14-6 shows a page from the payroll book, which is set up for you to do a monthly recapitulation of payroll deductions. It provides room for three months or one quarter. Although some payroll books may be organized differently, all will have a place for you to keep track of cumulative deductions of taxes.

Figure 14-6. This is a "recapitulation" page from a payroll book, where you can record cumulative monthly and quarterly taxes

Karen Jones		Payroll Period Ending 4/8/76	
Gross Pay	$55.90	F.O.A.B.	$3.27
		Withholding	.70
	- 4.27	N.Y.S.	.30
		Total Ded.	$4.27
Net Pay	$51.63		

Figure 14-5. If you don't use special payroll checks, attach a stub like this one to each employee's paycheck.

MONTHLY RECAPITULATION OF PAYROLL DEDUCTIONS

MONTH OF _____ 19___

F. O. A .B

TOTAL PAYROLL FOR MONTH
LESS EXEMPTION WAGES $ _____

1st Week _____
2nd " _____
3rd " _____
4th " _____
5th " _____

TOTAL TAXABLE WAGES $ _____

combined employer
employee Tax is   % $ _____

FEDERAL WITHHOLDING TAX

1st Week _____
2nd " _____
3rd " _____
4th " _____
5th " _____

TOTAL WITHHOLDING TAX $ _____

TOTAL F. O. A. B. & WITHHOLDING $ _____

STATE WITHHOLDING TAX

1st Week _____
2nd " _____
3rd " _____
4th " _____
5th " _____

TAX AT _____ %

OTHER DEDUCTIONS

1st Week _____
2nd " _____
3rd " _____
4th " _____
5th " _____

TOTAL $ _____

MONTH OF _____ 19___

F. O. A .B

TOTAL PAYROLL FOR MONTH
LESS EXEMPTION WAGES $ _____

1st Week _____
2nd " _____
3rd " _____
4th " _____
5th " _____

TOTAL TAXABLE WAGES $ _____

combined employer
employee Tax is   % $ _____

FEDERAL WITHHOLDING TAX

1st Week _____
2nd " _____
3rd " _____
4th " _____
5th " _____

TOTAL WITHHOLDING TAX $ _____

TOTAL F. O. A. B. & WITHHOLDING $ _____

STATE WITHHOLDING TAX

1st Week _____
2nd " _____
3rd " _____
4th " _____
5th " _____

TAX AT _____ %

OTHER DEDUCTIONS

1st Week _____
2nd " _____
3rd " _____
4th " _____
5th " _____

TOTAL $ _____

MONTH OF _____ 19___

F. O. A .B

TOTAL PAYROLL FOR MONTH
LESS EXEMPTION WAGES $ _____

1st Week _____
2nd " _____
3rd " _____
4th " _____
5th " _____

TOTAL TAXABLE WAGES $ _____

combined employer
employee Tax is   % $ _____

FEDERAL WITHHOLDING TAX

1st Week _____
2nd " _____
3rd " _____
4th " _____
5th " _____

TOTAL WITHHOLDING TAX $ _____

TOTAL F. O. A. B. & WITHHOLDING $ _____

STATE WITHHOLDING TAX

1st Week _____
2nd " _____
3rd " _____
4th " _____
5th " _____

TAX AT _____ %

OTHER DEDUCTIONS

1st Week _____
2nd " _____
3rd " _____
4th " _____
5th " _____

TOTAL $ _____

Note that, on the recapitulation page, there's a place to list "combined employer employee tax," for FOAB. Employers are required to contribute the same amount as the employee, so if the employee tax rate is 5.85 percent, the total taxes to be paid would be 11.7 percent of the employee's wages. Finally, there's a place to list the total FOAB, plus withholding taxes. This is the figure to be used to determine if your taxes must be deposited monthly or quarterly.

As explained fully in the *Employer's Tax Guide*, these taxes may be paid quarterly, unless the cumulative amount of undeposited taxes is $200 or more at the end of any month. If the total taxes due (employee's FOAB, plus employer's FOAB, plus federal withholding) by the end of the first or second month, are over $200, they must be deposited within 15 days after the end of the month.

Deposits of payroll taxes must be made at any authorized commercial bank or a Federal Reserve Bank. Your own bank may be authorized to take these deposits. If not, it can recommend one that is. Figure 14-7 shows Federal Tax Deposit Form 501, which must accompany each deposit. Send this form along with your check. If your total withholding and FOAB don't accumulate to $200 by the end of any quarter, however, it's not necessary to make a deposit.

FORM 941. At the end of each quarter you must fill out and send in Form 941, which lists names of employees, social security numbers, taxable FICA wages, withholding taxes, and totals. This form is due the last day of the following month, and must be accompanied by a check for any taxes that weren't deposited at an authorized commercial or Federal Reserve Bank.

In the sample shown in Figure 14-8, you'll note that you must list each employee and his total taxable FICA wages before deductions. On line 14, the taxable FICA wages paid are multiplied by 11.7 percent,

Figure 14-8. (Opposite page) *This is a sample Form 941 as it might be filled out by a typical employer.*

Figure 14-7. (Below) *This is Federal Tax Deposit Form 501, that must accompany each tax deposit to an authorized commercial or Federal Reserve Bank.*

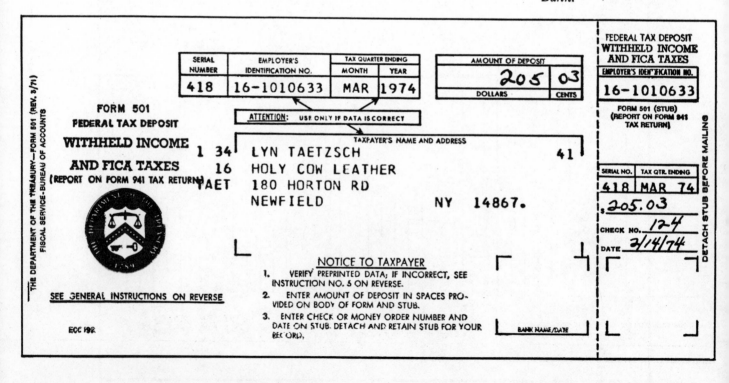

which is the combined amount paid by employee and employer. This is added to the total income tax withheld on line 13 to get the total taxes on line 19. In the sample case, all the taxes had already been deposited at an authorized commercial bank, so no further payments were due.

UNEMPLOYMENT TAXES. You must pay federal unemployment taxes if you employ four or more employees on at least some portion of one day in each of 20 or more calendar weeks. The 20 weeks don't have to be consecutive. If you're liable, this tax is due on or before January

Form **941** (Rev. April 1974) Department of the Treasury Internal Revenue Service	**Employer's Quarterly Federal Tax Return**	

Schedule A—Quarterly Report of Wages Taxable under the Federal Insurance Contributions Act—FOR SOCIAL SECURITY

List for each nonagricultural employee the WAGES taxable under the FICA which were paid during the quarter. If you pay an employee more than $13,200 in a calendar year report only the first $13,200 of such wages. In the case of "Tip Income" see instructions on page 4. IF WAGES WERE NOT TAXABLE UNDER THE FICA MAKE NO ENTRIES IN ITEMS 1 THROUGH 9 AND 14 THROUGH 18.

1. Total pages of this return including this page and any pages of Form 941a ▶ **1**	2. Total number of employees listed ▶ **8**	3. (First quarter only) Number of employees (except household) employed in the pay period including March 12th ▶		
4. EMPLOYEE'S SOCIAL SECURITY NUMBER 000 00 0000	**5. NAME OF EMPLOYEE** (Please type or print)	**6. TAXABLE FICA WAGES** Paid to Employee in Quarter (Before deductions) Dollars / Cents	**7. TAXABLE TIPS REPORTED** (See page 4) Dollars / Cents	
399-48-7891	Louise Liebherr	592. 90	
049-40-8827	David Hutchinson	863. 00	
173-40-0174	David Warden	803. 75	
153-44-7664	John Cowan	910. 80	
228-62-5702	William Wright	619. 50	
088-40-5587	Rebecca Stevens	71. 00	
050-50-0752	Robin Munson	91. 80	
166-48-0773	William Wilson	20. 70	

If you need more space for listing employees, use Schedule A continuation sheets, Form 941a.
Totals for this page—Wage total in column 6 and tip total in column 7 ⟶ **3973.45**

8. TOTAL WAGES TAXABLE UNDER FICA PAID DURING QUARTER. $ 3973.45

   (Total of column 6 on this page and continuation sheets.) Enter here and in item 14 below.

9. TOTAL TAXABLE TIPS REPORTED UNDER FICA DURING QUARTER. $ 0

   (Total of column 7 on this page and continuation sheets.) Enter here and in item 15 below. (If no tips reported, write "None.")

YOUR COPY

Name ....   Date Quarter Ended ....

Address ....   Employer Identification No. ....

IMPORTANT.—Keep this copy and a copy of each related schedule or statement.

Before filing the return be sure to enter on this copy your name, address, and identification number, and the period for which the return is filed.

10. Total Wages And Tips Subject To Withholding Plus Other Compensation . . . . . ▶	3973	45
11. Amount Of Income Tax Withheld From Wages, Tips, Annuities, etc. (See instructions) . . .	267	30
12. Adjustment For Preceding Quarters Of Calendar Year		—
13. Adjusted Total Of Income Tax Withheld . . . . ▶	267	30
14. Taxable FICA Wages Paid (Item 8) . . $ 3973.45 .... multiplied by 11.7% = TAX	464	89
15. Taxable Tips Reported (Item 9) . . . $ .... multiplied by 5.85% = TAX		0
16. Total FICA Taxes (Item 14 plus Item 15) . . . . ▶	464	89
17. Adjustment (See instructions)		—
18. Adjusted Total Of FICA Taxes . . . . ▶	464	89
19. Total Taxes (Item 13 plus Item 18)	732	19
20. TOTAL DEPOSITS FOR QUARTER (INCLUDING FINAL DEPOSIT MADE FOR QUARTER) AND OVERPAYMENT FROM PREVIOUS QUARTER LISTED IN SCHEDULE B (See instructions on page 4)	732	19

Note: If undeposited taxes at the end of the quarter are $200 or more, the full amount must be deposited with an authorized commercial bank or a Federal Reserve bank. This deposit must be entered in Schedule B and included in item 20.

21. Undeposited Taxes Due (Item 19 Less Item 20—This Should Be Less Than $200). Pay To Internal Revenue Service And Enter Here		0
22. If Item 20 Is More Than Item 19, Enter Excess Here ▶ $ And Check If You Want It ☐ Applied To Next Return, Or ☐ Refunded.		
23. If not liable for returns in succeeding quarters write "FINAL" here ▶ and enter date of final payment of taxable wages here ▶		

See "Where to File" on Page 2.

31 for the preceding year. Form 940 (see Figure 14-9) must be filled out and the balance due (on line 18) sent along with the form. If your quarterly unemployment taxes amount to more than $100, they must be paid quarterly.

This federal unemployment tax must be paid by the employer, not deducted from the employee's wages. But some of the unemployment taxes you pay to your state government may be deducted from the federal unemployment taxes. On the sample shown, $405.86 was paid in New York State unemployment taxes. The amount of $306.97 was allowed as a deduction from the gross federal tax (line 14), making the final balance due the IRS $65.94. Detailed instructions on how to compute this are given on the back of Form 940.

Figure 14-9. (Opposite page) This is a sample Form 940, which should accompany the payment of federal unemployment taxes.

Form 940
Department of the Treasury
Internal Revenue Service

Employer's Annual Federal Unemployment Tax Return

1973

Schedule A—Computation of Credit Against Federal Unemployment Tax

Name of State (1)	State reporting number as shown on employer's State contribution returns (2)	Taxable payroll (As defined in State act) (3)	Experience rate period (4)		Experience rate (5)	Contributions had rate been 2.7% (col. 3 × 2.7%) (6)	Contributions payable at experience rate (col. 3 × col. 5) (7)	Additional credit (col. 6 minus col. 7) (8)	Contributions actually paid to State (9)
			From—	To—					
N.Y.		11274							405.86
Totals ▶		11274							

10. Total tentative credit (Column 8 plus column 9) 405.86

11. Enter 2.7% of the amount of wages shown in Item 13 below 306.97

12. Credit allowable (Item 10 or 11 whichever is smaller). Enter here and in Item 15 . . . .   306.97

KEEP THIS COPY
FOR YOUR RECORDS

You must retain this copy, and a copy of each related schedule or statement for a period of 4 years after the date the tax is due or paid, whichever is the later. These copies must be available for inspection by the Internal Revenue Service.

13. Total taxable wages paid during calendar year (From Schedule B, on other side) . . . .   11369 | 25

14. Gross Federal tax (3.28% of Item 13) . . . .   372 | 91

15. Less: Credit (State taxes paid and additional credit) from Item 12, Schedule A . . . .   306 | 97

16. Item 14 less Item 15 . . . .   65 | 94

17. Total Federal tax deposited (From Schedule C, on other side)   0

18. Balance Due (Item 16 less Item 17). Pay to "Internal Revenue Service" . . . . ▶   65 | 94

19. If no longer in business at end of year, write "FINAL" here ▶

Important.—Before filing the return be sure to enter on this copy your name, address, and identification number.

STATE UNEMPLOYMENT TAXES. Each state has unemployment taxes. Because the rules vary in each state, you should check with the authorities to find out your obligations. Usually, the rate of tax charged is partially based on your previous unemployment experience, *i.e.*, the amount of unemployment your ex-employees have collected. This is why it's important not to allow employees who quit to collect unemployment insurance without just cause. Your rates may go up if you allow this. In some states the employee is assessed for unemployment taxes through payroll deductions.

STATE AND CITY WITHHOLDING TAXES. Contact your state and city authorities to find out their requirements for the withholding taxes from your employees' pay. Most state tax withholding forms will be similar to those used by the federal government. If the requirements differ from those for federal withholding tax returns, make sure your records give you the necessary information.

FORM W-2. At the end of the year you'll be required to provide every employee with a W-2 form listing total wages and taxes deducted for the year. This must be given to employees not later than January 31 of the following year. If an employee leaves your employ before the end of the year, however, the statement should be given to him within 30 days after his last wages were paid.

In the sample W-2 form shown in Figure 14-10, "Item 1" is the total federal income tax withheld for the year. "Item 2" lists total wages paid. "Item 3" lists FICA or social security taxes withheld (from the employee, not the total paid by employee and employer). "Item 4" lists the total FICA wages, which in most cases will be the same as Item 2. "Items 6, 7 and 8" are provided for state or local income tax information.

Figure 14-10. (Below) A W-2 form must be given to each employee at the end of every year. Here's an example of how an employer might fill one out.

Figure 14-11. (Opposite page) This W-3 Transmittal Form is used to transmit copies of the W-2 forms to the IRS.

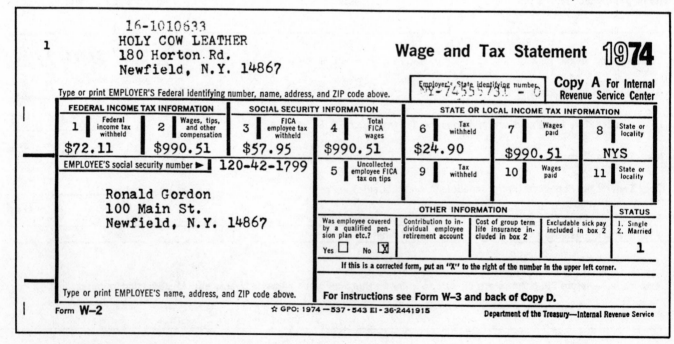

At the top of the form, type in your store name and address and your Employer's Federal and State identifying numbers. Also list the employee's name and address, his social security number, and his marital status. These forms come in sets, with copies for you, the employee, the federal government, the state government, and copies for the employee to file with his federal and state tax returns.

Figure 14-11 shows a W-3 transmittal form, which is used to transmit copies of the W-2 forms to the IRS. Detailed instructions on filling out these forms are provided in the instruction booklets you'll receive.

BE BUSINESSLIKE IN MEETING YOUR PAYROLL TAX OBLIGATIONS. Make sure that you file tax reports when they're due, and pay the tax on time. Mark your calendar at least five days in advance of each deposit and filing date to give yourself time to prepare the forms. Failure to file or pay taxes when due can bring penalties (fines or jail sentences, or both) and interest on the late payments. Even if a company is incorporated, in many cases the officers of the company can be held personally responsible for taxes due by their corporation. So find out about your tax responsibilities early, and set up your records to handle them.

Form W-3 — Transmittal of Income and Tax Statements

(Magnetic tape or disk pack filers: See the revenue procedures that apply to magnetic tape or disk pack transmittal of returns.)

Department of the Treasury — Internal Revenue Service — 1974

Enter number of documents	Form W-2	Form W-2P	Form 1099R	Original	Corrected	With taxpayer identifying number	Without taxpayer identifying number
15	15	0	0	X		X	

PAYER'S identifying number ▶ 16-1010633

Holy Cow Leather
180 Horton Rd.
Newfield, N.Y. 14867

Type or print PAYER'S name, address and ZIP code above.

Under penalties of perjury, I declare that I have examined this return, including accompanying documents and to the best of my knowledge and belief, it is true, correct, and complete. In the case of documents without recipients' identifying numbers I have complied with the requirements of the law by requesting such numbers from the recipients, but did not receive them. I assume full responsibility for the accuracy of Forms W-2 that reflect excludable sick pay.

Signature _____ Title Owner Date 1/15/75

15 Shrinkage

"Shrinkage" is the industry term for losses due to shoplifting and employee theft. This problem is much more serious than you might think, and growing worse all the time. Estimates of retail theft losses range from about 0.7 percent of sales for a well-managed department store to about 4.5 percent for a loosely controlled operation. According to one estimate, dishonest employees account for about two thirds of the retail theft. The other one third is due to shoplifting. In this chapter we're going to discuss methods to curb both types of shrinkage.

EMPLOYEE INTEGRITY. Obviously the store with the greatest proportion of honest employees suffers the least from theft loss. But too many retailers take integrity for granted. All too often, the biggest crook turns out to be the most trusted employee, who has been with the company "umpteen" years. Because this employee is so knowledgeable and well-trusted, he's in a better position to steal than anyone else. All it takes to get him started is one weak moment, one time of need, one dishonest friend, or one temptation that's too hard to resist. So after you've taken every precaution to ensure that the people you hire are honest, it's important to run your store in a way that will encourage them to stay honest.

In Chapter 13 we pointed out that an applicant may be very clever at pulling off an impressive interview. But don't let this impression dull your caution. Run a reference check on *every* new employee. When you compromise your standards of character and integrity, you also compromise your profit position.

STANDARDS AND INCENTIVES. It's important for you to set an atmosphere that will encourage honesty. This means you must display the same moral conduct you expect from your employees. Return overshipments or overpayments promptly. When you set rules, have them apply to *everyone*. If an employee catches you in even a minor dishonest act, he's encouraged in the same direction.

Set high standards and shoot for excellence. Let your employees know that you're shooting for "zero shortage." Even if you feel a reasonable write-off due to pilferage is all right, keep it a secret and hammer away at shortage control even when losses diminish.

Treat your employees with respect and dignity. Set reasonable goals, and provide the resources they need for success. Be fair in rewarding outstanding success. If the poor-performing salesclerks are rewarded as much as the top producers, resentment is likely to build up. Set reasonable rules of conduct, and enforce them rigidly. Loosely administered rules are worse than no rules at all.

Finally, you should remove the temptation to steal. One organization of counter-service restaurants is noted for its good employee relations. It treats people fairly and displays faith in their integrity. But it also provides uniforms *without pockets*. Once you remove the opportunity to steal, half the battle is won.

WAYS EMPLOYEES STEAL AND WHAT TO DO ABOUT THEM.
Refunds and returns provide dishonest employees several ways to steal. One way is to give refunds on goods that actually were never returned. In one store many returned items were marked down to a fraction of cost because of damage. It was easy for clerks to get authorization to buy "as is" merchandise. When they were armed with an okay, they substituted first-grade items for "as is" stock. To prevent this kind of theft, insist on a merchandise inspection by someone other than the person who made the sale. Match items to the return vouchers and then return the merchandise to stock as quickly as possible.

The popular salesperson is a great asset—if he or she is popular for the right reason. In one case, customers stood in line to be waited on by a particular saleswoman. They refused to be served by anyone else. Why? She switched tickets for many "special" customers, giving them substantial mark-downs. Store losses amounted to about $300 a week—not including $25 a week in increased commissions for the crook. So find out for yourself why a popular salesperson is so well-liked. Pay special attention to the salesperson who's visited by too many personal friends.

HANDLING CASH.
This is an area where employees sometimes find ways to steal. One way is to not ring up sales which are paid for by cash in the exact amount. Many times a customer doesn't ask for a receipt or sales slip. Another way is to have cooperative friends who "buy" merchandise without paying for it. This merchandise may later be returned for a refund. The employee and his friends share the proceeds. To detect this type of theft, keep a sharp eye open for signals— nods, winks, and gestures—between cashiers and customers. Pay special attention to cashiers when they're surrounded by clusters of people, and watch for items bypassed when ringing up sales.

If your employee's duties include paying bills and handling checks, these areas also provide opportunity for theft. The employee can make out checks to nonexistent companies for goods or services. Then he cashes the checks himself. Another method is to raise the amount of a check after it's been approved. To prevent this kind of theft, don't have the same employee in charge of both authorizing and issuing checks. Require each check to be verified by an invoice, keep carbon copies of the checks, and spot check the amounts to be sure they match.

SHOPLIFTING METHODS. Professional shoplifters are sleight-of-hand experts. They come equipped with coats and capes that have hidden pockets and slits or zippered hiding places. Hands emerge unseen to snatch articles directly from open displays. They're also adept at palming small items with the cover-up aid of loose handkerchiefs and gloves. Some thieves have been known to step behind counters, pose as salesclerks, and collect money from customers. Others pick up packages or handbags that store patrons have carelessly laid aside in their preoccupation with shopping.

Ticket switching is another method used by shoplifters. This is especially difficult to handle, because it's almost impossible to prove the guilt of a ticket switcher. There's also the hazard of false arrest counter-charges.

WHEN YOU CATCH A SHOPLIFTER. Call the police. Failure to prosecute first offenders encourages shoplifting. When every merchant in town follows the policy of prosecuting every shoplifter, the word gets around. Hardened professionals will avoid the town and amateurs will think twice before yielding to temptation.

PROTECTIVE PERSONNEL AND DEVICES. Some large stores use uniformed guards and plainclothesmen. In a small store where you have to rely solely on your own people, convex wall mirrors can be helpful. They allow your staff to see around corners and keep several aisles under observation at once.

Anti-shoplifting signs displayed prominently warn potential thieves. Electronic devices that expose the shoplifter are on the market. One example is an electronic pellet or wafer attached, usually, to an expensive garment so it cannot be removed without tearing the merchandise. If a shopper tries to remove the garment from the store, the pellet sends out signals. The cashier removes the pellet with special shears when the customer purchases the garment. But if the cashier forgets to remove the pellet, an innocent shopper may be stopped outside and falsely accused.

To prevent ticket switching, try the following:

1. Use tamper-proof gummed labels that rip apart when an attempt is made to remove them.

2. Use hard-to-break plastic string for soft goods tickets.

3. When tickets are stapled on, use special staple patterns that are recognizable by your staff.

4. Conceal extra price tickets on the merchandise.

5. If you use simple and basic pricing methods, don't write ticket prices in pencil. Use a rubber stamp or pricing machine.

PHYSICAL LAYOUT OF YOUR STORE. Your store's layout can encourage or discourage shoplifting. High fixtures and tall displays, which give visual protection to the shoplifter, will encourage him. Design the layout of your shop so you and your sales clerks can easily see what's going on in all sections of the store. Keep small, high-priced items out of reach, preferably in locked cases. If fire safety regulations allow it, lock all exits not to be used by customers. And always close and block-off unused check-out aisles.

WHAT YOU AND YOUR EMPLOYEES MUST DO. Be alert for people wearing loose coats, capes, or bulky dresses. Watch people carrying large purses, packages, umbrellas, and shopping bags. Be especially alert for "teams"—thieves who pretend not to know each other. One of the team will attract your attention while his partner picks up the merchandise and makes a quick exit.

If you have a clothing store, keep a check on the number of garments taken into the dressing room. Otherwise a shoplifter may try on an item and, if they think no one is watching, walk out wearing it. Or one might enter the dressing room with a shopping bag and hide the stolen garments in it. By having a limit on the number of garments allowed in the dressing room at one time, and enforcing this limit, you'll be able to prevent this type of shoplifting.

Don't give the impression that you mistrust your customers, but always be alert to their movements. When busy with one customer, acknowledge other customers with a polite remark, such as, "I'll be with you in a minute." Such attention will please ordinary customers, but make shoplifters feel uneasy.

APPREHENSION AND ARRESTS. It's best to apprehend shoplifters outside of your store. This strengthens your case against the shoplifter and avoids scenes that might interfere with store operation. If the merchandise is of substantial value, however, and you feel that the shoplifter may get away with the stolen goods if you allow him to get beyond the premises, apprehend him in the store. In some states it's sufficient if a shoplifter is observed concealing merchandise on his or her person.

A good way to stop a suspect is to speak to him and identify yourself. Then say, "I believe you have some merchandise in your bag that you've forgotten to pay for. Would you mind coming back to the store to straighten out this matter?" Never physically touch the suspect, because this could be construed as roughness. Be especially gentle with an elderly person in order to avoid his becoming shocked and having a possible heart attack.

As a general rule, be very certain before apprehending a suspected shoplifter or you'll risk a false arrest charge. Many states have passed shoplifting laws which deal with apprehending shoplifters. Check with your lawyer or local police to find out about the laws in your state.

ARE YOU BEING RIPPED-OFF? By keeping careful records and controls on sales and inventory, as discussed in Chapter 9, you'll be aware of the amount of shrinkage that is occurring in your store. Once you're aware that there is a problem, you can take steps to correct it. If you discover a serious shrinkage loss which you're unable to control by the methods listed earlier in this chapter, consider hiring a professional investigator to uncover employee and customer theft. The well-trained professional knows what to look for, where to look, and what steps to take to trip up a hard-core thief. He'll report his findings to you with documented evidence.

In many towns, merchants are forming protective associations that establish uniform procedures for handling retail theft and that cooperate to curb shoplifting in their towns. Lists are kept of previous offenders, and successful methods and experiences are shared. You can also get advice, assistance, and information from a retail credit bureau, a better business bureau, the police department, and the district attorney's office.

16 Financial Record-keeping

One obvious reason you'll need to keep records is that the IRS requires you to. You may feel that the government has overburdened you, but keeping records actually is to your advantage. A simple, well-organized system of records, regularly kept up, can save you time by bringing order out of disorder. Many studies have found a close relationship between inadequate records and business failures. Good records give you information you need to make the decisions which will keep your business profitable.

CASH OR ACCRUAL? These are two basic bookkeeping methods recognized by the IRS. If you keep your books on a cash basis, no income or expense is recorded until cash is actually paid out or received. In the accrual method, however, income and debts are recorded as soon as they're incurred. For example, using the accrual method, if you buy $100 of merchandise on 30-day terms, you'd enter the $100 expenditure in your books when you receive the invoice. In the cash method, you'd enter the $100 only when you actually wrote out a check and paid the bill.

The IRS allows either method to be used if it's used consistently. But where inventories play an important part in your business, the accrual method *must* be used in recording sales and purchases. Since, in the case of a retail store, inventories *are* an important part of your assets, you'll have to use the accrual method in recording purchases and sales. The cash system can be used for expenses and income other than sales.

THE CHANGE FUND. Since you'll be making change in your daily sales transactions, it's important to have a change fund that is set at a fixed amount. This amount is kept in the cash register at the end of each day for use the next day. The receipts for the day are taken out and deposited in the bank, leaving the change fund intact for the following day. For example, if you have a $50 change fund, and sales for the day are $250, your total in the cash register will be $300. You'll deposit $250 in the bank, leaving the $50 change fund for the next day.

PETTY CASH. A petty cash fund is useful for small miscellaneous purchases that come up during the day. You may want to keep $10, $25, or even $50 in this fund, depending on your needs. Each time money is taken from the fund, fill out a Petty Cash Slip like the one shown in Figure 16-1. Keep these slips with the petty cash (in a cash box separate from the register). When the fund gets low, write a check to petty cash and use this to bring the total back up to the original amount. When you do this, mark the used petty cash slips "complete" and file them in an envelope for future use. They will be the back-up for the check you write to bring the balance up to its full amount (see below).

```
┌─────────────────────────────────────────────────────────┐
│                                                           │
│  Amount──────────────         No.─────────                │
│                                                           │
│         RECEIVED OF PETTY CASH                            │
│                                                           │
│                       ─────────────────────19───          │
│                                                           │
│  For ──────────────────────────────────────────          │
│                                                           │
│  Charge to─────────────────────────────────────          │
│                                                           │
│  ─────────────────────────────────────────────           │
│                                                           │
│  Approved by              Received by                     │
│                                                           │
│  ─────────────────        ─────────────────────          │
│    Form No. 700-24 "RENCO QUALITY"                        │
└─────────────────────────────────────────────────────────┘
```

Figure 16-1. This is a sample Petty Cash Slip, which can be purchased at your local stationery store.

DAILY SUMMARY. At the end of each day, count the actual cash on hand and balance it against the total of the receipts recorded for the day. This is done by making a Daily Summary of Sales and Cash Receipts, as shown in Figure 16-2. If you have more than one cash register, separate summaries should be done for each and then combined.

Item 1 on the summary is Cash Sales. This is the total sales, from sales slips or cash register tape, made that day. Miscellaneous Receipts in item 2 might include refunds from suppliers for overpayments and advertising rebates or allowances. Miscellaneous Receipts should be itemized on the back of the Summary for later entry in T-accounts (see below). Item 3 is the total of 1 and 2.

Item 4 is found by actually counting the coins, bills, and checks in the register. From item 4 you must deduct item 5, your Change Fund, which remains in the cash register. Remember that this is the amount you started the day with. Item 6 is the Total Cash to be Deposited in the bank. This figure should equal item 3—Total Receipts. If it does, you have reconciled your cash receipts and can stop at this point.

But your Daily Summary won't always come out right. If items 3 and 6 don't agree, subtract item 7 (which is the same as 3) from item 6. The difference will be your shortage or overage, items 8 and 9. If you have an overage or a shortage, recheck your figures carefully. Overages could be caused by neglecting to record or ring up a sale, recording a sale for too small an amount, or giving a customer too little change. Shortages could be caused by recording too large an amount for a sale,

Figure 16-2. The Daily Summary is used for recording Cash Receipts and Sales.

DAILY SUMMARY

Cash Receipts

1. Cash Sales		$435.00
2. Miscellaneous Receipts		15.00
3. Total Receipts to be Accounted For		450.00

Cash On Hand

4. Cash in Register:		
Coins	25.00	
Bills	374.00	
Checks	95.00	
Total Cash in Register		494.00
5. Less: Change Fund		50.00
6. Total Cash to be Deposited		444.00
7. Total Receipts to be Accounted For		450.00
8. Cash Short (item 7 greater than item 6)		6.00
9. Cash Over (item 7 less than item 6)		—

Total Sales

10. Cash Sales		$435.00

giving a customer too much change, or taking money from the cash register without recording it.

As soon as you've finished your Daily Summary, make your deposit at the bank and keep a duplicate deposit slip with the summary as evidence that the deposit was made.

If you have credit customers who buy on open account, your Daily Summary should include a place to record such transactions. See Figure 16-3 for an example of such a Daily Summary. Note the addition of Collections on Account (item 2), Charge Sales (item 12), and Total Sales (item 13).

RETURNS AND REFUNDS. To protect yourself against unauthorized returns, returns of merchandise purchased elsewhere, or refunds of too great an amount, set up a policy with specific rules, including the following:

1. The original cash-register slip or sales check must be presented when merchandise is returned.

2. No refunds will be made after a specific length of time.

3. No cash refunds will be made on charge purchases.

4. All returns must be approved by you or someone you authorize to do so.

RECORDING RETURNS OR REFUNDS ON THE DAILY SUMMARY. If you use sales checks instead of a cash register, a credit sales

---

DAILY SUMMARY

Cash Receipts

1. Cash Sales $435.00
2. Collections on Account   100.00
3. Miscellaneous Receipts   15.00
4. Total Receipts to be Accounted For   550.00

Cash On Hand

5. Cash in Register:
   Coins   25.00
   Bills   474.00
   Checks   95.00
       Total Cash in Register   594.00
6. Less: Change Fund   50.00
7. Total Cash Deposit   544.00
8. Total Receipts to be Accounted For   550.00
9. Cash Short (item 8 greater than item 7)   6.00
10. Cash Over (item 8 less than item 7)   —

Total Sales

11. Cash Sales   435.00
12. Charge Sales (Sales slips #161-170)   140.00
13. Total Sales $575.00

Figure 16-3. This Daily Summary provides a place for recording Collections on Account and Charge Sales.

check marked "cash refund" should be made out when the cash is refunded to the customer. The amount of this refund should be deducted from the Cash Sales figure on the Daily Summary.

If you use a cash register with a key for return-sales, the return sale is rung up. Some cash registers subtract return sales directly from sales. In this case, the total in the cash register at the end of the day is net sales and can be entered on the Daily Summary as is. Other cash registers show only the total returned sales, which must be subtracted from the cash register total to get net sales.

If you don't have many return sales and refunds, and they don't add up to much money, you can treat them as petty cash payments and make out a petty cash slip for them. In this case they'll be treated as any other petty cash disbursement.

SALES TAXES. If your city, county, or state have retail sales taxes, you may be subject to collecting them. Some states exempt certain items such as clothes and food. Check with your chamber of commerce or local sales tax office for information about sales tax requirements in your city, county, and state.

If you're required to collect them, the sales tax percentage will have to be figured on every applicable purchase made in your store. You can get a printed chart to help in your computations. Or use a modern cash register, which is set up to compute sales taxes and print them on the register tape. If you don't use such a cash register, list the sales tax on each sales slip so you'll have a record of it. The sales taxes you collect will have to be paid periodically to your state government. See Figure 16-4 for an example of the kind of form you'll have to fill out when paying your sales taxes.

Figure 16-4. This is a New York State and Local Sales and Use Tax Return form. You may be required to file a similar form in your state.

ST-100

New York State Department of Taxation and Finance 42

New York State and Local Sales and Use Tax Return

Page 1

Under Articles 28 and 29 of Tax Law

March 1, 1972 - May 31, 1972

Use Pre-addressed Form and Return Envelope for filing your return.
Keep duplicate for your records.

Enter name, address, ZIP code and identification number if not shown correctly below.

Holy Cow Leather
Attn: Lyn Paetzsch
Apt. 5, 192 Pinckney Rd.
R. D. #7
Ithaca, New York 14850

NY-7455231

Complete page 2 of this form before making entries below.

SUMMARY OF BUSINESS ACTIVITY	GROSS SALES AND SERVICES A (to nearest dollar)	TAXABLE SALES AND SERVICES B (to nearest dollar)	PURCHASES SUBJECT TO USE TAX C (to nearest dollar)

ENTER TYPE OF BUSINESS

If this return reports sales taxes for more than one business location, check here. ☐

Summary of Taxes Due

1	Sales and Use Taxes (total column (e), page 2 and amounts from Schedules A, B and N, if any)			
2	(a) Credits (attachments required)			
	(b) Prepayments (attach Form ST-330)			
	(c) Total Credits and Prepayments	▶ ▶ ▶		
3	Sales and Use Taxes Due (line 1 less line 2(c))			
4	Add: Late Filing Charge			
5	Amount Due including Late Filing Charge (line 3 plus line 4) Pay this amount ▶			

Attach remittance payable to "New York State Sales Tax Bureau" and mail to your New York State District Tax Office on or before June 20, 1972.

SIGNATURE OF VENDOR

For office use only

TITLE   DATE

SIGNATURE OF PREPARER (IF OTHER THAN VENDOR)   DATE

ADDRESS

ST-100 (3/72)

Did you complete the other side of this form?

COMPUTING SALES TAXES. If all your sales are subject to sales tax, and a separate accounting for sales tax collections is not required by law, use this method to compute your sales taxes when due:

1. Divide total sales by 1 plus the sales tax rate to get the sales-only figure.

2. Multiply the sales-only figure by the sales tax rate to get the sales tax.

Example: Total sales = $12,022.50 divided by 1.05 (tax rate 5%) = $11,450.00 (sales only). Then $11,450 times 0.05 (tax rate 5%) = $572.50 (sales tax). Check: $11,450 (sales only) plus $572.50 (sales tax) = $12,022.50 (total sales).

If only part of your sales is subject to sales tax, record taxable sales and sales tax collections separately. If you use sales slips, total the tax-exempt sales and taxable-sales collections separately. If you use a cash register with keys for taxable sales and sales tax, you can ring up taxable sales as they're made. Your register tape will show you the total tax-exempt sales, taxable sales, and sales taxes collected.

If all your sales are subject to sales tax, there's no need to list sales taxes on the Daily Summary. But if only part of your sales are subject to sales taxes, add lines 14 and 15 to your Daily Summary, as shown in Figure 16-5. This way you'll have a record of each day's taxable sales and sales taxes.

DAILY SUMMARY

Cash Receipts

1. Cash Sales	$435.00
2. Collections on Account	100.00
3. Miscellaneous Receipts	15.00
4. Total Receipts to be Accounted For	550.00

Cash On Hand

5. Cash in Register		
Coins	25.00	
Bills	474.00	
Checks	95.00	
Total Cash in Register		594.00
6. Less: Change Fund		50.00
7. Total Cash Deposit		544.00
8. Total Receipts to be Accounted For		550.00
9. Cash Short (item 8 greater than item 7)		6.00
10. Cash Over (item 8 less than item 7)		—

Total Sales

11. Cash Sales	435.00
12. Charge Sales (Sales slips #161-170)	140.00
13. Total Sales	$575.00
14. Sales Subject to Sales Tax	115.00
15. Sales Tax Collected	4.60

Figure 16-5. This Daily Summary provides a place to record Sales Subject to Sales Tax and Sales Tax Collected.

DOUBLE ENTRY BOOKKEEPING. In this chapter we're assuming your business is fairly small and that you do most of your own record-keeping. We've kept the process as simple as possible, and in fact we've eliminated a step often used in larger or more complex businesses—the Daily Journal. If you plan to set up your own books, you can get additional information from the following sources:

> *Financial Recordkeeping for Small Stores*
> Small Business Administration
> Washington, D.C.

> *Fundamental Accounting Principles, 6th ed.*
> Pyle, William W., and John Arch White.
> Homewood, Illinois: Richard D. Irwin, Inc. 1972

You may, however, wish to hire an accountant to set up your bookkeeping systems for you. If so, study this and Chapter 17 carefully, anyway, so you'll know as much as possible about the subject. Choose an accountant who's had experience with retail stores, and make sure the systems he sets up for you will give you the information you need to run your store properly. If possible, choose an accountant recommended by successful retail store managers in your area.

The mechanics of double-entry bookkeeping basically involves setting up "T-accounts," on which the left side of the page records debits and the right side records credits. The idea of "double-entry" means that every dollar you spend or receive is entered twice; once on the debit side of an account, and once on the credit side of another account.

The principle behind entering everything twice is this: if you spend $100 on some stock for your store, you've depleted your cash resources. But you've also increased your business's resources—in particular, its inventory. So the $100 must be entered in two places to show the decrease in cash and the increase in inventory.

The sample T-accounts in Figure 16-6 illustrates how to record two utility payments. In the first transaction on June 7, a telephone bill of $30.42 was paid. On the Utilities account, "6/7" is entered under Date, "telephone" under Item, and "$30.42" under Debit. To complete the *double* entry, this $30.42 must be entered as a credit on another T-account. By listing the $30.42 under the credit column of the Cash account, the entry is balanced out.

The second transaction in Figure 16-6 is the payment of an electric and gas bill. It's recorded under Debit on the Utilities account and under Credit on the Cash account. The important thing is to be consistent. All expenditures for operating costs and purchases for your store must be entered on the debit side of those T-accounts and on the credit side of the Cash account.

SETTING UP T-ACCOUNTS. One T-account every business needs is a Cash account. Here you'll record everything that comes in under Debit and everything you spend under Credit. See Figure 16-7 for an example of a Cash account. Note that the debit side lists the cash sales

UTILITIES

DATE	ITEM	DEBIT	DATE	ITEM	CREDIT
6/7	Tel - MAY	30.42			
6/9	ELEC. & GAS	40.17			

CASH

DATE	ITEM	DEBIT	DATE	ITEM	CREDIT
			6/7	TEL. - MAY	30.42
			6/9	ELEC. & GAS	40.17

CASH

DATE	ITEM	DEBIT	DATE	ITEM	CREDIT
6/1	CASH SALES	205.00	6/1	RENT	350.00
6/2	" "	195.00	6/2	PETTY CASH	42.00
6/3	" "	150.00	6/8	HUDSON CARD CO.	195.00
6/4	" "	215.00		ZOCKO CO.	148.00
	REFUND - ZOCKO CO	15.00		GO GAME CO.	200.00
6/5	CASH SALES	230.00	6/15	PAYROLL	248.56

for each day, plus refunds from suppliers. The credit side lists all payments made for stock purchases, petty cash, salaries, and so forth.

The opposite of the cash credit listings are Cost account debit listings. For each item listed under Cash credit, there must be an account where you list it as a debit. Some cost accounts that you'll find useful in the operation of a retail store are: Stock Purchases, Freight, Utilities, Rent, Promotion, Supplies, and Payroll. Basically, you'll need to cover every major area in which you spend money. For more detailed information, these accounts can be broken down further. For example, rather than having one payroll account, you can have one each for Salaries, Social Security Taxes, Unemployment Insurance, Employee Withholding Taxes, Workmen's Compensation, and Disability Insurance. To cover occasional items that don't fit any particular category, set up an account called "Miscellaneous Expenditures."

The opposite of Cash debit listings are Receivables and Sales Credit listings. If all your income is from cash sales, you'll only need one account called "Sales." You would then record each day's net sales (minus returns) from the Daily Summary on the credit side of the Sales account and the debit side of the Cash account. See Figure 16-8 for an example of these two accounts.

Figure 16-6. (Left) These sample T-accounts for Utilities and Cash illustrate the recording of two transactions.

Figure 16-7. (Below, left) This illustration of a Cash account illustrates that income is recorded on the debit side and expenditures on the credit side.

Figure 16-8. (Below) As shown in these Sales and Cash accounts, cash sales should be recorded on the credit side of Sales and on the debit side of Cash.

SALES

DATE	ITEM	DEBIT	DATE	ITEM	CREDIT
			6/1	CASH SALES	205.00
			6/2	" "	195.00
			6/3	" "	150.00
			6/4	" "	215.00

CASH

DATE	ITEM	DEBIT	DATE	ITEM	CREDIT
6/1	CASH SALES	205.00			
6/2	" "	195.00			
6/3	" "	150.00			
6/4	" "	215.00			

If you have customers who charge merchandise on open accounts, you'll need another T-account to handle this information—Accounts Receivable. When a credit sale is made, the amount should be listed on the debit side of Accounts Receivable and the credit side of sales. When payments are made on credit sales, they should be listed on the credit side of Accounts Receivable and the debit side of Cash. This information can be taken from the Daily Summaries. Figure 16-9 illustrates the recording of the collections on account and charge sales from the Daily Summary in Figure 16-3.

Figure 16-9. This illustration of the Accounts Receivable, Sales, and Cash accounts shows how to record Charge Sales and Collections on Account.

ACCOUNTS RECEIVABLE

DATE	ITEM	DEBIT	DATE	ITEM	CREDIT
7/3	CHARGE SALES	140.00	7/3	COLLECTIONS ON ACCOUNT	100.00

SALES

DATE	ITEM	DEBIT	DATE	ITEM	CREDIT
			7/3	CHARGE SALES	140.00

CASH

DATE	ITEM	DEBIT	DATE	ITEM	CREDIT
7/3	COLLECTIONS ON ACCOUNT	100.00			

MISCELLANEOUS RECEIPTS AND PETTY CASH SLIPS. Miscellaneous receipts from the Daily Summary should be recorded in the appropriate T-account. For example, if you receive a refund from a supplier for an overpayment of an invoice, this should be listed on the credit side of Stock Purchases and the debit side of Cash. See Figure 16-10 for an illustration.

When completed Petty Cash Slips are filed in an envelope, as discussed above, they should be summarized on the front of the envelope so you'll know which accounts to list them under—Office Supplies, Sales (refunds), Miscellaneous Expenses, and so forth.

ACCOUNTS PAYABLE. Since you're using the accrual method of accounting, stock purchases should be recorded as soon as you receive the invoice, not when you make the payment. In order to do this and keep your records straight, you'll need a T-account called "Accounts Payable." When you get an invoice for merchandise, record the amount on the debit side of Stock Purchases and the credit side of Accounts Payable. Note that since you haven't paid any cash yet for this merchandise, it can't be recorded on the Cash account at this time. Later, when you pay the invoice, list the amount on the credit side of Cash and the debit side of Accounts Payable. See Figure 16-11 for an illustration of such transactions.

Figure 16-10. This illustration shows how refunds from suppliers should be recorded: on the credit side of Stock Purchases and on the debit side of Cash.

STOCK PURCHASES

DATE	ITEM	DEBIT	DATE	ITEM	CREDIT
			7/2	REFUND - GEM JEWELRY	22.00

CASH

DATE	ITEM	DEBIT	DATE	ITEM	CREDIT
7/2	REFUND - GEM JEWELRY	22.00			

ACCOUNTS PAYABLE

DATE	ITEM	DEBIT	DATE	ITEM	CREDIT
6/8	HUDSON CARD CO.	195.00	5/3	HUDSON CARD CO.	195.00
	ZOCKO CO.	148.00	5/5	ZOCKO CO.	148.00
	GO GAME CO.	200.00	5/10	GO GAME CO.	200.00

STOCK PURCHASES

DATE	ITEM	DEBIT	DATE	ITEM	CREDIT
5/3	HUDSON CARD CO.	195.00			
5/5	ZOCKO CO.	148.00			
5/10	GO GAME CO.	200.00			

CASH

DATE	ITEM	DEBIT	DATE	ITEM	CREDIT
			6/8	HUDSON CARD CO.	195.00
				ZOCKO CO.	148.00
				GO GAME CO.	200.00

BALANCE COLUMNS. It's a good idea to add balance columns to your T-accounts for monthly and yearly cumulative totals. This way you'll be able to tell at a glance what your monthly sales are, how much cash you have on hand, what you've spent on expenditures, and how much you owe in Accounts Payable.

To get the Cash Account balance, subtract the credits from the debits. Your Cash Account balance should match the total of your checking account balance, plus cash and checks on hand. Periodically reconcile your checking account balance with your Cash Account balance. See Figure 16-12 for an illustration of a Cash account with balance columns.

Figure 16-11. This illustration of Accounts Payable, Stock Purchases, and Cash shows how to record merchandise receipts and payments.

Figure 16-12. This Cash account illustrates how a Balance Column is used to keep a running monthly balance. Note that debits are added to the balance and credits are subtracted.

CASH

DATE	ITEM	DEBIT	DATE	ITEM	CREDIT	BAL.
			5/31			2,452.30
6/1	CASH SALES	205.00	6/1	RENT	350.00	
6/2	" "	195.00	6/2	PETTY CASH	42.00	
6/3	" "	150.00	6/8	HUDSON CARD CO.	195.00	
6/4	" "	215.00		ZOCKO CO.	148.00	
	REFUND-ZOCKO CO.	15.00		GO GAME CO.	200.00	
6/5	CASH SALES	230.00	6/15	PAYROLL	248.56	
6/6	" "	250.00	6/16	TEL.-MAY	35.20	
6/8	" "	180.00	6/18	ELEC. & GAS	42.68	
6/9	" "	135.00	6/20	GEM JEWELRY	529.00	
6/10	" "	201.00		GEORGE'S	422.00	
6/11	" "	215.00		ARCO. MFG.	982.00	
6/12	" "	202.00	6/23	INSURANCE PMT.	85.00	
6/13	" "	198.00	6/30	PAYROLL	248.56	
6/15	" "	203.00				
	REFUND GO GAME CO.	2.15				
6/16	CASH SALES	198.00				
6/17	" "	142.00				
6/18	" "	168.00				
6/19	" "	207.00				
6/20	" "	259.00				
6/21	" "	210.00				
6/23	" "	245.00				
6/24	" "	298.00				
6/25	" "	186.00				
6/26	" "	243.00				
6/27	" "	207.00				
6/28	" "	229.00				
6/30	" "	201.00				4,313.45

On all cost accounts, such as Rent, Payroll, and Stock Purchases, figure your balance by adding the debits and subtracting the credits. Figure 16-13 illustrates a Stock Purchases account, with monthly and cumulative totals filled in. Note that the refund listed in the credit column is subtracted from the purchases (debits).

OWNER'S WITHDRAWAL. When you or your partners take money out of the business for your personal use, or "salary," you should record this in a Draw account. Suppose there are two partners in the business, Karen and Richard. The business is doing so well that each partner can withdraw $400 a month. Set up one account as "Karen's Draw" and another as "Richard's Draw." When each partner is paid, the transaction should be listed as a debit in the Draw account and a credit in the Cash account.

Figure 16-14 illustrates the recording of partners' withdrawal in these accounts: Karen's Draw, Richard's Draw, and Cash. On April 1 each partner took $400. This is entered in the debit column of each partner's Draw account and the credit column of the Cash account. On May 1 each partner took another $400, which is similarly recorded. Note that the balance for each partner is now $800.

SALES TAX T-ACCOUNTS. If any of your sales are subject to sales taxes, you'll need a Sales Taxes Payable account and a Sales Taxes account. Enter the daily, weekly, or monthly taxable sales and sales taxes collected (using the above methods of computation or recording from the Daily Summary) on the credit side of Sales Taxes Payable and the debit side of Sales Taxes, as shown in Figure 16-15.

When you pay your sales taxes, enter the payments on the debit side

Figure 16-13. Wherever you have an interest in monthly totals, it's a good idea to add a Monthly Balance Column in addition to a Cumulative Balance Column, as shown on this Stock Purchases account.

STOCK PURCHASES

DATE	ITEM	DEBIT	DATE	ITEM	CREDIT	MONTHLY BAL.	CUM. BAL.
							14,520.89
5/3	HUDSON CARD CO	195.00	5/14	REFUND WHISCO	30.25		
5/5	ZOCKO CO.	148.00					
5/10	GO GAME CO.	200.00					
5/12	GEM JEWELRY	529.00					
5/15	ARCO MFG.	982.00					
5/22	GEORGE'S	422.00					
5/25	HUDSON CARD CO.	305.40					
5/29	WHISCO	48.00				3,105.15	17,626.04
6/1	ZOCKO CO.	306.00					

KAREN'S DRAW

DATE	ITEM	DEBIT	DATE	ITEM	CREDIT	BAL.
4/1	APRIL DRAW	400.00				400.00
5/1	MAY DRAW	400.00				800.00

RICHARD'S DRAW

DATE	ITEM	DEBIT	DATE	ITEM	CREDIT	BAL
4/1	APRIL DRAW	400.00				400.00
5/1	MAY DRAW	400.00				800.00

CASH

DATE	ITEM	DEBIT	DATE	ITEM	CREDIT	BAL
			4/1	KAREN'S DRAW	400.00	
				RICHARD'S "	400.00	
			5/1	KAREN'S "	400.00	
				RICHARD'S "	400.00	

Figure 16-14. These three accounts illustrate how to keep track of money withdrawn from the business by the owner or partners.

of Sales Taxes Payable and the credit side of Cash, as shown in Figure 16-16. Note the reduced balance on the Sales Taxes Payable account after a payment has been made.

RECORDING TRANSACTIONS. Record the information in your T-accounts at regular intervals, rather than trying to do it daily or as expenditures are made. Weekly or monthly recording would be a reasonable way to handle it. By making all payments for purchases and rent by check, you can get the information to record payments from your check stubs. Other forms you'll need are invoices from suppliers, Daily Summary forms, and petty cash envelopes.

When you record each item as a debit, make one check mark on the check stub, Daily Summary, invoice, or petty cash envelope. Then when you enter the item as a credit on its corresponding T-account, make another check mark. This way you'll be certain that each item has been recorded twice.

Keep recorded documents separate from those that haven't been. You might file everything in a "book work" folder until it is used for recording. Then, after the items have been double-checked, file each one

SALES TAXES PAYABLE

DATE	TAXABLE SALES	DEBIT		DATE	TAXABLE SALES	CREDIT	MONTHLY BAL.	CUM. BAL.
				2/7	340.00	13.60		
				2/14	205.00	8.20		
				2/21	118.00	4.72		
				2/28	389.00	15.56	42.08	42.08
				3/6	270.00	10.80		
				3/13	430.00	17.20		
				3/20	303.00	12.12		
				3/27	119.00	4.76	44.88	86.96

SALES TAXES

DATE	TAXABLE SALES	DEBIT		DATE	TAXABLE SALES	CREDIT	MONTHLY BAL.	CUM. BAL.
2/7	340.00	13.60						
2/14	205.00	8.20						
2/21	118.00	4.72						
2/28	389.00	15.56					42.08	42.08
3/6	270.00	10.80						
3/13	430.00	17.20						
3/20	303.00	12.12						
3/27	119.00	4.76					44.88	86.96

in the proper folder: Daily Summaries, Accounts Payable, Petty Cash, and Paid Bills.

You can purchase standard ledger books or columnar pads, which make it easy to keep T-accounts. You should be able to find a varied assortment of accounting pads, and paper in your local stationery store. I prefer the analysis pads that have numbered lines and columns; they are available with two to 25 columns. For the Daily Summary, you may want to have a form mimeographed once you decide what basic information you'll need on your form. Then you can simply write in the date and record the amounts on each line.

MERCHANDISE WITHDRAWN BY OWNER. While it's understandable that you and your family may take merchandise from your store for personal use, a record must be made of these withdrawals. Not to

Figure 16-15. If any of your sales are subject to sales taxes, set up a Sales Taxes Payable account and a Sales Taxes account, as shown here.

SALES TAXES PAYABLE

DATE	TAXABLE SALES	DEBIT		DATE	TAXABLE SALES	CREDIT	MONTHLY BAL	CUM. BAL.
				2/7	340.00	13.60		
				2/14	205.00	8.20		
				2/21	118.00	4.72		
				2/28	389.00	15.56	42.08	42.08
				3/6	270.00	10.80		
				3/13	430.00	17.20		
				3/20	303.00	12.12		
				3/27	119.00	4.76	44.88	86.96
4/1	2174.00	86.96						—
				4/3	204.00	8.16		
				4/10	119.00	4.76		

CASH

DATE	ITEM	DEBIT		DATE	ITEM	CREDIT	BAL.
				4/1	SALES TAX PAYMENT	86.96	

Figure 16-16. When sales tax payments are made, they should be recorded on the debit side of Sales Taxes Payable and on the credit side of Cash, as illustrated here.

record them is illegal, and will also distort your records and cause inventory shortages. But your withdrawals shouldn't be recorded as ordinary sales, either, because this method would increase your income tax unnecessarily.

The best procedure is to treat these withdrawals as a deduction from purchases. For example, if you take an item that has a wholesale cost of $50, list this $50 under the credit side of Stock Purchases and the debit side of your Draw account. Also be sure to deduct the items you take from your inventory list.

FILING SYSTEMS. Your business will accumulate quite a few papers, forms, and letters, which you'll need to keep track of. A two- or four drawer file cabinet and folders will store these materials where they can be located quickly. To find a used file cabinet, look in your daily newspaper under "Items for Sale." You can often get them at end-of-the-year school sales, from companies going out of business, or, if you want a new one, at an office equipment store.

Set up an 8½-x-11-inch manila folder for each heading under which you'll have things to file. For example, if your business correspondence is light, make a folder labeled "Correspondence" for all letters received and copies of letters sent (make certain you keep a copy of every business letter sent out). If you find that you correspond heavily with certain people, make separate folders for them.

Keep suppliers in general or individual folders. For example, you may want to keep one folder for filing all utility bills, but make an individual folder for each company that supplies merchandise for your stock. Whatever headings you make, the important thing is that they help you find what you need when you need it.

A 3-x-5-inch card file kept on your desk or near the phone is a handy place to keep names, addresses, and telephone numbers of your suppliers, landlords, credit customers, and other people you'll deal with on a regular basis. You might want to keep customer information in a separate file.

SUMMING UP. The record-keeping methods and materials discussed in this chapter will help you keep track of what's happening in your business. They provide a simple, efficient way to record what you spend and what you take in. Once you have this information accumulated, it'll be available for profit and loss analysis (Chapter 17) and figuring your income taxes (Chapter 18).

17 Profit or Loss?

Once your business is in operation, you'll want to know what kind of progress it's making. Is your business making a profit? Is the net value of your business increasing? Is your stock turning over fast enough?

An analysis of your progress will be required information when you apply for a bank or small business association loan. It will enable you to fill out the required forms of credit associations to help establish a good credit rating for your business. It also provides the necessary information for completing income tax returns. And finally, this analysis will provide a source of information that can help you increase your profits if you put it to work constructively.

ASSETS, LIABILITIES, AND EQUITY. Anything a business owns that has a monetary value is an *asset* of the business. Cash, merchandise, supplies, amounts owed by customers (accouts receivable), land, buildings, furniture and fixtures, delivery equipment, and so on, are assets.

Anything the business owes is a *liability*. Liabilities might include amounts owed to suppliers (accounts payable) or to the bank (notes payable), taxes already incurred but not yet due for payment, wages earned by employees since the last payday, and anything else that the business owes.

Equity, or capital, is the amount that really belongs to the owner of the business—the difference between the assets and the liabilities. For example, if you start your business by depositing $10,000 from your savings into your business account, the business now has assets of $10,000 cash, no liabilities, and your owner equity, or capital, is $10,000.

Let's suppose you next purchase $15,000 worth of merchandise for stock. You pay $5,000 cash for it and owe the other $10,000 to your suppliers. Now your assets are $5,000 cash, and $15,000 worth of merchandise. Your liabilities are the $10,000 owed your suppliers. Your equity, however, is still $10,000:

Assets=Liabilities+Equity

5,000
15,000
$20,000= $10,000+ $10,000

This listing of owner's assets, liabilities, and equity is called a Balance Sheet. As your business progresses, a balance sheet will be useful to show you the net worth, or your equity in the business. Balance sheets are also used when applying for a loan, and on credit applications.

Figure 17-1 shows how a Balance Sheet might look after a store was in operation for a year. The cash listed includes money in checking accounts, uncashed checks, cash in the cash register, and petty cash. The inventory is valued at wholesale (not retail) cost. Chapter 18 discusses the various ways of valuing inventory for income tax purposes. The $500 for supplies includes miscellaneous office supplies, other paper supplies, cleaning equipment, etc. The furniture and fixtures have been valued at $2,000 after a year's depreciation (see below). Prepaid insurance includes payments made in advance on insurance policies.

Under Liabilities, the accounts payable includes all money owed to suppliers for goods already received. Notes payable is the outstanding balance on a bank loan. Taxes payable are sales and income taxes owed, but not yet paid.

The total assets less the total liabilities give an owner's equity of $21,900. Or, looked at another way—liabilities plus the owner's equity equals the assets. Doing a balance sheet at the end of the year will show you the real growth of your business, because it includes all the business assets and liabilities. But to evaluate this growth properly, you should take into consideration the amount of money you withdrew from the business during the year for personal use, or owner's salary. Obviously the more you withdraw, the less your owner's equity will be at the end of the year.

You should also take into consideration how much capital investment you put into the business to start with. If you invested $50,000, took out nothing for your personal use during the year, and had an owner's equity of $30,000 at the end of the year, the business obviously made a loss and not a profit. This is a gross example, but it illustrates the importance of considering all pertinent factors in your analysis.

BALANCE SHEET: As of 12/31/77

ASSETS		LIABILITIES	
Cash	5,000	Accounts Payable	4,000
Inventory	25,000	Notes Payable	6,400
Supplies	500	Taxes Payable	500
Furniture & Fixtures	2,000		10,900
Prepaid Insurance	300		
		Owner's Equity	21,900
	$32,800		
		Total Liabilities & Owners Equity	$32,800

Figure 17-1. This is an illustration of a Balance Sheet, showing Assets, Liabilities, and Owner's Equity.

INCOME STATEMENTS. An income or operating statement showing your store's profit or loss should be made at the end of every month. While a Balance Sheet shows the worth of a business on a specific date, an Income Statement shows the profit or loss which occurred during a particular period.

In order to prepare a monthly Income Statement, you'll need to know the value of your inventory as of the last day of the month. You may wish to take a physical inventory, or estimate your inventory, or use the information from a perpetual inventory system. (See Chapter 9 for a more thorough discussion of inventories.) You'll also need the monthly balances from all the T-accounts discussed in Chapter 16.

A sample income statement format is shown in Figure 17-2. Note that it has a place to record a particular month, plus the cumulative information for that year. Net sales can be taken directly from your Sales T-account. The cost of goods sold is figured by adding your beginning inventory (item 2—this is the previous month's ending inventory) to your total Merchandise Purchases for the month (item 3) to get Merchandise Available For Sale (item 4). Your Ending Inventory (item 5) is subtracted from item 4 to give you the Cost Of Goods Sold (item

Figure 17-2. This is an Income Statement form for profit and loss analysis.

INCOME STATEMENT

Month of _____, 19__ and __ months ended _____, 19__

	This Month Amount	Percent of Sales	Year to Date Amount	Percent of Sales
1. Net Sales	$ ____	100	$ ____	100
Less Cost of Goods Sold:				
2. Beginning Inventory	____		____	
3. Merchandise Purchases	____		____	
4. Merchandise Available for Sale	____		____	
5. Less Ending Inventory	____		____	
6. Cost of Goods Sold	____	____	____	____
7. Gross Margin	____	____	____	____
Less Expenses:				
8. Salaries and Wages	____		____	
9. Rent	____		____	
10. Utilities	____		____	
11. Repairs and Maintenance	____		____	
12. Delivery Expense	____		____	
13. Supplies	____		____	
14. Promotion	____		____	
15. Depreciation	____		____	
16. Bad Debts	____		____	
17. Taxes	____		____	
18. Insurance	____		____	
19. Interest	____		____	
20. Other Expense	____		____	
21. Total Expenses	____	____	____	____
22. Operating Profit (Loss)	____	____	____	____

6). By subtracting the Cost Of Goods Sold (item 6) from Net Sales (item 1), you get your Gross Margin (item 7).

Items 8 through 20 are various expenses that are totaled on line 21. By subtracting Total Expenses (item 21) from Gross Margin (item 7), you get your Operating Profit or Loss (item 22). The expenses listed are simply suggested items. You may not have some of them, but you may have others which aren't listed. These expenses should accurately reflect costs incurred for that month. For example, if you pay half a year's rent in January, only one month's rent should be listed in the January Income Statement and on each month's statement thereafter.

Salaries and wages should reflect monies paid or owed for work done through the end of the month. If, for example, at the end of January, employees have earned salaries for which they'll be paid in February, this amount should be included in January's statement. The same holds true for taxes and insurance.

DEPRECIATION. The furniture, fixtures, delivery trucks, and so on, that your business purchases will probably last for more than one year. Items such as this should be "depreciated" on your income statement. They in fact *must* be depreciated for income tax purposes. The IRS allows several depreciation methods to be used, but the simplest is the "straight line" method: take the cost of the item, subtract its "salvage value," and divide by the number of years of its useful life. For example, if you purchase office furniture for $1,000, expect it to last for 10 years, and to be able to sell it at the end of that time for $100, you should allocate a depreciation expense on this furniture of $90 per year

$$\$1,000 \text{ minus } \$100 = \$900 \text{ divided by } 10 = \$90$$

To keep track of depreciation on your fixtures, furniture, and equipment, set up two T-accounts, one called "Depreciation," the other "Fixtures, Furniture & Equipment Purchases." When you make a purchase, enter it on both the debit side of Fixtures, Furniture & Equipment Purchases and the credit side of your Cash T-account. When you write off a percentage of the amount for depreciation at the end of the month or year, enter it on both the credit side of Fixtures, Furniture & Equipment Purchases and the debit side of the Depreciation account. This is illustrated in Figure 17-3.

If the monthly depreciation for your business's assets amount to very little, you may wish to compute the depreciation once a year only. At that time Uncle Sam requires you to depreciate these assets. Chapter 18 covers this aspect of depreciation more fully.

PERCENTAGES. In Figure 17-2 you'll note there's a place for you to fill in Percent of Sales for the Cost of Goods Sold, Gross Margin, Total Expenses, and Operating Profit or Loss. To figure these percentages, divide the dollar amount of the item by the amount of net sales. For example, if Net Sales were $10,000 and Cost of Goods Sold was $6,000, the Percent of Sales would be 60 percent.

Figure 17-3. This illustration of Furniture, Fixtures, & Equipment Purchases account; Cash account; and Depreciation account; shows how to record depreciation.

FURNITURE, FIXTURES, & EQUIP. PURCHASES

DATE	ITEM	DEBIT	DATE	ITEM	CREDIT	MONTHLY BAL.	CUM. BAL.
1/4	DESK	400.00				400.00	400.00
			2/1	Depreciation - DESK	3.33		

CASH

DATE	ITEM	DEBIT	DATE	ITEM	CREDIT	BAL.
			1/4	DESK	400.00	

DEPRECIATION

DATE	ITEM	DEBIT	DATE	ITEM	CREDIT	MONTHLY BAL	CUM. BAL
2/1	DESK	3.33					

$6,000 divided by $10,000 = 0.60 = 60 percent

Once you know your percentage cost of goods sold expenses, you can compare your store with similar businesses to see how well you're doing. You can also compare your figures month-to-month to see what changes occur. By computing the percentages of each individual expense, such as Promotion or Salaries, you can observe the increase or decrease in these expenses from month to month and the corresponding change in sales and profits.

YEAR TO DATE. For the first month of the year, the figures for the Year to Date will be identical to those for the month. For all other months, each year to date figure will equal the current month's figures plus the year to date figure from the preceding month's statement.

The exceptions to this will be the inventory figures. The Beginning Inventory figure (item 2) in the Year to Date column should remain the same throughout the year. It will always be the beginning inventory at the start of the year. For a new store this figure will be 0. Merchandise Available for Sale (item 4) in the Year to Date column will always be the beginning inventory plus the year to date merchandise purchases (cumulative monthly purchases). Ending Inventory (item 5) in the Year to Date column should be the same as that in the month's column.

See Figure 17-4 for this example of a sample situation. January sales were $8,000 and February sales were $10,000, adding up to $18,000 on the February statement's Year to Date column. The Beginning Inven-

INCOME STATEMENT

Month of Jan., 1976 and 1 months ended Jan. 31, 1976

	This Month		Year to Date	
	Amount	Percent of Sales	Amount	Percent of Sales
1. Net Sales	$ 8,000	100	$ 8,000	100
Less Cost of Goods Sold:				
2. Beginning Inventory	25,000		25,000	
3. Merchandise Purchases	3,000		3,000	
4. Merchandise Available for Sale	28,000		28,000	
5. Less Ending Inventory	24,000		24,000	
6. Cost of Goods Sold	4,000	50	4,000	50

INCOME STATEMENT

Month of Feb., 1976 and 2 months ended Feb. 29, 1976

	This Month		Year to Date	
	Amount	Percent of Sales	Amount	Percent of Sales
1. Net Sales	$10,000	100	$18,000	100
Less Cost of Goods Sold:				
2. Beginning Inventory	24,000		25,000	
3. Merchandise Purchases	5,000		8,000	
4. Merchandise Available for Sale	29,000		33,000	
5. Less Ending Inventory	23,500		23,500	
6. Cost of Goods Sold	5,500	55	9,500	52.8

tory at the start of the year is $25,000. This is the figure used in the Year to Date column. Merchandise Purchases are added to get the Year to Date figure ($3,000 January + $5,000 February = $8,000). Ending Inventory for year to date is the same as the month's, $23,500. To get Cost of Goods Sold, subtract item 5 from item 4 to get $9,500 for year to date ($33,000 - $23,500). Note that this equals the cumulative Cost of Goods Sold for January and February ($4,000 + $5,500). Also note that percentages must be computed separately for year to date figures. In Figure 17-4 the percentage of sales of the cost of goods sold was 50 percent for January, 55 percent for February, and 52.8 percent for Year to Date.

Figure 17-4. These sample Income Statements for January and February illustrate some of the differences in recording the "Year to Date" figures as opposed to the "This Month" figures.

TURNOVER. You may want to use the information on your income statement to figure out your stock turnover for the month or year. To do this, add your Beginning Inventory and the Ending Inventory and divide by 2 to get your average inventory. For the example shown in Figure 17-4, the average inventory for January would be $24,500 ($25,000 + $24,000 = $49,000 ÷ 2 = $24,500); for February $23,750 ($24,000 + $23,500 = $47,500 ÷ 2 = $23,750); for year to date $24,250 ($25,000 + $23,500 = $48,500 ÷ 2 = $24,250).

To get turnover per month, divide the cost of goods sold by this average inventory figure. In year to date, divide this result by the number of months included. In the above example, January's turnover rate would be 0.16 ($4,000 ÷ $24,500); February's would be 0.23 ($5,500 ÷ $23,750), and year to date's would be 0.20 ($9,500 ÷ $24,250 ÷ 2). Once you've got turnover rate *per month*, multiply this by 12 to get turnover per year; for example, 0.20 x 12 = 2.4. This means the turnover for the year would be almost two and a half times if the trend continued throughout the year.

DEPARTMENTAL OPERATING RECORDS. If you sell several different types of merchandise you may want to set up your records by department rather than throwing all the data in one pot. The advantage is to see which departments are making the most money for you and which are making the least, or even losing money. To do this, you'll have to separate sales by departments and purchases by departments. You may even want to separate freight, sales costs, and other expenses by department.

Once you've decided what departments you'll want to keep separately, set up all the forms shown with separate columns for each department. But don't go so far that you complicate your record-keeping beyond what you can handle and what will be useful to your operation.

SUMMING UP. A Balance Sheet and Income Statement are important devices for analyzing the progress of your business. They're also required when borrowing money, getting credit, or filling out your income tax returns. Use the information above to set up the kind of statements that will benefit your operation, or call in an accountant to help you develop the analytical tools best suited to your needs.

18 Income Taxes

The type of federal income tax return you file will depend upon the form of your business organization (see Chapter 3). If your business is operated as an individual proprietorship you'll report your business operations on Schedule C, to be attached to the Form 1040 you file as an individual. If your business is a partnership, the business must file a Form 1065. No federal income tax has to be paid by the partnership, but the individual partners must report their shares of the profit or loss of the partnership on Form 1040. If your business is a corporation, the corporation must file a Form 1120 and pay a tax on the taxable income reported. You must report any salaries paid to you by the corporation on Form 1040.

PROFIT OR LOSS. The profit or loss shown on your yearly Income Statement (see Chapter 17) should match the profit or loss you show on your federal income tax return. All operating costs and other business expenses are allowable business deductions. If your business is making a profit, each quarter you'll have to file a Declaration of Estimated Tax. If the profit from your business is your only income, you should also file a Schedule SE for Computation of Social Security Self-Employment Tax.

SCHEDULE C. This is the form to use to report your business operations if you are a sole proprietor. (Form 1065 for partnerships requires the same basic information about your business as Schedule C.) Figures 18-1 and 18-2 show the front and back of Schedule C filled out for a fictitious retail store. (While these forms may change slightly from year to year, the information required is the same.) We'll start with Schedule C-1 on the bottom front of Schedule C (Figure 18-1).

COST OF GOODS SOLD. Copy the figures from your Yearly Income Statement on Schedule C-1. On line 1 list your beginning inventory, and on line 2 list purchases (less items withdrawn for personal use). Add lines 1 and 2 to get line 6. On line 7 list your ending inventory.

SCHEDULE C
(Form 1040)
Department of the Treasury
Internal Revenue Service

Profit or (Loss) From Business or Profession
(Sole Proprietorship)
Partnerships, Joint Ventures, etc., Must File Form 1065.
▶ Attach to Form 1040. ▶ See Instructions for Schedule C (Form 1040).

1974

Name(s) as shown on Form 1040 | Social security number

A Principal business activity (see Schedule C Instructions) ▶ *retail* ; product ▶ *Gifts*

B Business name ▶ *HOUSE OF GIFTS*   C Employer identification number ▶ *10-001-12*

D Business address (number and street) ▶ *100 MAIN ST.*

City, State and ZIP code ▶ *SOMEWHERE CITY, SOMEWHERE 00001*   **C**

E Indicate method of accounting: (1) ☐ Cash (2) ☒ Accrual (3) ☐ Other ▶ _____

	Yes	No
F Were you required to file Form W-3 or Form 1096 for 1974? (See Schedule C Instructions.)	X	
If "Yes," where filed ▶ *ANYWHERE CITY, ANYWHERE STATE*	/////	/////
G Was an Employer's Quarterly Federal Tax Return, Form 941, filed for this business for any quarter in 1974?	X	
H Method of inventory valuation ▶ *COST (FIFO)* .... Was there any substantial change in the manner of determining quantities, costs, or valuations between the opening and closing inventories? (If "Yes," attach explanation)		X

Income

1 Gross receipts or sales $ *141,200* Less: returns and allowances $ *1,200* ... Balance ▶		*140,000*
2 Less: Cost of goods sold and/or operations (Schedule C-1, line 8)		*78,000*
3 Gross profit		*62,000*
4 Other income (attach schedule)		
5 Total income (add lines 3 and 4)		*62,000*

Deductions

6 Depreciation (explain in Schedule C-3)		*200*
7 Taxes on business and business property (explain in Schedule C-2)		*10,200*
8 Rent on business property		*3600*
9 Repairs (explain in Schedule C-2)		*350*
10 Salaries and wages not included on line 3, Schedule C-1 (exclude any paid to yourself)		*15,600*
11 Insurance		*400*
12 Legal and professional fees		*500*
13 Commissions		
14 Amortization (attach statement)		
15 (a) Pension and profit-sharing plans (see Schedule C Instructions)		
(b) Employee benefit programs (see Schedule C Instructions)		
16 Interest on business indebtedness		*1,300*
17 Bad debts arising from sales or services		
18 Depletion		
19 Other business expenses (specify):		
(a) *OWNER'S EXPENSE ACCOUNT*	*235*	
(b) *PROMOTION*	*2,500*	
(c) *FREIGHT*	*2,000*	
(d) *UTILITIES*	*600*	
(e) *SUPPLIES*	*2,200*	
(f) *TRASH REMOVAL*	*300*	
(g) *MISCELLANEOUS EXPENSES*	*2,400*	
(h)		
(i)		
(j)		
(k) Total other business expenses (add lines 19(a) through 19(j))		*12,235*
20 Total deductions (add lines 6 through 19)		*44,385*
21 Net profit or (loss) (subtract line 20 from line 5). Enter here and on Form 1040, line 28. ALSO enter on Schedule SE, line 5(a)		*17,615*

SCHEDULE C-1.—Cost of Goods Sold and/or Operations (See Schedule C Instructions for Line 2)

1 Inventory at beginning of year (if different from last year's closing inventory, attach explanation)	*20,000*
2 Purchases $ *80,500* Less: cost of items withdrawn for personal use $ *500* Balance ▶	*80,000*
3 Cost of labor (do not include salary paid to yourself)	
4 Materials and supplies	
5 Other costs (attach schedule)	
6 Total of lines 1 through 5	*100,000*
7 Less: Inventory at end of year	*22,000*
8 Cost of goods sold and/or operations. Enter here and on line 2 above	*78,000*

Subtract 7 from 6 to get line 8, "Cost of Goods Sold." See Figure 18-3, the Yearly Income Statement for the fictitious store we're using, to see how this information is taken from the statement.

SCHEDULE C-2. This schedule (on the back of Schedule C) is used to explain lines 7 and 9 from the front of Schedule C. Line 7 is for taxes that are deductible as business expenses, such as real property tax (on property used in your business), sales taxes (if you include them in gross sales), and payroll taxes. Note that our sample store listed sales taxes and payroll taxes.

Line 9 on Schedule C is the total amount spent on repairs, including labor and supplies, which don't add to the value or utility of the property, or appreciably prolong its life. Our sample store had its counters refinished during the year and the cost of these repairs listed on Schedule C-2 and line 9, was $350.

DEPRECIATION. Schedule C-3 (Figure 18-2) is used to record depreciation. Your only concern here will probably be depreciation on furniture and fixtures. If your business owns a delivery truck or other vehicle, this should be depreciated, also. If you own the building your store is in, this will also be depreciated. Our sample store had only $2,000 in furniture and fixtures on which to claim depreciation. It used the "straight line" method of computing depreciation.

To use the "straight line" method, first take the cost of the property and subtract its "salvage value." This is the amount the property will be worth when you eventually sell it. Then figure the useful life of the property, *i.e.*, the number of years you'll be able to use it in your business. Divide the number of years into the "cost less salvage value" in order to get a yearly depreciation figure. For example:

> Cost of furniture & fixtures: $2,000
> Less salvage value: 200
> $1,800
> Useful life: 9 years
> Depreciation: $1,800 ÷ 9 = $200 per year

There are other depreciation methods allowed by the IRS. There's also an additional first-year depreciation allowance that can be taken on certain property. For information on these items, see Publication 334, *Tax Guide For Small Business*. Whatever depreciation methods used, however, the total of all your annual depreciation deductions cannot exceed your cost (less salvage value) of a property.

EXPENSE ACCOUNT INFORMATION. Schedule C-4 is where you'll list expense account information. As the owner of your own retail store, these expenses will probably be minimal—perhaps some travelling expenses for trade shows, and visits to a supplier. You can't claim daily travel expenses to your place of business. For business trips away from home, you can claim meals, lodging, baggage charges, telephone and telegraph, tips, cleaning and laundry, and transportation.

Figure 18-1. This is the front of Schedule C for computing Profit or Loss from Business or Profession (for sole proprietorships).

Schedule C (Form 1040) 1974

Page **2**

SCHEDULE C–2.—Explanation of Lines 7 and 9

Line No.	Explanation	Amount	Line No.	Explanation	Amount
7	SALES TAXES	$5,600			$
	PAYROLL TAXES	4,600			
9	COUNTERS REFINISHED	350			

SCHEDULE C–3.—Depreciation (See Schedule C Instructions for Line 6) If you need more space, you may use Form 4562.

Note: If depreciation is computed by using the Class Life (ADR) System for assets placed in service after December 31, 1970, or the Guideline Class Life System for assets placed in service before January 1, 1971, you must file Form 4832 (Class Life (ADR) System) or Form 5006 (Guideline Class Life System). Except as otherwise expressly provided in income tax regulations sections 1.167(a)–11(b)(5)(vi) and 1.167 (a)–12, the provisions of Revenue Procedures 62–21 and 65–13 are not applicable for taxable years ending after December 31, 1970. (See Publication 534.)

Check box if you made an election this taxable year to use ☐ Class Life (ADR) System and/or ☐ Guideline Class Life System.

a. Group and guideline class or description of property	b. Date acquired	c. Cost or other basis	d. Depreciation allowed or allowable in prior years	e. Method of computing depreciation	f. Life or rate	g. Depreciation for this year
1 Total additional first-year depreciation (do not include in items below) ⟶						
2 Depreciation from Form 4832 (See Note above)						
3 Depreciation from Form 5006						
4 Other depreciation:						
Buildings						
Furniture and fixtures . . .	1/1/73	2,000	200	st. line	9 YRS	200 00
Transportation equipment . .						
Machinery and other equipment .						
Other (specify)						
5 Totals		2,000				200 00
6 Less amount of depreciation claimed in Schedule C–1, page 1						
7 Balance—Enter here and on page 1, line 6						200 00

SCHEDULE C–4.—Expense Account Information (See Schedule C Instructions for Schedule C–4)

Enter information with regard to yourself and your five highest paid employees. In determining the five highest paid employees, expense account allowances must be added to their salaries and wages. However, the information need not be submitted for any employee for whom the combined amount is less than $25,000, or for yourself if your expense account allowance plus line 21, page 1, is less than $25,000.

	Name	Expense account	Salaries and Wages
Owner			
1			
2			
3			
4			
5			

Did you claim a deduction for expenses connected with:

(1) Entertainment facility (boat, resort, ranch, etc.)? . . . ☐ Yes ☐ No (3) Employees' families at conventions or meetings? . . . ☐ Yes ☐ No

(2) Living accommodations (except employees on business)? ☐ Yes ☐ No (4) Employee or family vacations not reported on Form W–2? ☐ Yes ☐ No

If you use your own car, keep track of the mileage and claim 15 cents a mile (check a current *IRS Tax Guide* for allowances).

Put the total expenses claimed in Schedule C-4 and on line 19 on page 1 of Schedule C. Note that you don't have to submit expense information on Schedule C-4 if your expense account allowance plus your net profit was lower than $25,000. In this case, simply list it under line 19, as our sample store did.

SCHEDULE C, FRONT. On line A you should list your principal business activity, "retail," and product. For example, if you sell clothing, write "apparel." If you sell several products, choose a descriptive term that would best describe them. On line B list your business name, on line C your Employer Identification Number (see Chapter 14), and on line D your business address.

On line E you must indicate the method of accounting you're using. As mentioned in Chapter 16, retail stores must use the accrual method, because inventories are involved. So check box 2. If you had employees during the year, your answer to line F and G would be "yes." (See Chapter 14.)

On line H you're asked to list the "method of inventory valuation." If you match the goods in your inventory with their invoices to find the cost of each inventoried item, this is called the "specific identification method." However, if the costs of some items have varied over the year, you may wish to use the following methods.

The "first in first out (FIFO) method" is based on the assumption that the items first purchased or produced are the first sold. For example, if you purchased 100 units of item X during the year, and had 10 units left at the end of the year, you'd assign these 10 units the cost of the last 10 which you purchased.

In valuing your inventory you may use (1) *cost* or (2) *cost or market, whichever is lower*. Whether you use method 1 or method 2, you must apply this to your whole inventory. The "lower of cost or market" (2) means that you compare the market value of each item on hand at the inventory date with its cost, and use the lower valuation as its inventory value. If you use this method, you must separately evaluate each item in your inventory.

Any goods in your inventory that are unsalable at normal prices because of damage, imperfections, shopwear, changes of style, or similar causes, should be valued at selling prices less direct costs of disposition. This should be done whether you use the "cost" or "cost or market, whichever is lower" basis of valuing your inventory. Our sample retail store used the FIFO-cost method of accounting to value its inventory.

INCOME. Lines 1 through 5 show your gross profits and total income. On line 1 list your total sales less returns and allowances. On line 2 fill in the "Costs of goods sold," from line 8 on Schedule C-1. Subtract line 2 from 1 to get gross profit (line 3). If your business earned any other income, line 4 is the place to list it. Our sample store had none. Line 5 is the total of lines 3 and 4.

Figure 18-2. This is the back of Schedule C, which contains Schedule C-2, C-3, and C-4.

DEDUCTIONS. Lines 6 through 19 cover deductions, or operating expenses. List your total depreciation (Schedule C-3) for the year on line 6. On line 7 copy the amount of total taxes, from Schedule C-2. On line 8 list your total rent expenses. On line 9 copy the total cost of repairs from schedule C-2. Salaries are listed on line 10, and insurance costs on line 11. If you incurred any legal or professional fees for lawyers, accountants, and consultants, list these on line 12. If you paid your employees commissions in addition to salaries, list these on line 13.

Line 14, "Amortization," and line 18, "Depletion," will probably not apply to your business, but they're discussed in the *Tax Guide for Small Business.* Line 15 covers employee pension and profit-sharing plans and employee benefit programs. Our sample store had no such programs. If you have a pension or profit-sharing plan, use Form 4848 or 4848A to compute your deductions for your contributions to the plan. Then use the deductible amount you contributed to your employees' plan on line 15a of Schedule C. The amount you pay to your own plan should be entered on line 42 of Form 1040. For more complete information on this, see the *Tax Guide.*

On line 16 list any interest you've paid during the year on loans for your business. If you sell merchandise on credit, and thereby have an Accounts Receivable (see Chapter 16), you may have incurred some bad debts, which can be written off on line 17. Our sample store didn't sell merchandise on credit and had no bad debts.

Line 19 is used to list any other business expenses not accounted for. Our sample store lists costs for owners expense account, promotion, freight, utilities, supplies, trash removal, and miscellaneous expenses. Note that now every expense item from the year's Income Statement in Figure 18-3 has been listed on Schedule C. Add 19(a) through (j) to get (k) "total other business expenses." Add lines 6 through 19 to get total deductions (line 20). Subtract line 20 from line 5 to get net profit (line 21). This amount should be entered on Form 1040, line 28.

FORM 1040. Figures 18-4 and 18-5 show the front and back of Form 1040, giving the business income (line 21, Schedule C) listed on line 28 on the back of Form 1040. If you have other income (other than wages, dividends, and interest), list it on the appropriate space on lines 29 through 37. Then add lines 28 through 37 and list the total on line 38. Enter this amount on the front of Form 1040, line 12.

If your business shows a loss, rather than a profit, indicate this by putting a minus sign in front of the amount, and list it on Form 1040 as explained above. In the case of a loss, it should be subtracted from any other income you might have had that year, or from your spouse's if you file a joint return. For example, if you and your spouse earned $12,000 in salaries and had a total business loss of $2,000, this would bring your total income, line 13 of Form 1040, to $10,000.

SCHEDULE SE. Schedule SE shown in Figure 18-6 is used to compute your social security self-employment tax. If you earned wages of $13,200 or more, (this figure may change from year to year) which were

INCOME STATEMENT

From January 1, 1974 to December 31, 1974

Net Sales	$140,000	(+ $1,200 re-
Less Cost of Goods Sold		turns and allow-
Beginning Inventory	20,000	ances)
Merchandise Purchases	80,000	(+ $500 withdrawn
Merchandise Available for Sale	100,000	for personal use)
Less Ending Inventory	22,000	
Cost of Goods Sold	78,000	
Gross Margin	62,000	
Less Expenses:		
Depreciation	200	
Sales Taxes	5,600	
Payroll Taxes	4,600	
Rent	3,600	
Repairs	350	
Salaries	15,600	
Insurance	400	
Legal & Professional Fees	500	
Interest on Business Indebtedness	1,300	
Owner's Expense Account	235	
Promotion	7,500	
Freight	1,000	
Utilities	600	
Supplies	1,200	
Trash Removal	300	
Miscellaneous Expenses	1,400	
Total Expenses	44,385	
Operating Profit (Loss)	17,615	

Figure 18-3. This is the Income Statement from which the information was taken to fill out the sample Schedule C in Figures 1 and 2.

subject to social security taxes, i.e., your employer deducted them from your pay, then you don't have to fill in this form. If you didn't, and your income from your business was $400 or more, you're required to fill in this form.

If you file a joint tax return with your spouse, but you are the sole proprietor of your business, only you can file a Schedule SE to get this social security coverage. If you both have self-employment income, each of you must file a separate Schedule SE.

The sample Schedule SE shown in Figure 18-6 assumes the taxpayer's income was solely from his business (self-employment). That is, he earned no wages that were subject to social security tax deductions. Note that the only income listed is the $17,615 on Part II(a), which is taken from line 21, Schedule C. This amount also goes on line 6, "Total," and line 8, "Adjusted net earnings."

Bring this total down to Part III, line 12(b), and line 13, "Total net earnings." Since this taxpayer earned no "FICA" wages, line 15 is left blank. Line 16 is $13,200, the same as line 14. Since the taxpayer's income was more than $13,200, $13,200 is entered on line 17. Since line 17 is $13,200, the social security self-employment tax is $1,042.80 (line 18). If line 17 was less than $13,200, it would be multiplied by .079 to get line 18.

Figure 18-4. This is the front of Form 1040, US Individual Income Tax Return, with lines 12, 13, 15, and 19 filled in.

Form **1040**   **US**   Department of the Treasury—Internal Revenue Service
Individual Income Tax Return   **1974**

For the year January 1–December 31, 1974, or other taxable year beginning ...., 1974, ending ...., 19........

Please print or type	Name (If joint return, give first names and initials of both)	Last name	COUNTY OF RESIDENCE	Your social security number
	Present home address (Number and street, including apartment number, or rural route)			Spouse's social security no.
	City, town or post office, State and ZIP code		Occu-pation Yours ▶ Spouse's ▶	

Filing Status (check only one)

1 ☐ Single
2 ☐ Married filing joint return (even if only one had income)
3 ☐ Married filing separately. If spouse is also filing give spouse's social security number in designated space above and enter full name here ▶
4 ☐ Unmarried Head of Household (See instructions on page 5)
5 ☐ Widow(er) with dependent child (Year spouse died ▶ 19   )

Exemptions   Regular / 65 or over / Blind
6a Yourself . . . ☐ ☐ ☐   Enter number of boxes checked ▶
b Spouse . . . ☐ ☐ ☐
c First names of your dependent children who lived with you _____
d Number of other dependents (from line 27) . . . . Enter number ▶
7 Total exemptions claimed . . . . ▶

8 Presidential Election Campaign Fund . . ▶   Do you wish to designate $1 of your taxes for this fund? . . ☐ Yes ☐ No   If joint return, does your spouse wish to designate $1? . . ☐ Yes ☐ No
Note: If you check the "Yes" box(es) it will not increase your tax or reduce your refund.

Income (Please attach Copy B of Forms W-2 here)

9	Wages, salaries, tips, and other employee compensation (Attach Forms W-2. If unavailable, see instructions on page 3.) . . .	9	
10a	Dividends (See instructions on pages 6 and 13)$................, 10b Less exclusion $.............., Balance ▶ (If gross dividends and other distributions are over $400, list in Part I of Schedule B.)	10c	
11	Interest income. [If $400 or less, enter total without listing in Schedule B / If over $400, enter total and list in Part II of Schedule B] .	11	
12	Income other than wages, dividends, and interest (from line 38)	12	17,615 00
13	Total (add lines 9, 10c, 11, and 12)	13	17,615 00
14	Adjustments to income (such as "sick pay," moving expenses, etc. from line 43) .	14	
15	Subtract line 14 from line 13 (adjusted gross income)	15	17,615 00

● If you do not itemize deductions and line 15 is under $10,000, find tax in Tables and enter on line 16.
● If you itemize deductions or line 15 is $10,000 or more, go to line 44 to figure tax.
● CAUTION. If you have unearned income and can be claimed as a dependent on your parent's return, check here ▶ ☐ and see instructions on page 7.

Tax, Payments and Credits

16	Tax, check if from: ☐ Tax Tables 1–12 ☐ Schedule D ☐ Tax Rate Schedule X, Y, or Z ☐ Schedule G OR ☐ Form 4726	16	
17	Total credits (from line 54)	17	
18	Income tax (subtract line 17 from line 16)	18	
19	Other taxes (from line 61)	19	4,042 80
20	Total (add lines 18 and 19)	20	
21a	Total Federal income tax withheld (attach Forms W-2 or W-2P to front)	21a	
b	1974 estimated tax payments (include amount allowed as credit from 1973 return)	b	
c	Amount paid with Form 4868, Application for Automatic Extension of Time to File U.S. Individual Income Tax Return	c	
d	Other payments (from line 65)	d	
22	Total (add lines 21a, b, c, and d)	22	

Pay amount on line 23 in full with this return. Write social security number on check or money order and make payable to Internal Revenue Service.

Balance Due or Refund (Please attach Check or Money Order here)

23	If line 20 is larger than line 22, enter BALANCE DUE IRS . . . . . ▶	23	
	(Check here ▶ ☐ , if Form 2210, Form 2210F, or statement is attached. See instructions on page 7.)		
24	If line 22 is larger than line 20, enter amount OVERPAID . . . . . ▶	24	
25	Amount of line 24 to be REFUNDED TO YOU . . . . . . ▶	25	
26	Amount of line 24 to be credited on 1975 estimated tax. ▶	26	

If all of overpayment (line 24) is to be refunded (line 25), make no entry on line 26.

Sign here
Under penalties of perjury, I declare that I have examined this return, including accompanying schedules and statements, and to the best of my knowledge and belief it is true, correct, and complete. Declaration of preparer (other than taxpayer) is based on all information of which he has any knowledge.

▶ Your signature   Date   ▶ Preparer's signature (other than taxpayer)   Date

▶ Spouse's signature (if filing jointly, BOTH must sign even if only one had income)   Address (and ZIP Code)   Preparer's Emp. Ident. or Soc. Sec. No.

Figure 18-5. This is the back of Form 1040 with lines 28, 38, 55, and 61 filled in.

Form 1040 (1974)   Page **2**

	(a) NAME	(b) Relationship	(c) Months lived in your home. If born or died during year, write B or D.	(d) Did dependent have income of $750 or more?	(e) Amount YOU furnished for dependent's support. If 100% write ALL.	(f) Amount furnished by OTHERS including dependent.
Other Dependents					$	$

27 Total number of dependents listed in column (a). Enter here and on line 6d . . . . ▶

Part I   Income other than Wages, Dividends, and Interest

28 Business income or (loss) (attach Schedule C)	28	17,615	00
29 Net gain or (loss) from sale or exchange of capital assets (attach Schedule D)	29		
30 Net gain or (loss) from Supplemental Schedule of Gains and Losses (attach Form 4797) . .	30		
31 Pensions, annuities, rents, royalties, partnerships, estates or trusts, etc. (attach Schedule E) . .	31		
32 Farm income or (loss) (attach Schedule F)	32		
33 Fully taxable pensions and annuities (not reported on Schedule E—see instructions on page 8)	33		
34 50% of capital gain distributions (not reported on Schedule D—see instructions on page 8) .	34		
35 State income tax refunds (does not apply if refund is for year in which you took the standard deduction—others see instructions on page 8).	35		
36 Alimony received	36		
37 Other (state nature and source—see instructions on page 8) ▶...............................			
	37		
38 Total (add lines 28, 29, 30, 31, 32, 33, 34, 35, 36, and 37). Enter here and on line 12 . . ▶	38	17,615	00

Part II   Adjustments to Income

39 "Sick pay." (From Forms W-2 and W-2P. If not shown on Forms W-2 or W-2P, attach Form 2440 or statement.)	39		
40 Moving expense (attach Form 3903)	40		
41 Employee business expense (attach Form 2106 or statement)	41		
42 Payments as a self-employed person to a retirement plan, etc.—see instructions on page 9 .	42		
43 Total adjustments (add lines 39, 40, 41, and 42). Enter here and on line 14 . . . . . ▶	43		

Part III   Tax Computation (Do not use this part if you use Tax Tables 1–12 to find your tax.)

44 Adjusted gross income (from line 15)	44		
45 (a) If you itemize deductions, check here ▶ ☐ and enter total from Schedule A, line 41 and attach Schedule A			
(b) If you do not itemize deductions, check here ▶ ☐ and enter 15% of line 44, but do NOT enter more than $2,000. ($1,000 if line 3 checked)	45		
46 Subtract line 45 from line 44	46		
47 Multiply total number of exemptions claimed on line 7, by $750	47		
48 Taxable income. Subtract line 47 from line 46	48		

(Figure your tax on the amount on line 48 by using Tax Rate Schedule X, Y, or Z, or if applicable, the alternative tax from Schedule D, income averaging from Schedule G, or maximum tax from Form 4726.) Enter tax on line 16.

Part IV   Credits

49 Retirement income credit (attach Schedule R)	49		
50 Investment credit (attach Form 3468)	50		
51 Foreign tax credit (attach Form 1116)	51		
52 Credit for contributions to candidates for public office—see instructions on page 9 . .	52		
53 Work Incentive (WIN) credit (attach Form 4874)	53		
54 Total credits (add lines 49, 50, 51, 52, and 53). Enter here and on line 17 . . . . . ▶	54		

Part V   Other Taxes

55 Self-employment tax (attach Schedule SE)	55	1,042	80
56 Tax from recomputing prior-year investment credit (attach Form 4255)	56		
57 Tax from recomputing prior-year Work Incentive (WIN) credit (attach schedule)	57		
58 Minimum tax. Check here ▶ ☐, if Form 4625 is attached	58		
59 Social security tax on tip income not reported to employer (attach Form 4137)	59		
60 Uncollected employee social security tax on tips (from Forms W-2)	60		
61 Total (add lines 55, 56, 57, 58, 59, and 60). Enter here and on line 19 . . . . . . ▶	61	1,042	80

Part VI   Other Payments

62 Excess FICA tax withheld (two or more employers—see instructions on page 9)	62		
63 Credit for Federal tax on special fuels, nonhighway gasoline and lubricating oil (attach Form 4136)	63		
64 Credit from a Regulated Investment Company (attach Form 2439)	64		
65 Total (add lines 62, 63, and 64). Enter here and on line 21d . . . . . . ▶	65		

Foreign Accounts Did you, at any time during the taxable year, have any interest in or signature or other authority over a bank, securities, or other financial account in a foreign country (except in a U.S. military banking facility operated by a U.S. financial institution)? ▶ ☐ Yes ☐ No
If "Yes," attach Form 4683. (For definitions, see Form 4683.)

☆ U.S. GOVERNMENT PRINTING OFFICE : 1974—O—548-293   E.I. 13-2687299

SCHEDULE SE
(Form 1040)
Department of the Treasury
Internal Revenue Service

Computation of Social Security Self-Employment Tax

► Each self-employed person must file a Schedule SE.
► Attach to Form 1040. ► See Instructions for Schedule SE (Form 1040).

1974

- If you had wages, including tips, of $13,200 or more that were subject to social security taxes, do not fill in this form.
- If you had more than one business, combine profits and losses from all your businesses and farms on this Schedule SE.

Important.—The self-employment income reported below will be credited to your social security record and used in figuring social security benefits.

NAME OF SELF-EMPLOYED PERSON (AS SHOWN ON SOCIAL SECURITY CARD) | **Social security number of self-employed person ►**

Business activities subject to self-employment tax (grocery store, restaurant, farm, etc.) ►

- If you have only farm income complete Parts I and III. ● If you have only nonfarm income complete Parts II and III.
- If you have both farm and nonfarm income complete Parts I, II, and III.

Part I Computation of Net Earnings from FARM Self-Employment

A farmer may elect to compute net farm earnings using the OPTIONAL METHOD, line 3, instead of using the Regular Method, line 2, if his gross profits are: (1) $2,400 or less, or (2) more than $2,400 and net profits are less than $1,600. However, lines 1 and 2 must be completed even if you elect to use the FARM OPTIONAL METHOD.

REGULAR METHOD
1 Net profit or (loss) from: { (a) Schedule F, line 54 (cash method), or line 74 (accrual method). . |
{ (b) Farm partnerships . . . . |

2 Net earnings from farm self-employment (add lines 1(a) and (b)) . . . . |

FARM OPTIONAL METHOD
3 If gross profits { (a) Not more than $2,400, enter two-thirds of the gross profits . . . }
from farming¹ are: { (b) More than $2,400 and the net farm profit is less than $1,600, enter $1,600 . }

¹ Gross profits from farming are the total gross profits from Schedule F, line 28 (cash method), or line 72 (accrual method), plus the distributive share of gross profits from farm partnerships (Schedule K–1 (Form 1065), line 15) as explained in instructions for Schedule SE.

4 Enter here and on line 12(a), the amount on line 2, or line 3 if you elect the farm optional method .

Part II Computation of Net Earnings from NONFARM Self-Employment

REGULAR METHOD
5 Net profit or (loss) from:

(a) Schedule C, line 21. (Enter combined amount if more than one business.) . | 17,615 | 00

(b) Partnerships, joint ventures, etc. (other than farming) . . . . . . |

(c) Service as a minister, member of a religious order, or a Christian Science practitioner. (Include rental value of parsonage or rental allowance furnished.) If you filed Form 4361, check here ☐ and enter zero on this line . . . . . |

(d) Service with a foreign government or international organization . . . . |

(e) Other (See Form 1040 instructions for line 37.) Specify ► _____ |

6 Total (add lines 5(a), (b), (c), (d), and (e)) . . . . | 17,615 | 00

7 Enter adjustments if any (attach statement) . . . . |

8 Adjusted net earnings or (loss) from nonfarm self-employment (line 6, as adjusted by line 7) . . . | 17,615 | 00

If line 8 is $1,600 or more **OR** if you do not elect to use the Nonfarm Optional Method, omit lines 9 through 11 and enter amount from line 8 on line 12(b), Part III.

Note: You may use the nonfarm optional method (line 9 through line 11) only if line 8 is less than $1,600 and less than two-thirds of your gross nonfarm profits,² and you had actual net earnings from self-employment of $400 or more for at least 2 of the 3 following years: 1971, 1972, and 1973. The nonfarm optional method can only be used for 5 taxable years.

² Gross profits from nonfarm business are the total of the gross profits from Schedule C, line 3, plus the distributive share of gross profits from nonfarm partnerships (Schedule K–1 (Form 1065), line 15) as explained in instructions for Schedule SE. Also, include gross profits from services reported on lines 5(c), (d), and (e), as adjusted by line 7.

SE

NONFARM OPTIONAL METHOD
9 (a) Maximum amount reportable, under both optional methods combined (farm and nonfarm) . . | $1,600 | 00

(b) Enter amount from line 3. (If you did not elect to use the farm optional method, enter zero.) . . |

(c) Balance (subtract line 9(b) from line 9(a)) . . . . |

10 Enter two-thirds of gross nonfarm profits² or $1,600, whichever is smaller . . . . . . |

11 Enter here and on line 12(b), the amount on line 9(c) or line 10, whichever is smaller . . . . . |

Part III Computation of Social Security Self-Employment Tax

12 Net earnings or (loss): (a) From farming (from line 4) . . . . |

(b) From nonfarm (from line 8, or line 11 if you elect to use the Nonfarm Optional Method) . . . | 17,615 | 00

13 Total net earnings or (loss) from self-employment reported on line 12. (If line 13 is less than $400, you are not subject to self-employment tax. Do not fill in rest of form.) . . . . | 17,615 | 00

14 The largest amount of combined wages and self-employment earnings subject to social security tax for 1974 is . . . | $13,200 | 00

15 (a) Total "FICA" wages as indicated on Forms W–2 . . . . |

(b) Unreported tips, if any, subject to FICA tax from Form 4137, line 9 . . |

(c) Total of lines 15(a) and (b) . . . . |

16 Balance (subtract line 15(c) from line 14) . . . . | 13,200 | 00

17 Self-employment income—line 13 or 16, whichever is smaller . . . . | 13,200 | 00

18 If line 17 is $13,200, enter $1,042.80; if less, multiply the amount on line 17 by .079 . . . . | 1,042 | 80

19 Railroad employee's and railroad employee representative's adjustment from Form 4469, line 10 . . |

20 Self-employment tax (subtract line 19 from line 18). Enter here and on Form 1040, line 55 . . . | 1,042 | 80

☆ U.S. GOVERNMENT PRINTING OFFICE: 1974—O–548-261 230427710

Figure 18-6. This is an illustration of Schedule SE, Computation of Social Security Self-Employment Tax.

The amount on line 20 (same as line 18) should be entered on Form 1040, line 55, as shown in Figure 18-5. It will be added to your total taxes owed (line 19, Figure 18-4). For more information on self-employment taxes, see the *Tax Guide* and ask your IRS office for Publication 533.

ESTIMATED TAXES. If you expect to make a profit on your business the following year, and the taxes you expect to pay are over $100, you're probably required to file a Form 1040-ES (Figure 18-7) by April 15 of the following year. Form 1040-ES comes with a worksheet (Figure 18-8), which you keep for your records.

The worksheet allows you to compute your estimated tax based on earnings, exemptions, and deductions, similar to Form 1040. Once you've estimated your tax, fill out the Form 1040-ES, Voucher 1. You can pay the whole tax at this time, or in four monthly installments in April, June, September, and January.

If your profit picture changes during the year and you find that your estimated taxes won't be what you originally thought, a space is provided on the worksheet for you to work out amended computations. Adjustments in your payments can be made with each quarterly declaration voucher.

As a new business, it may be very tough to figure out whether you'll make a profit the following year, and if you will, how much that profit might be. It's probably best to wait until you actually start making a profit. For example, if you open your store in February and start showing a profit by August of that same year, you can then file a 1040-ES "Declaration of Estimated Tax for Individuals" by September 15. For full details on estimated taxes, see the *Tax Guide,* and also get Publication 421, *Optional Self-Employment Tax Table,* from the IRS.

Figure 18-7. This is Voucher 1 from a Form 1040-ES for filing estimated income taxes.

CITY AND STATE INCOME TAXES. If you're subject to city or state

---

Form **1040-ES** Department of the Treasury Internal Revenue Service	**Estimated Tax Declaration–Voucher for Individuals—1975** (To be used for making declaration and payment)	Voucher **1** (Calendar year—Due April 15, 1975)

°A. Estimated tax for the year ending .... (month and year) **$**

°B. Overpayment from last year credited to estimated tax for this year **$**

If fiscal year taxpayer, see Instruction 11.
* Do not file this declaration–voucher if your total estimated tax for the year is less than $100.00.

Return this voucher with check or money order payable to the Internal Revenue Service. For where to file your declaration–voucher, see Instruction 5.

1. Amount of this installment ... ▷ $
2. Amount of overpayment credit from last year (all or part) applied to this installment (See Instruction 9) . ▷
3. Amount of this installment payment (line 1 less line 2) .... ▷ $

File this original declaration–voucher even if line 3 is zero.

Sign here ▷
Your Signature

Spouse's signature (if joint declaration)

Please type or print

Your social security number

Spouse's number, if joint declaration

First name and middle initial (of both spouses if joint declaration)

Last name

Address (Number and street)

City State, and ZIP code

1975 Estimated Tax Worksheet (Keep for your records—Do not file)

Name	Social Security Number

1 Enter amount of Adjusted Gross Income expected in 1975 (See Instruction 2) . . . .

TAX TABLE USERS OMIT LINES 2, 3, 4, AND 5. FIND TAX IN TAX TABLES 1–12 IN
1974 INSTRUCTIONS FOR FORM 1040 OR FORM 1040A AND ENTER ON LINE 6

2 If you expect to itemize deductions, enter estimated total of those deductions. If you do not expect to itemize deductions, enter 15% of line 1 (limited to $2,000 ($1,000 if married filing separately)) . . . .

3 Line 1 less line 2 . . . .

4 Exemptions ($750 for each, including additional exemptions for age and blindness) . . . .

5 Line 3 less line 4. This is your estimated taxable income . . . .

6 Tax (Compute tax on the amount on line 5 by using appropriate Tax Rate Schedule X, Y, or Z on page 4, or tax on the amount on line 1 from 1974 Tax Tables 1–12 (See "Caution" in Instruction 2)) . . . . . .

7 Credits: retirement income, foreign tax, investment, political contributions, and work incentive (WIN) . . .

8 Line 6 less line 7 . . . .

9 Tax from recomputing a prior year investment credit (See Form 4255) and work incentive (WIN) credit . .

10 Estimate of 1975 self-employment income $..................; if $14,100 or more, enter $1,113.90; if less, multiply the amount by .079. If joint declaration and both have self-employment income, make separate computations .

11 Add lines 8, 9, and 10 . . . .

12 Estimated income tax withheld and to be withheld during 1975 plus credit for Federal tax on gasoline, special fuels, and lubricating oil (See Form 4136) . . . .

13 Estimated tax (line 11 less line 12). Enter here and in Block A on declaration–voucher. If $100 or more, file the declaration–voucher; if less, no declaration is required . . . .

14 Computation of installments:

If declaration is due to be filed on: { April 15, 1975, enter ¼ / June 15, 1975, enter ⅓ / September 15, 1975, enter ½ / January 15, 1976, enter amount } of line 13 here and on line 1 of original and subsequent declaration–vouchers } . . . . .

Note: *If your estimated tax should change during the year, you may use the amended computation below to determine the amended amounts to enter on your declaration–voucher.*

Amended Computation		Record of Estimated Tax Payments				
(Use if your estimated tax substantially changes after you file your first declaration–voucher.)		Voucher number	Date (a)	Amount (b)	1974 overpayment credit applied to installment (c)	Total amount paid and credited from Jan. 1 through the installment date shown. Add (b) and (c) (d)
1 Amended estimated tax. Enter here and in Block A on declaration–voucher						
2 Less: (a) Amount of last year's overpayment elected for credit to 1975 estimated tax and applied to date .		1				
(b) Payments made on 1975 declaration .		2				
(c) Total of lines 2(a) and 2(b)		3				
3 Unpaid balance (line 1 less line 2(c)) . .		4				
4 Amount to be paid (line 3 divided by number of remaining installments). Enter here and on line 1 of declaration–voucher. . . .		Total . . . . . ▶				

Page **2**   Detach here

income taxes, these forms usually follow the federal income tax forms and shouldn't be too difficult to figure out. Check with your local and state tax offices for information and required forms.

Your city or state may also require you to pay "unincorporated business taxes" in addition to personal income taxes. And of course, if you are incorporated, your corporation will have at least federal, if not city and state, taxes to pay.

SHOULD YOU BE YOUR OWN TAX ACCOUNTANT? If your business is a corporation, nonfamily partnership, or in any way more complex than the simple examples shown in this chapter, you'll probably need to have a tax accountant handle your tax forms. You may already

*Figure 18-8. This is the Work-
sheet from Form 1040-ES.*

have engaged an accountant to set up your books and record-keeping procedures when you start your business. Use the same person at tax time.

Even if your business is small and simple, you may still want to have an accountant handle your tax forms. But if you're used to doing your own taxes, enjoy pouring through the IRS publications, and have your records in top shape, maybe you can handle it yourself. In any case, you should learn as much as you can about taxing procedures, exemptions, and deductions in order to be a fully informed manager of your business. Whenever you hire a professional, it helps to know as much as you can about what the professional is doing. So when you hire a tax accountant, don't just sit back until it's time to sign the bottom line of the forms. Check them carefully. Ask questions. Find out exactly what's being done on your behalf.

19 Banking and Loans

When starting a business, it's important to choose the right bank and establish good relations with your banker early in the game. Besides the normal day-to-day banking services you'll require, you may find it necessary to borrow money from time to time. Good financial planning and a strong relationship with your banker will facilitate your securing extra funds when you need them.

WHICH BANK IS FOR YOU? You may choose to open your business checking account in the bank that you used before going into business. The advantage is that you've already established a relationship with the bank and may already know one of the bank's officers. But before you go ahead, find out what services the bank offers for small businesses. Some services your bank might provide are:
1. Credit references on customers or potential customers
2. Financial, investment, and estate advisory services
3. Loans
4. Check certification
5. Safe deposit boxes
6. Night depositories
7. Check reconciliation services
8. Payroll accounting services

You should choose a bank near your place of business, if at all possible, to reduce the risks involved in carrying cash receipts to the bank. If you do have to carry cash for any distance, ask your banker's advice about how you can cover the theft and personal liability risks that are involved.

If possible, choose a bank that is familiar with your type of business. This will help them to understand and evaluate your requirements and financial status more quickly.

Another good idea is to use the bank that most of your customers use. This will help you because checks will clear the bank more quickly, and credit information on customers will be more readily available to you.

Since most businesses need to borrow money sooner or later, an important issue is what the bank's requirements are on loans. Ask your banker these questions about business loans:

1. Is collateral required?
2. How much collateral?
3. How long does it take to have a loan approved?
4. Does the bank have limitations on the number of small loans or types of businesses to which it will grant loans?
5. What are the repayment terms?
6. What supporting informational reports do you have to make?
7. Is it necessary for you to maintain certain balances before the bank can consider loans?

EARN YOUR BANKER'S RESPECT. You'll earn your banker's respect by managing your business properly and keeping him informed about your operation. Show good faith by keeping your word and observing the bank's policies. When a financial problem arises, don't try to evade the issue. Let your bank in on it. The bad image you'll create by trying to hide trouble is worse than the actual condition might warrant.

Provide your banker with financial information on your business. Right from the start, even before borrowing is necessary, file copies of your income statements and balance sheets with your banker. Supplying factual information on your company's finances helps to build your reputation for integrity.

Once you're in business, invite your banker to visit the store. Show him the operation and introduce him to your sales clerks and other members of the business. Tell him about your suppliers, how you receive and maintain stocks, and your merchandising techniques. Talk to him about your future plans so he can offer advice and suggest ways in which the bank can help you meet these needs.

FINANCIAL PLANNING. By making the cash forecasts outlined in Chapter 3, you should have a good idea what your money requirements will be in your business. If you see that you're going to be short of cash, show these plans to your banker *early*. Also show him income statements and balance sheets to back up your business's sound financial footing. If you can show proof that your business is making a profit, it will seem likely to him that it will continue to do so.

You may require a loan to start your business. If you've got limited savings to invest, it's better to borrow the additional money early, rather than wait until you reach a financial crisis. If your cash forecast indicates you'll need more capital by the third month of your operation, don't wait until then to apply for a loan. Show your banker the figures and your plans before you start.

WHY BORROW MONEY? Lack of sufficient operating capital is a frequent cause of business failures. It's important to have enough cash to start your business properly, get it through its initial growth period, carry it through "bad times," and enable it to expand when the opportunity is right. If you've got limited starting capital—which would mean not enough funds to properly stock your store, or get you the best location, and so forth—it's a good idea to get a loan and start out properly. Why throw $10,000 of your savings into a poorly set up operation that might fail, when you could borrow another $10,000 and do the job right? Don't try to start your business with less capital than you need. With the proper beginning, your store's success will enable you to pay back the loan. So if extra capital will make the difference between success and failure, borrow the money.

Because most new businesses require an initial growth period, it's important to have the capital to take you through this period and avoid a financial crisis. You'll also need extra capital for the normal slow times.

Another time when you might require a loan is when your business increases or you expand your facilities, or both. When sales increase, it'll be necessary to purchase more inventory. You'll need extra capital to do this. At some point you may find you need more space, or a decorative renovation. Again, you'll need money.

BANK LOANS. If you don't have the capital resources yourself, or through members of your family or friends, the first place to try to get a loan is through your bank. The least expensive type of loan is a short-term note. For example, you might borrow $2,000 on a 90-day note at 9½ percent interest. This means you would pay back the $2,000, plus interest, at the end of 90 days. Short-term notes carry you through short periods of need; for example, when you need extra cash to purchase your Christmas inventory.

Long-term notes are usually paid in monthly installments, have larger interest rates, and often require collateral. You might borrow $10,000 for five years at 11½ percent interest, using your store's fixtures and inventory as collateral. You'd make regular monthly payments on the loan throughout those five years.

LOAN SOURCES IN THE FEDERAL GOVERNMENT. If you can't get a loan directly from your bank, there are small-business loan sources available in the federal government. The Small Business Administration offers several types of loans:

1. Business loans to assist small firms to finance construction, conversion, or expansion; to purchase equipment, facilities, machinery, supplies, or materials; and to acquire working capital. These loans can be direct or in participation with banks (in which case your banker can help you apply for it).

2. Economic opportunity loans to assist small firms operated by those who have marginal or submarginal incomes, or those who have been denied equal opportunity (Title IV of the Economic Opportunity Act).

3. Disaster loans to assist disaster victims to rebuild homes or business establishments damaged in SBA-declared disaster areas.

4. Economic-injury loans to assist small concerns suffering economic injury from: (a) a major or natural disaster declared by the Pres-

ident or Secretary of Agriculture; (b) federally aided urban renewal or highway construction programs; (c) inability to market or process a product because of disease or toxicity resulting from natural or undetermined causes; (d) U.S. trade agreements.

Veterans business loans are available to eligible World War II and Korean conflict veterans for the purchase of property other than real estate, such as inventory, equipment, and machinery, or for working capital required for engaging in business or purchasing a gainful occupation. The loan application is made to a bank and approved by your nearest Veterans Administration office.

APPLYING FOR AN SBA LOAN. Whether you apply for your SBA loan directly from the SBA or through your bank, certain forms and other written requirements are needed to back up your request. To start with, they'll want to know:

1. *How much money you need*
2. *For how long*
3. *For what reason*

Figure 19-1 shows a sample list of items to be purchased with an SBA loan.

You'll have to provide the SBA with copies of balance sheets and income (operating) statements for every year of the business, and a current balance sheet (within the last three months). If your business is new, or if past operating statements don't indicate enough profit to cover the loan, prepare a Projected Operating Statement for the following year, indicating what you expect sales, costs, and profit to be (see Figure 19-2).

You'll also be asked to fill out a Personal Financial Statement (Figures 19-3 and 19-4) that should include the assets and liabilities of your spouse, if any. In fact, you'll find that banks and the SBA usually will require that husband and wife apply for the loan jointly, even if only one is the proprietor of the business.

For each manager of the business, write up a description of education, technical training, employment, and business experience. (See Figure 19-5.)

You should also write up a history and description of the business, explaining when and how it was started, what its purpose is, and its

Loan Request: $15,000

To be used for:

$5,000   **renovations, which include breaking through wall to back room, which will add 400 additional square feet selling space**

$2,000   **fixtures and display materials**

$6,000   **inventory purchases to fill additional selling space**

$2,000   **working capital**

Figure 19-1. This is a sample explanation of what an SBA loan would be used for.

Figure 19-2. This is a sample Projected Income or Operating Statement which the SBA would require you to submit if you had just started or weren't in business long enough to show a regular profit.

**PROJECTED
INCOME (OPERATING) STATEMENT
January 1, 1977 through December 31, 1978**

Net Sales		**$95,000**
Less Cost of Goods Sold:		
Inventory at beginning of period	15,000	
Merchandise purchases	50,000	
Merchandise available for sale	65,000	
Less inventory at end of year	21,000	
Cost of Goods Sold		44,000
Gross Margin		51,000
Operating Expenses:		
Salaries	11,650	
Rent	3,600	
Promotion	5,000	
Sales Taxes	2,850	
Utilities	400	
Insurance	300	
Supplies	700	
Interest payments	1,500	
Total Operating Expenses		26,000
Net Profit or Loss		**$25,000**

growth and development. (See Figure 19-6.) Finally, write a short statement of the benefits your company will receive from the loan. (Figure 19-7.)

Other items you may be required to furnish are insurance on the manager or managers of the business until the loan is repaid, and a chattel mortgage on the fixtures and inventory that are used to secure the loan. Your banker or SBA representative will explain the various aspects of the loan requirements and tell you which ones you're responsible for. Ask him questions about any item you don't understand.

SUMMING UP. Plan your cash needs well in advance so you won't be caught short of working capital. Choose your bank carefully and establish strong relations with your banker. Use small short-term loans for short periods of need. Pay back these small loans on time to demonstrate financial stability and create a sound credit standing.

Use long-term installment loans for larger needs. If your bank turns down your loan request, check the possibility of Veterans Administration or SBA-backed loans. Prepare your loan requests carefully, providing financial statements and other supporting data, including plans for repayment of the loan. Having enough capital when you need it can make the difference between failure and success in your business.

Figure 19-3. This is the front of a Personal Financial Statement used by the SBA.

PERSONAL FINANCIAL STATEMENT	Return to:	For SBA Use Only
As of_____ , 19 ___.	Small Business Administration	SBA Loan No.

Name and Address, Including ZIP Code *(of person and spouse submitting Statement)*	This statement is submitted in connection with S.B.A. loan requested or granted to the individual or firm, whose name appears below:
	Name and Address of Applicant or Borrower, Including ZIP Code
SOCIAL SECURITY NO. _____	
Business *(of person submitting Statement)*	

Please answer all questions using "No" or "None" where necessary

ASSETS	LIABILITIES
Cash on Hand & In Banks . . . . $_____	Accounts Payable . . . . $_____
Savings Account in Banks . . . . _____	Notes Payable to Banks . . . . _____
U. S. Government Bonds . . . . _____	*(Describe below - Section 2)*
Accounts & Notes Receivable . . . . _____	Notes Payable to Others . . . . _____
Life Insurance-Cash Surrender Value Only . . _____	*(Describe below - Section 2)*
Other Stocks and Bonds . . . . _____	Installment Account (Auto) . . . . _____
(Describe - reverse side - Section 3)	Monthly Payments $_____
Real Estate . . . . _____	Installment Accounts (Other) . . . . _____
(Describe - reverse side - Section 4)	Monthly Payments $_____
Automobile - Present Value . . . . _____	Loans on Life Insurance . . . . _____
Other Personal Property . . . . _____	Mortgages on Real Estate . . . . _____
(Describe - reverse side - Section 5)	*(Describe - reverse side - Section 4)*
Other Assets . . . . _____	Unpaid Taxes . . . . _____
(Describe - reverse side - Section 6)	*(Describe - reverse side - Section 7)*
	Other Liabilities . . . . _____
	(Describe - reverse side - Section 8)
	Total Liabilities . . . . _____
	Net Worth . . . . _____
Total . . . . $_____	Total . . . . $_____

Section I. Source of Income	CONTINGENT LIABILITIES
(Describe below all items listed in this Section)	
Salary . . . . $_____	As Endorser or Co-Maker . . . . $_____
Net Investment Income . . . . _____	Legal Claims and Judgments . . . . _____
Real Estate Income . . . . _____	Provision for Federal Income Tax . . . . _____
Other Income *(Describe)* . . . . _____	Other Special Debt . . . . _____

Description of items listed in Section I _____

Life Insurance Held *(Give face amount of policies - name of company and beneficiaries)* _____
_____
_____

SUPPLEMENTARY SCHEDULES

Section 2. Notes Payable to Banks and Others

Name and Address of Holder of Note	Amount of Loan		Terms of Repayments	Maturity of Loan	How Endorsed, Guaranteed, or Secured
	Original Bal.	Present Bal.			
	$	$	$		

Figure 19-4. This is the back of the Personal Financial Statement. This statement should include the assets of you and your spouse (if any).

Section 3. Other Stocks and Bonds: Give listed and unlisted Stocks and Bonds *(Use separate sheet if necessary)*

No. of Shares	Names of Securities	Cost	Market Value Statement Date	
			Quotation	Amount

Section 4. Real Estate Owned. *(List each parcel separately. Use supplemental sheets if necessary. Each sheet must be identified as a supplement to this statement and signed). (Also advises whether property is covered by title insurance, abstract of title, or both).*

Title is in name of

Type of property

Address of property (City and State)

Original Cost to (me) (us) $_____
Date Purchased   _____
Present Market Value $_____
Tax Assessment Value $_____

Name and Address of Holder of Mortgage (City and State)

Date of Mortgage   _____
Original Amount $_____
Balance $_____
Maturity   _____
Terms of Payment   _____

Status of Mortgage, i.e., current or delinquent. If delinquent describe delinquencies

Section 5. Other Personal Property. *(Describe and if any is mortgaged, state name and address of mortgage holder and amount of mortgage, terms of payment and if delinquent, describe delinquency.)*

Section 6. Other Assets. *(Describe)*

Section 7. Unpaid Taxes. *(Describe in detail, as to type, to whom payable, when due, amount, and what, if any, property a tax lien, if any, attaches)*

Section 8. Other Liabilities. *(Describe in detail)*

(I) or (We) certify the above and the statements contained in the schedules herein is a true and accurate statement of (my) or (our) financial condition as of the date stated herein. This statement is given for the purpose of: *(Check one of the following)*

☐ Inducing S.B.A. to grant a loan as requested in application, of the individual or firm whose name appears herein, in connection with which this statement is submitted.

☐ Furnishing a statement of (my) or (our) financial condition, pursuant to the terms of the guaranty executed by (me) or (us) at the time S.B.A. granted a loan to the individual or firm, whose name appears herein.

_____ Signature   _____ Signature   _____ Date

Cecily Jones, the proprietor and manager of The Mod Shop, has completed 21 credits in business administration, including basic accounting, marketing, and management, at Ourcity Community College. She has also participated in seminars conducted by the Small Business Administration in Ourcity.

Cecily Jones's business experience includes two years working as a sales clerk for Ourcity Department Store, where she was promoted to Assistant Buyer after six months. She also spent three years working at The Grope Shop, where she started as Assistant Manager and was promoted to Manager after one year. In this job she got direct retail experience in buying, planning promotions, record-keeping, sales, and supervising two other employees.

Figure 19-5. This is a sample description of a store manager's education and business background. This is necessary to convince the SBA that the person managing the store is capable of doing so.

Cecily Jones opened The Mod Shop in Ourcity in January, 1976. The shop carries high-fashion clothes and accessories which appeal primarily to the teenage and college market. With two colleges, a university, and a community college all located in or on the outskirts of Ourcity, there's quite a large group from which the store's clientele is drawn.

The Mod Shop is located within walking distance of one college and the university, but there's ample parking in the area and many customers come from other areas of the city to shop there.

Cecily opened The Mod Shop with $10,000 of her own savings, plus a $5,000 loan from her parents. She started the shop with $8,000 worth of inventory and used $2,500 for fixtures and renovations. The rest of the money was used as working capital.

In one year The Mod Shop has shown gross sales of $65,000 and the inventory has increased from $8,000 to $15,000. Cecily has paid back $1,500 of the loan to her parents, and earned a net profit of $8,500.

Figure 19-6. Here's a sample history of a store applying for a loan.

The Mod Shop's initial selling space was 800 square feet, but the store has three large back rooms. Since only two of these rooms are necessary for storage and office space, Cecily would now like to convert one of them into additional selling space. This would give her an opportunity to expand her accessory lines, offer more depth in her clothing assortments, and eliminate the crowded conditions which now exist. The $15,000 loan would enable Cecily to make these changes in The Mod Shop.

Figure 19-7. This is a sample explanation of how the SBA loan will help the business.

20 The Personal Side of Your Business

The first 19 chapters of this book have concentrated on what you can *do* to open and operate a successful retail store. But this chapter is going to focus on *you*—your personality, your dreams, your needs, and your relations with the other people in your life. Because, in a sense, you *are* your business. Its problems will be your problems. Its losses will be your losses. And accordingly, its success will be your success.

HAVE YOU GOT WHAT IT TAKES TO BECOME A SUCCESSFUL ENTREPRENEUR? An entrepreneur has been defined as one who organizes, manages, and assumes the risks of a business or enterprise. A successful entrepreneur, of course, is one who does these things successfully. Studies have been made of people who are successful entrepreneurs, in order to find the common denominators among them. The Small Business Administration uses the self-evaluation test shown in Figure 20-1 to help people evaluate themselves in terms of their entrepreneurial personalities.

How do you rate on this scale? Are you a self-starter? Can you get along with all kinds of people? Are you a leader who will be able to inspire employees? Can you handle responsibility? Are you a good organizer? Do you have a large capacity for hard work? Can you make decisions? Do people trust you? Can you stick with your business on a long-term basis to make it work? How good is your health?

THE EFFECTIVE ENTREPRENEUR. In their book, *The Effective Entrepreneur,** Charles Swayne and William Tucker have taken a close look at the makeup of successful entrepreneurs. They point out certain characteristics common to the majority of effective entrepreneurs who were studied:
1. *Positive attitude*
2. *Self-confidence*
3. *Goal-oriented*
4. *Action-oriented*

The Effective Entrepreneur, Swayne, Charles and Tucker, William, General Learning Press, Morristown, N. J. (07960) 1973.

Rating Scale for Personal Traits Important to a Business Proprietor

INSTRUCTIONS: After each question place a check mark on the line at the point closest to your answer. The check mark need not be placed directly over one of the suggested answers because your rating may lie somewhere between two answers. Be honest with yourself.

ARE YOU A SELF-STARTER?

| I do things my own way. Nobody needs to tell me to get going. | If someone gets me started, I keep going all right. | Easy does it. I don't put myself out until I have to. |

HOW DO YOU FEEL ABOUT OTHER PEOPLE?

| I like people. I can get along with just about anybody. | I have plenty of friends. I don't need anyone else. | Most people bug me. |

CAN YOU LEAD OTHERS?

| I can get most people to go along without much difficulty. | I can get people to do things if I drive them. | I let someone else get things moving. |

CAN YOU TAKE RESPONSIBILITY?

| I like to take charge of and see things through. | I'll take over if I have to, but I'd rather let someone else be responsible. | There's always some eager beaver around wanting to show off. I say let him. |

HOW GOOD AN ORGANIZER ARE YOU?

| I like to have a plan before I start. I'm usually the one to get things lined up. | I do all right unless things get too goofed up. Then I cop out. | I just take things as they come. |

HOW GOOD A WORKER ARE YOU?

| I can keep going as long as necessary. I don't mind working hard. | I'll work hard for a while, but when I've had enough, that's it! | I can't see that hard work gets you anywhere. |

CAN YOU MAKE DECISIONS?

| I can make up my mind in a hurry if necessary, and my decision is usually o.k. | I can if I have plenty of time. If I have to make up my mind fast, I usually regret it. | I don't like to be the one who decides things. I'd probably blow it. |

CAN PEOPLE TRUST WHAT YOU SAY?

| They sure can. I don't say things I don't mean. | I try to be on the level, but sometimes I just say what's easiest. | What's the sweat if the other fellow doesn't know the difference? |

CAN YOU STICK WITH IT?

| If I make up my mind to do something, I don't let anything stop me. | I usually finish what I start. | If a job doesn't go right, I turn off. Why beat your brains out? |

HOW GOOD IS YOUR HEALTH?

| I never run down. | I have enough energy for most things I want to do. | I run out of juice sooner than most of my friends seem to. |

5. *Thick-skinned*
6. *Selective curiosity*
7. *Competitive*
8. *Creative*

1. *Positive attitude.* This is basically the idea that you should be optimistic about your business plans and feel that success is possible.

Figure 20-1. This is the Rating Scale from the 3rd edition of Starting And Managing A Small Business of Your Own, *put out by the Small Business Administration, Washington, D.C.*

Are you the kind of person who is generally optimistic about the things you undertake in life? Do you look forward to good results, rather than expecting the worst? While you shouldn't blindly go ahead thinking faith is all that's necessary for success, it sure is an added bonus.

2. *Self-confidence.* How do you feel about yourself? Do you consider yourself to be a competent individual who can accomplish what you set out to do? Do you have confidence in your ability to learn new things, cope with new situations, and adapt as necessary to the conditions around you? While this self-confidence should certainly be tempered with realism, and an acceptance of your weaknesses as well as your strengths, you should basically feel that you've got what it takes to get the job done.

3. *Goal-oriented.* This means you should focus on the job to be done. There are people I know who have great ideas and great plans, but somehow they always seem to get bogged down in unessential details, and never move any closer to their goals. You should know exactly what your goals are, and this is one reason we stressed earlier the importance of making sales and expense plans for the future. Know where you want your store to be in one year, two years, and five years. If you're still in the very early planning stages, set the date when you plan to open your store, outline the things that must be done to achieve that goal, and then work at them one by one until you've accomplished what you started out to do.

4. *Action-oriented.* This goes hand in hand with goal-oriented. Once you've set your goal or goals, the next thing you've got to do is start moving toward them. Once again, some people are great at forming fantastic plans about the things they want to achieve. But if they simply sit around and talk about it, nothing happens. You've got to figure out what needs to be done to accomplish your goals, and then get right out there and do those things. People may accuse you of acting too quickly, making decisions too fast, but when you run your own business, decisions must be made daily on all kinds of things, and a fence-sitter will never accomplish anything. You should certainly try to make decisions based on the best information you can get, and you've then got to act on them—you can't sit around waiting for perfect answers, or hoping that somehow things "will take care of themselves." You've got to get out there and act.

5. *Thick-skinned.* When you're running your own business you can't afford to be overly sensitive to remarks from customers, associates, competitors, neighbors, relatives, and the like. Some people will be envious of what you're doing. Others will try to tell you you're doing it all wrong. And you'll never be able to please every customer who walks in your door. Even your family may place emotional pressure on you from time to time. And on top of this, your own plans will not always work out the way you figured. So you're going to be under a lot of tension at times, and you've got to be somewhat thick-skinned to ride through it.

6. *Selective curiosity.* Reading this book is one proof of your selective curiosity. You should want to find out everything you can relating

to your business. You should devour trade magazines, business sections of the newspaper, take related courses, read books, and so on. You should be selectively curious about anything that might improve you personally, or increase your knowledge and ability to do a better job to achieve your goals.

7. *Competitive*. Swayne and Tucker found that most of the successful entrepreneurs they studied were competitive in almost everything they did. They enjoyed competitive sports and games, such as tennis, chess, handball, table tennis, and squash; rather than fishing, hunting, skiing, surfing, swimming, and bowling. This, of course, was merely a trend, and I wouldn't worry about it if you hate tennis and love fishing. But if you do have a competitive streak in you, starting your own business may be another opportunity to express it.

8. *Creative*. The creativity meant here is not artistic creativity, but the ability to see a problem and create solutions. Or the ability to work with ideas that will improve and expand your business' success. As Swayne and Tucker point out, an effective entrepreneur can either be good at getting his own creative ideas and solutions, or good at utilizing the creative ideas of others. If you fit either category, you'll find it a great asset in starting your own business.

While the above list is by no means the final word in who will and who will not succeed in business, having some or many of these traits will probably help insure your success in running your own business. Unfortunately, no similar study has been made of the entrepreneurs who failed, so there's no list of traits common to the failures.

RISK AND UNCERTAINTY. When you work at a salaried job, you're pretty certain that a paycheck is going to be waiting for you at the end of the week. You put in your hours, do your work, and are rewarded. But in your own business, things are not as certain. You do all your homework, lay the groundwork, in fact do everything you can to insure success. That's what this book is all about. But bad weather, a dip in the economy, the opening of a competitor across the street—any number of unforseeable influences, not to mention a simple miscalculation on your part, can turn success into failure. Yes, there is some risk in starting your own business. You can minimize it by careful planning and preparation. It will lessen as you gain experience and age (more businesses fail in the early years of their operation than later on). But before going ahead, do you know whether you and your family can accept this risk and live with it?

You may be the kind of person who can take calculated risks. You may feel that if you fail, you can always start again. But how does your spouse feel? Will he or she be able to handle it? To give up his or her half of the family's life savings for your dream? To accept the lean times that might accompany the start of a business until it grows into a profit-making operation? Talk these problems over with your spouse first. Perhaps just filling him in on the careful plans and preparations will help him feel more secure about your enterprise. Perhaps you'll have to compromise, and leave a small amount of the nest egg intact in the savings account so your spouse will feel secure enough to back you in your project.

TIME. When you start your own business, you'll find that's where all your time will be spent. In contrast to the normal 40-hour work week, you'll be putting 60, 80, or more hours into a new business. And it still won't be enough. There will always be something else which could be done—paperwork to do, tradebooks to read, improvements to be made. When you aren't actually at work, you'll be thinking about your business. Conversation at the supper table will revolve around an interesting customer, a problem with an employee, overdue merchandise, and so on. You're liable to even dream about the store at night when you're trying to get the rest you need to cope with it the next day.

You may find it easy to devote all your time to the business. It's your baby, your *thing*. You wouldn't stay home Friday night even if you did have employees to handle it. You'd want to be right in the middle of the action. To *know* what's going on. To *control* what's going on. And in the early months or even years, you might not be able to afford to have enough employees to relieve you of a lot of the time spent in your shop. Every penny counts in those early days, and the more you do yourself, the less you'll have to pay someone else to do it.

So plan on devoting most of your waking hours to your business when it's in its initial stages, and prepare your family to accept this. Hopefully, your spouse will want to join you in many of the hours spent in the store. In this way you'll get to share some time together, and doubly enjoy your accomplishments. If you've got kids, arrangements may have to be made for sitters or nursery school. Since you won't be able to spend as much time in leisure activities with them as you used to, try to find ways to incorporate them into your business life. Are they old enough to help in the store? If they're too young, can they play in a corner while you're taking inventory on Sunday? One nice thing about a retail store is that it can be adapted very well to a family business, with all members sharing as they're able to in the work. Your children will become more aware of what it means to "bring home the bacon," and will develop an appreciation of the value of money earned.

TOO MANY COOKS. It's been said that "too many cooks spoil the broth." In the same way, too many people trying to make the same decisions in a business may lead to failure, not to mention arguments between the cooks. If you're operating your store as a husband and wife team, or with other friends or relatives, be certain to make it clear early in the game who will be responsible for what. Assign an area of the operation to each "partner"—where he'll have the final say. For example, let one person make buying decisions, another hire and train employees, another keep the records, another plan promotions. Group meetings can be held and ideas discussed, but the final decision should be up to one person. If you feel that you want to have the final say in *all* store decisions, then make this clear in the beginning.

Along this same line, it's nice to hire relatives in order to provide work for them, but only if it also fits the needs of your store. Don't try to support too many people on a new small business. And don't keep an incompetent relative on the payroll any longer than you would an incompetent stranger. You'll only end up by destroying the business.

PRESSURE. Sure, there's plenty of pressure in running your own business. Murphy's Law will probably hold true, that "everything that can possibly go wrong, will." In fact, you won't even be able to imagine the kinds of things that might go wrong. You'll be under pressure to make decisions, to solve problems, all the time. Merchandise won't arrive on time, an employee won't show up for work, your ad will appear wrong in the newspaper, your ad *won't* appear in the newspaper, your supplier will send you the wrong merchandise—on and on and on. But each day you'll cope with the problems. You'll make decisions. You'll see results. You'll revise your actions. You'll see more results.

Suddenly you'll realize that you're thriving on all this pressure. It's a challenge. The problems are different every day, and you're getting to see the direct results of your actions in sales totals that are rung up at the end of the day. And more importantly, you see the results in the net figures on your profit and loss statement. Yes, the work is hard. It demands all you've got to give it. You'll be using more of your skills, knowledge, ability, creativity, and sheer physical capacity than you ever have in your life—more than you even knew existed. But you'll find that you've got what it takes. And you'll discover that unique feeling of satisfaction that goes with it!

Appendix

IRS PUBLICATIONS
Available Free From Your IRS Office

17 Your Federal Income Tax
#334 Tax Guide for Small Business
#463 Travel, Entertainment and Gift Expenses
#505 Tax Withholding and Declaration of Estimated Tax
#506 Computing Your Tax Under the Income Averaging Method
#528 A Guide to Preparing Form 1040
#533 Information on Self-Employment Tax
#534 Tax Information on Depreciation
#535 Tax Information on Business Expenses
#536 Losses from Operating a Business
#538 Tax Information on Accounting Periods and Methods
#539 Withholding Taxes from Your Employees' Wages
#540 Tax Information on Repairs, Replacements and Improvements
#541 Tax Information on Partnership Income and Losses
#542 Corporations and the Federal Income Tax
#545 Income Tax Deductions for Interest Expense
#546 Income Tax Deductions for Taxes
#548 Tax Information on Deductions for Bad Debts
#552 Record-keeping Requirements and a Guide to Tax Publications
#556 Audits of Returns, Appeal Rights and Claims for Refund
#583 Record-keeping for a Small Business
#587 Tax Information on Operating a Business in Your Home

TRADE MAGAZINES (21 categories)

Agricultural equipment and supplies:

Ag Chem Magazine, Meister Publishing Co., 37841 Euclid Ave., Willoughby, Oh. 44094.
Custom Applicator, 3637 Park Ave., Memphis, Tn. 38111.
Farm Supplier, Mt. Morris, Il. 61054.

Auto and truck:

Auto Merchandising News, 1188 Main St., Suite 500, Bridgeport, Ct., 06604.
Automotive News, 965 E. Jefferson Ave., Detroit, Mi. 48207.
Commercial Car Journal, Chilton Way, Radnor, Pa. 19089.
Service Station & Garage Management, 109 Vanderhoof Ave., Suite 101, Toronto, Ont. M4G 2J2, Canada.
Shop Talk, P. O. Box 2586, Framingham, Ma. 01701.

Baking:

Pacific Bakers News, Route 2, Belfair, Wa. 98528

Book and book store trade:

Christian Bookseller, Gundersen Dr. & Schmale Rd., Wheaton, Il. 60187.
Publishers Weekly, 1180 Ave. of the Americas, NYC 10036.

Building interiors:

Decorating Retailer, 9334 Dielman Industrial Dr., St. Louis, Mo. 63132.
Kitchen Business, 1501 Broadway, NYC 10036.

Clothing and knit goods:

Earnshaw's Infants, Girls, Boyswear Review, 393 Seventh Ave., NYC 10001.
Hosiery & Underwear, 757 Third Ave., NYC 10017.
Tack'n Togs Merchandising, P. O. Box 67, Minneapolis, Mn. 55440.
Teens and Boys, 71 W. 35th St., NYC 10001.
Western Outfitter, 5314 Bingle Rd., Houston, Tx. 77018.

Confectionery and snack foods.

Candy Marketer, 777 Third Ave., NYC 10017.

Department store, variety, and dry goods:

Juvenile Merchandising, 370 Lexington Ave., NYC 10011.
Sew Business, 1271 Avenue of the Americas, NYC 10020.

Drugs, health care, and medical products:

Drug Topics, 550 Kinderkamack Rd., Oradell, N. J. 07649.
N. A. R. D. Journal, 1 E. Wacker Dr., Chicago, Il. 60601.

Equipment rental and leasing:

Rental Equipment Register, 2048 Cotner Ave., Los Angeles, Ca. 90025.

Florists, nurserymen, and landscaping:

Florist, 900 West Lafayette, Detroit, Mi. 48226.
Flower News, 549 W. Randolph St., Chicago, Il. 60606.

Groceries:

Convenience Store Journal, 1100 Jorie Blvd., Oak Brook, Il. 60521.
Deli News, P. O. Box 706, Hollywood, Ca. 90028.

Hardware:

Chain Saw Age, 3435 N. E. Broadway, Portland, Or. 97232.
Hardware Age, Chilton Way, Radnor, Pa. 19089.
Hardware Merchandising, 481 University Ave., Toronto 1, Ontario, Canada.

Home furnishings and appliances:

Casual Living Magazine, Time & Life Bldg., 1271 Ave. of the Americas, NYC 10020.
China Glass and Tablewares, 1115 Clifton Ave., Clifton, N. J. 07013.
Consumer Electronics, 155 East 78th St., NYC 10021.
Gift & Tableware Reporter, 1515 Broadway, NYC 10036.
Gift & Decorative Accessories, 51 Madison Ave., NYC 10010.
Mart Magazine, Berkshire Commons, Pittsfield, Ma. 01201.
Retailer & Marketing News, P. O. Box 57149, Dallas, Tx. 75207.

Jewelry:

Modern Jeweler, 15 W. 10th St., Kansas City, Mo. 64105.

Music:

Music Trades, 80 West St., P. O. Box 432, Englewood, N. J. 07631.
Musical Merchandise Review, Peacock Business Press, 200 S. Prospect Ave., Park Ridge, Il. 60068.

Office equipment and supplies:

Geyer's Dealer Topics, 51 Madison Ave., NYC 10010.
Office Products, Hitchcock Building, Wheaton, Il. 60187.
Office World News, 645 Stewart Ave., Garden City, N.Y. 11530.

Paint:

American Paint & Wallcoverings Dealer, 2911 Washington Ave., St.
    Louis, Mo. 63103.

Pets:

Pet Age, 2561 North Clark St., Chicago, Il. 60614.
Pets/Supplies/Marketing, 1 E. First St., Duluth, Mn. 55807.

Sporting goods:

American Bicyclist & Motorcyclist, 461 Eighth Ave., NYC 10001.
Selling Sporting Goods, 717 N. Michigan Ave., Chicago, Il. 60611.
The Shooting Industry, 8150 N. Central Park Blvd., Skokie, Il. 60076.
Skiing Trade News, One Park Ave., NYC 10016.
Sports Merchandiser, 1760 Peachtree Rd., N.W., Atlanta, Ga. 30309.

Toys, novelties, hobbies, and crafts:

Model Dealer Magazine, 733 Fifteenth St., N.W., Washington, D.C.
    20005
Profitable Craft Merchandising, News Plaza, Peoria, Il. 61601.
Souvenirs & Novelties, Bldg. 30, 20-21 Wagaraw Rd., Fair Lawn, N.J.
    07410.
Toy & Hobby World, 124 E. 40th St., NYC 10016.

Miscellaneous:

The Antiques Dealer, 1115 Clifton Ave., Clifton, N.J. 07013.
The Army/Navy Store Magazine, 475 Park Ave. S., NYC 10016.
Health Foods Business, 475 Park Ave. S., NYC 10016.
Specialty Food Merchandising, 29 Park Ave., Manhasset, N.Y. 11030.
Specialty Salesman & Franchise Opportunities Magazine, 307 N
    Michigan Ave., Chicago, Il. 60601.
Boutique Fashions, 50 Hunt St., Watertown, Ma. 02172.
Handbags & Accessories, 80 Lincoln Ave., Stamford, Ct. 06904.
Womens Wear Daily, Fairchild Publications, Inc., 7 E. 12th St., NYC
    10003.

Bibliography

BOOKS

Your Business: A Handbook of Management Aids for the New York Businessman, 1972 ed. State of New York, Dept. of Commerce, 99 Washington Ave., Albany, N.Y. 12210.

How to Start Your Own Craft Business, Genfan, Herb and Taetzsch, Lyn, New York: Watson-Guptill Publications, October 1974.

Fundamental Accounting Principles, 6th ed. Pyle, William W. and White, John Arch, Homewood, Il.: Richard D. Irwin, Inc., 1972.

The Effective Entrepreneur, Swayne, Charles and Tucker, William, Morristown, N.J.: General Learning Press, 1973.

Marketing Channels, Boone, Louis E. and Johnson, James C., Morristown, N.J.: General Learning Press, 1973.

PERIODICALS

"Promoting Customer Traffic," Charlotte Ann Smith, *Western Outfitter* December 1974.

"Controlling Your Expenses," Guy Laird, *Western Outfitter* December 1974.

"The Family Business: Fathers & Sons," *Gifts & Decorative Accessories* October 1974.

"Please Handle Our Merchandise—You'll Love It," *Gifts & Decorative Accessories* October 1974.

"Store Planning," Ron Mumford w/L.C. Rutledge, *Western Outfitter* September 1974.

"Why Customers Do Not Come Back," Guy Laird, *Western Outfitter* September 1974.

"Better Public Relations," John A. Haskett, *Western Outfitter* February 1975.

"Six Systems For Building Profit," Joan Lutz and Kenneth Steinke w/Ron Mumford, *Western Outfitter* March 1974.

"What Can Be Done About Freight Losses?" Paul Harms w/Ron Mumford, *Western Outfitter* August 1974.

"Protect Yourself Against Employee Theft," Roger A. Hawson, *Western Outfitter* August 1974.

"Pumping Up Your Salesmen's Productivity," Guy Laird, *Western Outfitter* August 1974.

"The ABC's of Gift Display," *Gifts & Decorative Accessories* February 1974.

BOOKS AND PAMPHLETS
From Small Business Administration, Washington, D.C.:

Financial Record-Keeping for Small Stores.
Management Audit for Small Retailers.
Selecting Advertising Media.
Guides for Profit Planning.
Starting & Managing a Small Business of Your Own, 3rd ed.
A Handbook of Small Business Finance.

Small Marketers Aids:
\# 25   Are You Kidding Yourself About Your Profits?
\# 96   Checklist for Successful Retail Advertising
#106   Finding & Hiring The Right Employee
#107   Building Strong Relations With Your Bank
#108   Building Repeat Retail Business
#109   Stimulating Impulse Buying for Increased Sales
#113   Quality & Taste as Sales Appeals
#114   Pleasing Your Boss, the Customer
#115   Are You Ready for Franchising
#118   Legal Services for Small Retail & Service Firms
#119   Preventing Retail Theft
#120   Building Good Customer Relations
#123   Stock Control for Small Stores
#124   Knowing Your Image
#125   Pointers on Display Lighting
#129   Reducing Shoplifting Losses
#130   Analyze Your Records to Reduce Costs
#137   Outwitting Bad Check Passers
#140   Profit by Your Wholesalers' Services
#148   Insurance Checklist for Small Business
#150   Business Plan for Small Retailers

Management Aid #52:
"Loan Sources In The Federal Government."

Index